CONTENTS

RIG: Sections of a field in ploughing

B

Straw Into Gold

Here is David Toulmin's follow-up to his much-praised first
book, HARD SHINING CORN. This book is a miscellany of
rural life in North-east Scotland over the last half-century —
in fact, fiction and poetry. His short stories brim with life and
humour and his recollections, of such aspects of the development
of rural Scotland as the early cinemas and the first railway
lines in the North-east, are gems of social history which Toulmin
has managed to capture and which are here committed to
print before memory fades for all time.
David Toulmin is the pen-name of John Reid, who now lives
in Aberdeen after more than forty years working on the
land as a farm servant. His formal education ended on his 14th
birthday at a rural Aberdeenshire school, and he began work
the following day as a 'fee'd loon' for £6.50 per half-year.

What the critics said about Toulmin's HARD SHINING CORN:

*John Reid is a born writer, a natural, who recreates with
intense vividness the incredibly hard, rough life of farm workers
in north east Scotland . . . an artist to his calloused fingertips
. . . his pages brim with life; moving, tender, astonishing,
funny and grim. Gorki and Gogol would approve him.*
Maurice Wiggin in The Sunday Times

*a collectors piece of a book . . . in the same class as the best
of Grassic Gibbon's short stories of the Mearns.*
Diane Morgan in The Scotsman

*important as a piece of social history . . . a work of considerable
literary merit.*
Aberdeen Evening Express

A

Straw Into Gold

➤➤➤ ● ❮❮❮

A Scots Miscellany

DAVID TOULMIN

IMPULSE BOOKS

ABERDEEN

First published 1973 by Impulse
Publications Ltd., 28 Guild Street,
Aberdeen, Scotland

ISBN 0 901311 32 4

*To my three sons
Eric, Jackie and Graham
this work is dedicated*

*I make no apologies for this book being different from the last
one, but from the shorn stubble fields to the realms of stardust
may ye reap a hairst of golden surprises.*

David Toulmin

Printed in Scotland by
Holmes McDougall, Ltd.

LANG BREEKS!

WELL well, it would be my last crack at Aunt Sally, there was no doubt about that. I had smashed a lot of her clay pipes in my time but this would be the last of it. I can see her twisted old mouth yet, her chalky face and apple-red cheeks, her coconut hair, her hat all askew from the whacks she got.

I would be fourteen the day after the school picnic and starting work with Auld Weelum Mackenzie of Fernieden. And besides, I was wearing my father's trousers, and taking a drag at his pipe on the sly. I was getting that big I was beginning to look down my nose at the old man, and I looked rediculous in knee-length breeks. I had fine sturdy knees and I liked showing them off, but it just wouldn't do any more. I even asked for a kilt but mother said we couldn't afford it. But I think she was afraid of what the neighbours would say if I swanked about in a kilt, or that it would attract the girls prematurely, and then she'd be jealous.

I could still wear my socks with the coloured tops but nobody would see them under the old man's baggy trousers. First day I appeared in them at school the dominie fair sized me up. He had me out in the middle of the floor and walked round about me with his tongue in his cheek. I knew he wanted to take me down to size and making me look a fool in front of the class was one way of doing it.

He never did like me that dominie. I was always late and often absent and always seemed to rub him the wrong way.

"We don't keep cows in here," he cried, one morning I came in late chewing a Cocksfoot grass; and perhaps next day I would be minus a legging, or I had fallen into a peat bog through looking at the clouds. Sometimes I thought I had a loose screw 'cause something always ticked in my head when I ran, but mother said it was that blow I got on the head from Uncle Simon with the fencing mallet. Not that he meant it, but by the time I got my hand up to feel the bump it was as big as an egg.

But I knew my history and my geography and my Julius Caesar, and I was the most voracious reader in the school, and for these reasons the dominie had to put up with me, though at times he showed his resentment. He was always threatening to "go up in a blue flame," and it was a sore disappointment to most of us that it didn't happen.

But he shook his big hairy-knuckled fist in my face and said I wasn't a man yet. He had red hairs on his knuckles, like I've seen on a crab's legs, and eyes like a cat in a rabbit trap. Even the girls resented him. They said his wife had a dog's life and most of us believed it.

But my long trousers fair needled him. "I'll take you on ten years after this," he said, his toothbrush moustache bristling red. "If you would only come to school man, maybe I could make something of you. You have the makings of a scholar but you are a truant lout. You should be thrashed! Maybe your father isn't big enough to do it but by God I am. Get back to your seat and sit very quiet or I'll really get mad."

If he hadn't been such a tyrant maybe I'd have gone to school more often. But I wasn't afraid of him. Not a bit of it. So I was late as ever and stayed away when it suited me. He pinched my cheeks for it with his vice-grip thumbs and I felt like taking a swipe at his shins. And I couldn't help being the biggest boy in the school; trouble is I haven't grown an inch since then and my poor old father's trousers would still fit me.

But my old man had his faults as well. For years he had complained about my indolence and 'mischeef,' with emphasis on the 'chief' in mischief. Well of course I played truant, and the old man had just had his last warning from 'the wheeper-in,' in other words the Officer of Education, that unless he kept me at school he would be run in.

I ran on the old man's bicycle, smoked his pipe, wore his Sunday sark, threw stones, fired arrows, kissed the girls—what was the old man to do?

And damnit he was glad of me too. He was chauved to death in the byres and I ran home from school and sliced his turnips, carried straw, swept up; I even took his place for a fortnight when he was off with 'flu, so he could hardly hit a lad that did that for him—well, not often.

2

But I had talent that the old man couldn't see; gifts that might have landed him on easy street had he given me some encouragement. I was publishing my own monthly magazine of short stories (hand-written, of course) and sending them round the parish. I had begun a history of Roman Britain with illustrations that might have rivalled Gibbon's **'Decline and Fall.'** I was coming on as a strip cartoonist and poster artist and even the dominie had allowed me to design and paint the covers for the annual school magazines. He asked for a show of hands in my favour and it was unanimous.

I had the most unique puppet-theatre you ever heard of, all done with silhouettes and a wick lamp on a life-size screen; oncoming trains, stunting aeroplanes, ships at sea, sword fights, bathing beauties—the lot, and the neighbours used to give me threepence a time for a peep-show.

I built model herring drifters that floated on the miller's dam. I made a motor-coach, a binder, and a merry-go-round with swing chairs and painted ladies on the revolving panels. I could make almost anything from cardboard, a handful of pins and water colours. I had to because nobody could afford to give me toys. Anyway, I didn't want a mecanno set or a fretwork outfit because that was someone else's ideas. I wanted to be original and invent my own playthings. But a magic lantern at this stage would have been a real blessing.

I had a standing army of one hundred soldiers, every one a cardboard cut-out equipped and decorated with pencil and paint brush, even Highlanders in kilts. Sometimes I had a war, when I opened up on them with my pea-cannon, and the side left with most troops upright were the victors, and I coloured another part of the map red for a British victory, green, mauve or purple for an imaginary foe.

Compared with this as a geography lesson stamp collecting was a bore and I never touched them. But the old man frowned on my exploits: "Ye'll get plenty o' that when the time comes!" says he.

All this activity made me late for school. I sat up till after midnight preparing my shows; painting my posters, writing my magazine serials, sketching my cartoons. I had a camera-eye for detail on my silhouettes. I could give my patrons a girl's face in

3

close-up even to the eyelashes. A budding Mack Sennett I was when it came to spring-board diving. While my old man snored in the box-bed I was immersed in my late night studies. Sometimes on Fridays I read all night and went to bed when he rose.

What could the dominie teach me anyway? Geometry maybe? Algebra? Mathematics? A dreary lot, subjects probably that I would never have need for, not even as mental exercise 'cause I had plenty of that.

The dominie bored me and I disliked the brute. I had far more important things to learn than he could teach me. I was mad about Haley's Comet for instance and he never even mentioned the Solar System. And anyway when he asked the class a question I had my hand up first. And I could sketch a rough map of the world without a copy. I had read most of the books in the J. & P. Coates' library. The dominie even gave me a prize for general knowledge, second for gardening—gardening, heavens!

But nothing short of an earthquake or a tidal wave could get me up in the morning. I had to run all of three miles to school on a 'jammy piece,' through wet fields and over the moor, my books in a bundle under my arm, sometimes my slate when home to be scrubbed, never a moment to spare.

The only morning I got up early was to watch a total eclipse of the sun. I was up at six with my father to get it on show for my newsreel—a device I used that William Friese-Green would have shook my hand for.

I might have been a Walt Disney, a Beaverbrook, a Sam Goldwyn, a Bernard Shaw—but the old man had never heard of these men. They were only shadows, he said; they had no substance, they existed only on paper—never make a living that way lad!

The only people the old man knew were those that slaved their guts out for the neighbouring farmers. He could see these men, he could talk to them, he didn't have to go boring his head into books to find out what they had to say. He lived in a narrow world the old man and he couldn't read a book anyway, nor even write his name, or count his pay, not without mother looking over his shoulder to see that it was right.

4

LANG BREEKS!

Somebody said to the old man that that loon o' his could be on the stage yet. "Him on the stage!" said the old man, "none o' that for him; I had tae work afore his day and he'll hae tae dee the same. Na, na, he's nae gaun tae loaf aboot idle when he leaves the skweel!"

I don't blame the old man really but that was his philosophy. And when I started sending my stories to an editor and they came right back he really had me licked.

"Niver mak' money that wye ma loon, nae wi' a pincil ahin yer lug—wark is the only sure wye tae mak' a livin'; ye'll jist hae tae work like the rest o' us."

Maybe I could make my own way in the world. But what could I do without money, without influence, in my old man's trousers? And for once he had the old woman on his side. She didn't understand me either but I couldn't leave her, not without her blessing anyway.

Nobody understood me, or cared—and why should they? I was such an eccentric oddity, neurotic almost.

But there was still Auntie Sally and the school picnic. And there was this job with Auld Weelum Mackenzie of Fernieden. So I gets up on my toes and looks straight down my blower at the old man, real stern like, to make him look like a twirp, and I tells him flat I'm just not going to work on the farms. It was cheek I know, but a fellow has to put his foot down, even if he tramples his own toes in the process.

THE LOON'S FIRST FEE!

SO it was all settled. "Sieven powin," mither had said before we left the hoose, "nae a penny less! The loon's fourteen and he's worth that tae ony fairmer; aye, and mair, come tae that!" So I went with my father down through the fields to see old Weelum Mackenzie of Fernieden, the three-horse farm among the trees at the foot of the Berryhill. Somebody had told my old man that Weelum was looking for an orra loon tae sort the nowt and work the odd mare, old Bloom.

It was a fine June evening as we strode through the lush pasture, thrashing the white petals from the wet daisies, moistened with dew, so that they stuck to our black tackety boots like confetti at a wedding. We went down through the nowt, newly out from the byres, plucking at the fresh spring grass with their hard tongues, the sunhaze on their backs, too busy and content to bother us. The startled larks sprang up from their nests and sang above our heads, perhaps to distract us from their eggs and young. Peewits wheebled from the newly sprung cornfields, frightened at our approach, while the oyster-catchers were gossipping and running hither and thither on the greening turnip drills.

I was a bit flustered at the prospect of starting work on my own. I wasn't too keen and I had tried various ways to get out of it; away from the grun, the dubs and the sharn and the stink. Yet here I was on my way to get a chain round my neck like a stirk in a stall and earn my penny fee.

Old Weelum was in the farm close, throwing corn to the hens from a pail around the barn door. He saw us at the gate and laid down his pail and came to meet us.

"Aye aye Charlie," addressing my father, "that's a fine nicht."

"Aye, it is man," replied my old man, "this'll fairly bring on the neeps tae the hyow."

"Aye, juist the thing man."

Old Weelum then looked me up and down and stroked his stubbly chin, crinkling his blue eyes in a friendly smile. Not that

THE LOON'S FIRST FEE!

I was a stranger to old Weelum, for I ran through his parks every day to the school, sometimes calling in by for young Weelum to keep me company, though mostly it was an excuse to save me going round by the road.

"Ye've brocht the laddie wi' ye Charlie, I see."

"Oh aye, we heard ye wis needin' a loon tae sort the nowt and work the orra beast and thocht he micht suit ye."

"Juist that Charlie, juist that man." And Weelum pushed his cloth cap to the back of his grey head. "Weel I hinna fee-ed onybody yet. I was juist waitin' tae see gin I could get a loon leavin' the skweel at the simmer holidays. The last lad we had was gettin' owre big and needin' mair wages than I could affoord tae pey. That's juist the wye o't ye see: efter ye learn 'em tae work they juist up tail and aff tae somebody else for mair siller. That's juist the wye o't man."

Now I happened to know that the last loon hadn't been 'socht tae bide' because he had taken old Weelum's pocket-book from his jacket in the turnip shed, where Weelum had left it when he came home from the mart. In fact he was going to hash some neeps for the nowt and help the loon in the byre when his wife called him in for his tea. When his back was turned the loon put his hand in his maister's pooch and took the wallet. It contained £70 that Weelum had gotten for twa-three stirks at the market, paid in cash, and the loon thocht he had stumbled on a gold mine. Weelum got the bobby but it took them three days before they could get the loon to admit he took the money, and when finally cornered he handed it back. But it was a lesson for old Weelum, who had always trusted everybody, and after that he got a cheque book from his banker. I also knew that the last loon had been careless with Bloom when she bolted with a cart and smashed it, and it cost Weelum more than the loon's fee to repair the cart. Maybe the loon couldn't help it but I would bear it in mind if I had to work old Bloom. But Weelum never spoke ill of anybody and we heard nothing of all this from him.

My old man still had his hands in his trouser pockets. "Fit wages wid ye be offerin'?" he asked, looking bashful like at old Weelum.

7

"Lat's hear ye Charlie. Fat dae ye think yersel' ? "

"Fit aboot sievin powin Weelum?" And Weelum pursed his lower lip over his moustache, trying to make up his mind.

"Ye're juist stiff aneuch Charlie: ye see there's a month gaen by the term or the laddie leaves the skweel. That means sievin powin for the five months till Martinmass, and that's mair than I was coontin' on. Mind he winna hae a sair job and he'll be weel treatit in the hoose. We a' feed thegither in the kitchie and he'll get what's agyaun amang the rest o's."

"Aye aye, I ken that Weelum. I wasna thinkin' aboot that. But mind he's nae a greenhorn; he's been a lot wi' me in the byre up by, and he kens aboot the beasts."

Weelum rolled a pebble with his toe, thinking aboot the loon's experience 'up by,' as Charlie had put it, amang the nowt beasts.

"Fat wad ye say tae sax powin ten Charlie? Ten shillin's less than ye socht—and mind he's comin' tae a gweed hame: a cup o' tae afore bed-time, sleepin' in the hoose; man we dinna even rise in the mornin' wi' ither folk . . ."

"Weel it's like this Weelum: the gweed-wife said I wasna tae lat the loon awa' for less than sievin powin, that's the wye I'm sae thrawn!"

"Weel weel, but ye'll juist hae tae explain the thing tae her Charlie, maybe she never thocht on the five month instead o' sax the laddie wad hae tae work. There's only ten shillin's atween us and I think I'm bein' fair aneuch. I have tae gie my foreman thirty powin for the sax month, and he can ploo or dae onything; cut corn, thrash, big rucks or fill the barn. Losh man, we only get fifteen bob for a quarter o' corn, sievin and saxpence the bag, it hardly peys tae ploo nooadays."

At this moment the collie dog came out of the kitchen and began whacking my legs with his friendly tail. I bent down to fondle his silken head for Roy and I had met before in quite unusual circumstances. Weelum's face was a map of spidery wrinkles, smiling as he watched us, loon and dog. What he didn't know was that until lately I was terrified of dogs, even of Roy here, and that not so long ago, when I tried to saw down a tree for mither's fire in the wood above Fernieden, Weelum's collie came and watched me with his teeth bared. I was half through

8

the small tree and loth to leave it and yet terrified of the dog. I tried to shoo him away but he just stood there and snarled, while I thought of some way of getting rid of him. Then I had a brain wave, so I ran hame to mither and asked where was the bone that we had in the broth for Sunday? She said it was in the midden, and what would you be wantin' with a dead bone anyway? I said never you mind, trying to hide my cowardice, then ran to the midden for the bone and carried it to the wood on the Berryhill. I had hoped that Roy would be gone by the time I got back. But no, for there he sat, still watching the tree, bewitching it almost, you would have thought, his head to one side, my saw sticking in the rut. Perhaps the dog had more wit than I thought and knew I would be back. Anyway I tossed him the bone and he ran away with it quite contentedly, while I felled my tree and got it into lengths for carrying, for I was more afraid of that dog than I was of the gamekeeper, gun and all.

But now Roy and I were friends and we both watched while the two men bargained for my services.

"A' richt Weelum, we'll juist tak' it: sax powin ten as ye said; and as the loon disna need an insurance card till he's sixteen that'll save ye anither powin. And fa kens he could be somewye else or that time. But we winna fecht aboot ten shillin's gin ye treat the laddie weel."

"Nae fear o' that Charlie, nae fear o' that. We'll get on juist grand. Won't we loon?" And he crumpled my battered cap on my head with his work grained hand.

When we returned home mither was darning a sock on the tattie-chapper, though she sometimes used a ladle, the wooden chapper inside the sock to stretch it, the wool in her lap, her fingers busy with the needle.

My old man hung his sweaty cap on a rusty nail at the back of the inner door and sat down beside her at the fireside. "We couldna get sievin powin woman," he said, "ye forgot the laddie has still a month at the skweel efter the term, and aul Weelum Mackenzie wadna pay for his schoolin'."

"So I did," said mither, biting through the woollen thread with her teeth, "I forgot aboot that. A' the same the hungry brute could of gaen the loon the sieven powin. It'll hardly keep claes on his back onywye. He needs a decent suit for a start, and that'll tak' aboot fower powin; forbyes underclaes, socks and sheen, and he'll need a waterproof for comin' hame on a rainy nicht. You men folk dinna ken whaur the money goes and as little ye care. Hagglin' aboot ten shillin's. If I'd kent that I wad a fee-ed the loon masell!"

And so it was agreed, and in four weeks' time, when the school picnic was over, and I had bombarded the last Aunt Sally of my schooldays, and broken a few more clay pipes in her mouth, and the dominie had pinched my cheeks for the last time—on the day after my fourteenth birthday I would begin work as a fee-ed loon with old Weelum Mackenzie of Fernieden, picking the sprouts from the tatties at an earth-pit round the back of the steading. Looking back I must have been awfully anxious to start, because it was a Saturday (a whole day of course) thinking to have a break on Sunday before tackling a full week.

ROWENA TAKES A HOLIDAY

THERE was no kitchiedeem at Whunden. Auld Hosey Rankin said he couldna afford sic luxury. And no wonder when you thought of the bills he had to pay yon Dr. Dalzell who called once a fortnight in his Rolls Royce to examine his wife. Bathia Rankin was a cripple, maybe for life you might say since she fell down the loft stair with a pail of hen feed some years back, stone steps with an iron railing at the gable of the barn. Folk said she could have broken her neck or her back, never mind a broken thigh, which was bad enough for Bathia Rankin, cut down in the flower of life, in the midst of her child-bearing, still with a spark of life in her, and good for a man to look upon. Now she hobbled about on a stick and yon Doctor Dalzell said her hip couldn't be mended; but maybe he just didn't want to lose a good patient, because the guinea a time he charged for his visits helped to pay for those expensive cigars that he smoked. Bathia said that he never looked at the blue patch on her thigh, or even touched it, just stared at her white legs when the blankets were down, as if the sight of them did him a power of good.

And there was old Rowena, Hosey's spinster sister, who had lived most of her life with the family, ever since she had been jilted by yon scoundrel who had married her sister, though maybe Rowena was better off without him from what you had heard from folks out bye. But bein' denied bairns o' her ain Rowena had lavished affection on the geets at Whunden, young Hosey yonder and his two small sisters, Tess and Lena, spoiling them till they were speaking back to their parents long before their time.

So, as a fee-ed loon at Whunden one of the first jobs you got was scrubbing the flagstone floor in the kitchen, which was hardly what you was fee-ed for, but seein' there was no kitchiedeem, and with Chae Cantlay that was foreman milking the kye, and old Hosey feeding the hens and the swine, it seemed that the loon was the only body that could be spared for it, besides picking the sprouts off the tatties, and it was better than that.

11

You might have said that with Rowena about the place there was no need for a servant quine, and maybe that was so when Rowena was younger; but now she was too old and too fat for floor scrubbing. So, if the sky was overcast, or the foghorn moaning on the coast like a cow at the calving, neither a day for hay or harvest field, Rowena would rig you out with a sack or harn apron, a bar of Sunlight Soap, a pail of warm water and a scrubber, and you'd get down on your knees at the fireplace and scrub your way out at the back kitchen door.

And if it was a van day you had to hide under the kitchen table until the baker or the grocer or the butcher had gone. "Juist in case he comes in by," Rowena would say, "we dinna want a' the countraside tae ken we have the loon washin' oot the kitchie fleer!"

And you'd get a big jammy piece and a bowl of creamy milk for this obligement, and maybe a slab or two of Rowena's home-made toffee.

"And noo laddie, if you'd juist run tae the stack for a basket o' peats for the kitchie fire; my auld legs are that wobbly they'll hardly carry me . . . and if you'll jist ca' the deuks in frae the dam for fear they lay awa' in the mornin'. Losh aye. God bless ye laddie, ye're a great help in the hoose."

And so Rowena buttered you up no end, until old Hosey stuck his rosy face into the kitchen and said the sky had cleared: "God aye," says he, "there's a clear bore in the wast, abeen the swines' hoose; I think we'll hae a go at the hey!"

Rowena's room was fitted with a coal burning grate, so that peat was of little use to her, except when she ran out of coal, and then she would waddle over to the stack at the gable of the steading and fill her lap with black stickly peats, picking the best and avoiding all the big foggie divots that would burn better in the big kitchie grate under the swey. Rowena would then come panting back to the kitchen door, one chilblained hand holding the corners of her bulging apron, the other clutching the door jamb, while she heaved her huge bulk up the steps to the passage, ben the lobby to her ain room, warm and cosy, where she slept with the twa quines, Tess and Lena.

ROWENA TAKES A HOLIDAY

Rowena did most of the cooking over the peat fire in the kitchen, where her pots hung from the crooks on the swey, producing juicy clootie-dumplings and sago pudding that was sheer delight for a hungry loon, and rolly-polly made with a clart of rhubarb jam. And she could bake oat breid on her girdle with the best of them, besides scones and bannocks, and if she got you to yark at the long-handled churn for a while she'd make butter, though you couldna thole the buttermilk she offered you to drink in reward for your labour. And sometimes at night she'd pour a suppie rennet in the warm milk when Chae brought it in from the byre and next day you'd get yerned milk for dessert, which was a fair delight with a sprinkling of sugar, and whiles she'd let the milk curdle and make a hangman cheese, hanging it outside on a nail in the wall for nearly a week or it dried and hardened, though in hot weather she had to herd it against the blue-bottle flies that were attracted to the smell of it, and had a fancy to hatching their maggots through the gauze cloth.

The long bare table was scrubbed till the grain stuck out on the wood. It stood in front of the kitchen window and Rowena sat at the end nearest the door. It was furthest from the fire but in daylight it enabled Rowena to keep an eye on the farm road while she ladled out the broth or tattie-soup or handed round the plates of stovies. Spark the collie lay under the table, whacking your toes with his bushy tail, and between his barks and Rowena's quick eye you were soon aware of strangers in the farm close. Between them they could detect Doctor Dalzell's shining Rolls nearly a mile away, and Rowena would warn Bathia of his approach, and Bathia would hirple along the lobby and shed her clothes before he arrived, Rowena holding him up with some tittle-tattle at the door.

"He's a torment of a mannie that," Rowena would say, when he had gone ben the hoose, "ye never ken when he's comin', and for all the good he does he could stay away. But he never forgets tae send in his account though, na faith ye!" And she would spoon out the semolina pudding with great gusto, licking the spoon between each plateful, while the plates were passed from hand to hand along the table, right up to Chae Cantlay at the end nearest the fireplace, the head of the table, him being foreman, where he sat under a coloured painting of Burns at the plough.

Ben the hoose Bathia had hardly got her breath back when the doctor had her by the pulse. "You've been out of bed again," he snapped, squinting at his wrist watch; "you'll never get better at this rate, you'll have to rest that leg." He whipped down the blankets and looked at her legs, but never fingered the blue patch on her thigh. "It's here that it's sore!" Bathia ventured, caressing her swollen hip with her long fingers. "I know where it's sore woman; but what's the good of that when you wont do what you're told? Maybe we could get a clasp in there if you gave it half a chance to get the swelling down and get rid of the inflamation." Bathia winced under his withering gaze and pulled up the bedclothes. "But I don't want a clasp," she whimpered, "and I don't want to go to hospital; maybe it will heal with time." "Very well woman, have it your own way, but it will take an eternity and you haven't that time to spare."

"You mean I could die, doctor?"

"No no, you wont die woman; but unless you allow us to operate on that hip of yours you could be a cripple for the rest of your life!" And with that final warning Doctor Dalzell picked up his bag and snapped out of the room.

Rowena was waiting for him at the kitchen door, beaming like a full moon over the harvest stooks; but before she could say anything Doctor Dalzell cut her short with a curt "Good day!" put on his hat and departed, sweeping out of the muddy farm close in his great shining car.

"Nasty brute," said Rowena, seating herself again at the table.

The doctor wasn't more than a mile away when Bathia was back in the kitchen, her long black hair hanging down her back like a school-girl, and leaning on her stick. "What did he say the day?" Rowena asked. "Oh just the usual," Bathia sighed, "I've got to stay in bed or it heals."

"Ach," Rowena scorned, "Ye'll be there for a lifetime for all he knows or cares. You should hae been in hospital lang ago!"

ROWENA TAKES A HOLIDAY

"But ye ken I dinna want tae go tae hospital. He was speakin' aboot a clasp for my hip the day; but I dinna want that . . . I'll manage fine." Bathia sounded sure of herself, but the mist of tears in her soft brown eyes betrayed her.

Rowena handed her a plate of soup. "But if it's for your own good woman, you should be thankful for that. Maybe it's your own fault that the doctor mannie says that your hip won't heal unless you rest it."

Bathia couldn't sit down to her meals, so she sipped the hot soup standing in the middle of the floor, her staff hung on the back of a chair.

When Bathia had visitors she couldn't be bothered with the palaver of feeding them ben the hoose, mainly to save Rowena from extra work. So everyone was fed in the kitchen, be he factor or packman, and no matter what time of day you went into the old kitchie at Whunden the red enamelled tea-pot was never far from the peat ash, warm and full of welcome.

And when Bathia acted as hostess she leaned with her hand on the back of your chair, craning her neck over your shoulders and pressing her breasts into your back, spreading the trenchers of bread and cheese, scones and pancakes before her guests with her free hand, telling them to "Help themselves," while all the time her warm breath fanned the back of your neck and her long loose hair tickled your temples.

After dinner you went out with Chae to the stable while Bathia and Rowena had their nap before washing up. Bathia lay down on her leather-covered couch by the wall while Rowena sagged into her heavy armchair by the fireside. The bairns (when they weren't at school) went romping round the steading, playing 'hoosies' or 'beddies,' 'ring-a-ring-a-rosie,' 'hide-and-seek' or 'tackie roon the rucks.' But Chae barred the door to keep them out of the stable, for the quines liked to come and have a tease at you.

On Fridays everybody sat a whilie langer in the kitchie to get a bit squint at the **Broch Herald**. Chae had it first, him being foreman, for there might be a dance somewhere for him and his lass. Then you'd get a keek at it to see what was on at the Picture

15

House, or at French and Shand's "Empire" on the High Street. Bathia always read the Marriage, Birth and Death columns, and as she couldn't get peace to sit she read them standing in the middle of the floor. Old Hosey being only the farmer got a peep at the bit paperie last of all, maybe to see if anyone had a calf to sell or wanted to buy a few loads of neeps or hay depending on what he had to spare, and then he would retire to his cubby-hole at the top of the stairs. Here he slept at night with his young son, leaving the big bed downstairs to his wife, because nowadays she said she couldn't be doing with anyone in the bed with her since she injured her thigh. She had to have room to spread her legs she said, because of the pain.

Now there was no chaumer at the Whunden, so you slept in the fairmhoose, in an upstairs bedroom with a storm window that looked on to the garden, just along the passage from Hosey's cubby-hole. At an antrin time in the night you could hear Hosey creaking down the stairs to his wife, pretending to go to the earth-closet at the foot of the garden, and giving the front door a bit kick with his big toe to convince you; but by the time he was away you knew fine he was up to something, and if you could stay awake long enough you could hear him come creaking back up the stairs again.

But all this had stopped and there seemed to be a quietness between Hosey and his ailing wife. She was much younger than Hosey and folk said she had married him for his siller, and the thocht of being a farmer's wife, pretending to be in the family way to get him, stuffing her briest with a pillow-slip, and that it served her right getting a broken hip joint for getting up to such a trick. Her father had been the blacksmith out by in Haughfield yonder, and Bathia had plenty of lads before she met old Hosey at a "Meal-and-Ale" down at the Miller's place at Damneuk. And Hosey was glad to have the young limmer, bairn and all, had it materialised, for she was a lithesome change to his fat old sister at the Whunden. Some folk said it would be the death of him, but blind though he was in love old Hosey wasn't long in replacing the pillow-slip with something more substantial, and might have done even better had the randie not fallen down the loft stair,

something he found it harder to forgive than the pillow-slip affair
—that had only been the bait, but now he had swallowed the
hook as well he began to understand the meaning of misfortune.

And you would have thought for a time that there would be
fireworks between the old dame and the young wife at the Whunden, but in this you were disappointed, for they took to each other
like a cow with a mare's foal, never a natter between them; the
old woman at her wash-tub and Bathia dawdling a bairn on her
knee by the peat fire, a young Hosey Rankin to the very toe-nails,
and Rowena was glad of it that they wouldn't die childless after
all, and that there would be an heir to the Whunden.

After you had groomed a while at your roan mare, and Chae
had taken the body brush to Rose and Sally, to put a bit shine
on their hair, the pair of you lay down among the straw in the
spare stall, listening to the chap of an iron hoof on the cobblestones, or the snort of a mare over her water pail, or maybe you
was just dreaming that you had fallen in love and was likely to
have a wet dream when you hears old Hosey rattling the sneck
of the door at yoking time—"Come and get a drap tae lads afore
we start."

Not that old Hosey ever started anything, for he dodged around
real canny. But he was a good old soul compared with some
you'd known, and never fussy about yoking on the dot, and always
ready with a bowl of hot tea and a buttered scone when you came
out of the neep park to sort the nowt, your feet cold and numb
and your hands stinging with frost. There weren't many places
where a loon got that sort of treatment, so you were better not to
abuse it. "Ye're nae use tae me wi' a teem belly laddie," Hosey
would say, and you'd bite into the scone like you hadn't seen food
for a fortnight.

Now like all other human creatures Rowena had her dull days:
days when she sat listlessly in her chair, her feet and ankles
encased in high-laced boots and crossed in front of her on a
padded stool; her lower lip sagging like the stoup of a cream jug,
the tired old eyes peering over her spectacles, which had slid down
her nose, and her grey hair, uncombed and uncared for, hanging
about her face like an old rug thrown upon a dyke.

17

When in this mood even the foreman had to speak twice to Rowena before she took any notice, and that was saying something because Chae Cantlay was a great favourite with Rowena, like she was his mother almost, and knew all about the quine he went about with, or when he wanted a sark ironed, and as Chae didn't have a mother and had been at the Whunden since he was a loon you began to wonder if old Rowena was a spinster after all.

"I wasna listenin' Chae," or "I didna hear ye Chae," Rowena would mumble, startled out of her reverie, moving her thick cracked lips and her dry tongue. But she made no attempt to start a conversation and fell back into her chair while you drank your tea in silence.

A stranger body might have thought that Rowena was in a sulk, or that someone had offended her, but Chae knew the old spinster better than most and he blamed the wag who had jilted her for her sister those long long years ago. Surely she had been a sonsie lass in her day and she earned your secret sympathy. You couldn't say that she was bonnie, just sic like as your own granny, and yet old grandaw had married her.

But there were other days when Rowena was quite the opposite of despondent—days when she went about her tasks almost non-stop, her round jovial face bright and flushed with a resurgence of richer blood, her beady old eyes gleaming with mirth and her heavy mouth bursting with suppressed laughter. Even the bairns could sense her change of humour, and they would hang about her skirts hopefully, expecting peppermints or pandrops to be handed out forthwith, and this supplied she would 'hish' them off with a flap of her apron and a shake of her fist that sent them running for the door.

When Rowena slumped down in her chair at last a happy sigh escaped her, sometimes a grunt, as if she were an old sow who felt she had done her bit and had sunk down in her sty in restful contentment.

But Rowena was in the doldrums on the day that Bathia said to her: "You should tak' a holiday; I'll manage fine!" And come to think of it you had never seen either of these two women beyond the farm close, not even to the end of the cart road, because the vans brought all that they wanted and they did their shopping at the door. Old Hosey never had a motor car, or even a horse gig, and when he went to the marts to see his nowt sold he took the bus that went past the end of the road on market days.

So it was agreed that Rowena should have a holiday, when she would go and spend a fortnight with a married sister in the Broadsea, though not the one who had stolen her lad. Willie French sent a spanking horse and black cab out from the Broch to take her away, and everybody gathered round to see her off, Bathia and the bairns and old Hosey, while you watched with Chae from the stable door.

Rowena was dressed in her finest black and shining with sequins, a veiled hat to match and smelling strongly of mothballs. The driver assisted her into the cab, handed in her luggage and shut the door, like he was John Brown and she was Queen Victoria leaving Balmoral. John Brown climbed up to the dicky-board in front, took the leather reins in one hand and cracked his long whip with the other, and they were off, Rowena waving her silver-mounted umbrella handle from the carriage window, and Spark the collie barking at the highly polished wheels as they flashed silently out of the farmyard.

During the fortnight that Rowena was away you had to do other things besides floor scrubbing. For one thing you had to get down on your knees to whitewash the fireplace. Rowena usually whitewashed the arch twice a week and the low binks at the sides. The ironwork got rather more attention, especially if visitors were expected, when Rowena would get out her black-leading brushes and polish the lid of the ash-pit, the black swye that swung out on hinges above it, like a gate, and the huge black metal kettle that hung from the crook.

Last thing at night you had to 'rest' the peat fire, gathering all the embers together with the tongs and covering them with a shovel of ash from under the brander; and when you got up in the morning the fire was still a red glow, all you had to do was add more peat and blow the bellows, and you soon had the water boiling for the brose.

19

STRAW INTO GOLD

It was a slack period in the summer when you wasn't doing much in particular, and you had promised to help with the housekeeping until Rowena's return. Bathia would manage the cooking on her stick they said so you had to do most of the other chores. Up till then you had been scything yellow flowered tanzies and purple-headed thistles in the grass parks and old Hosey said he could spare you for a while. It was a job that wearied your legs and gave you nothing to think about and you almost welcomed the change, though it made you feel an awful Cissy working in the fairm hoose.

Bathia took to her bed occasionally, maybe a bit tired from hobbling about on her stick. Chae and old Hosey were in the fields most of the day, hacking with their hoes at the weeds in the turnip drills, and the bairns were at school, leaving you alone with Bathia in the old farm house, washing dishes and peeling potatoes.

Chae and Hosey had just gone to work and you was drying the dinner plates in the scullery when Bathia called to you from her downstairs bedroom, so you dried your hands on the towel and ran along the passage to see what she wanted.

Bein' a loon you was a bit shy at going into the room where your mistress slept, but she told you not to be fear't, that she was cold and wanted more fire put on. The room smelled strongly of scent and Bathia was in bed brushing her hair, her eyes strangely bright in her flushed face. Hosey had lit her fire in the morning but it had burned low. So you had a bit poke at the fire and put on a shovel of coal from the brass scuttle in the corner, besides some broken peat that was lying on the kerb. The lushness of the room made you feel a bit uneasy, you being a cottar bairn and little accustomed to anything more than the kitchen range: the thick red curtains on the window that looked into the farm close, the panelled wooden shutters fastened back to the walls, the wallpaper richly embossed and hung with coloured paintings, with expensive looking ornaments on the furniture.

But Bathia was watching you, where she lay on the four-poster bed, the hair-brush still in her hand, the tortoise-shell handle resting on the tasselled quilt. Her hair was down full length and hung about her shoulders in black mercurial strands, long enough to wrap around your neck, and Tess and Lena sometimes plaited it in two long ropes down her back, each standing on a kitchen chair while their mother leaned patiently with both hands on another. Lying there without her stick, her crippled body covered with blankets, you realised for the first excited moment in your young life that you were looking at a really beautiful woman; enough to make you blush and feel shy, especially so when she was your mistress. You was anxious to get back to your dish washing, but just as you meant to go she said she was thirsty and wanted a drink of water, while she reached over and laid the hair-brush on the small dressing-table at her bedside. So you brought the glass of water from the tap in the scullery and placed it in her hand. She took a small sip, hardly touching it, while her soft brown eyes wandered all over your face, pleading, beseeching, you knew not what, until she laid the tumbler on the dressing table. Then she asked if you would like to see her sore leg, but giving you little time to make up your mind about it she whipped down the blankets. You was fair astonished but couldn't help lavishing your eyes on her long white beautiful leg, her broad strong hip with the tiny blue veins running under the creamy softness of her skin, the first time you had ever seen such a sight. She took your nervous hand and placed it on her thigh, hot and soft and smooth and so exciting you didn't know where to look. She drew your hand across the bruise on her hip joint, which was rough and inflamed and slightly swollen. You was mesmerised and wanted to look but you was so afraid and bashful. Now she was pulling up her nightgown and you struggled to get your hand out of her grasp. Both her legs were now visible and she still held on to your wrist. You had no idea she was so strong, drawing your hand nearer her naked midriff, shameless in her strength of desire. Her head was rising from the pillow, pulling herself up with your wrist, until she had your knees against the bed, her free hand about your neck, her hot lips seeking yours, her eyes clear and beautiful. You couldn't have held out much longer, and would have fallen across her half-naked body, but suddenly she let you go and fell back on the pillow, pulling down her nightdress. She

21

was breathing heavily, excitedly, and you saw the pulse beating madly in her neck. Her eyes had changed and were clouding with anxiety, staring at the door, at Doctor Dalzell standing there with hat in one hand and brown leather bag in the other. "Well well," he challenged, "what have we here—another doctor?" But he wasn't joking. His face was white and stern.

With Rowena on holiday and the collie in the fields the silent Rolls had slipped unnoticed into the farm close. Bathia was blushing all over and pulled up the blankets over her thighs. "I was only showing the laddie my sore hip," she whimpered, "surely there was nae harm in that." But you didn't listen for more and ran past the doctor out of the room.

You never learned how Bathia got out of her embarrassment, or how much the doctor had seen, and being your mistress you didn't want to affront her further by asking awkward questions. She never mentioned the incident again and you worked on together in the kitchen as though nothing had happened, though sometimes she singed the sago pudding, perhaps at the thought of it.

In the second week of Rowena's absence Lena took sick in the night, ben in Rowena's room, across the passage from their mother at the foot of the stairs. Bathia was up in her nightdress and whacking on the bannister with her staff. Would Hosey send the boy down to help her with Lena that was sick on the bed? So Hosey got up from his cubby-hole and roused you from your sleep in the bed beside Chae and sent you downstairs to Bathia, perhaps the opportunity she had been waiting for.

So you got a glass of water for Lena and cleaned up the vomit and sat a while with the girls on the bed, Bathia watching you from the door, her eyes bright as beacons. How could you escape? Caught between two young girls of seven and eight and a sex-crazed mother. Yet you felt that if she touched you you would scream. After all you was only a loon and no match for Bathia. But you wouldn't betray her, a good kindly woman who treated you well in every way, except in showing her weakness, and you were the guardian of that. But temptation and fear had you by the throat and you could hardly wait until the girls fell asleep again.

The Grandfather clock in the hall struck three o'clock; three musical chimes that were so much a part of the night that it scarcely disturbed the silence. Tess never stirred but Lena quivered in the twylight of slumber while you still sat quietly on the bed. Your breathing came faster and your throat dried up while you pondered what to do. Bathia still stood by the door, her face soft and radiant in the warm glow of the paraffin lamp, her hair clustered to the breasts of her pale-blue nightdress, staff in hand, guarding against your escape. It would be so easy to put your hand on her mouth, take the staff away from her and put her back to bed; yet there was a magnetism of excitement which drew you towards her, breaking down your resistance, your will to escape; something mystifying for which you could hardly wait, and even as you sat there on the bed you felt it would be a pity if Bathia ignored you, now that she had teased you up with an inward fire.

A cock crowed outside in the darkness, quite near at hand but it seemed far away, lost on the wind that sighed and moaned among the trees in the garden. Lena turned over on her other side and you screwed the lamp nearly to darkness. You was losing patience with the girl and Bathia had turned to a statue in the shadows. But at last Lena was in dreamland and you slid from the bed in your stockinged feet, blew out the lamp and tip-toed towards the door.

Bathia was waiting for you, barring your escape; afraid of what you would do—perhaps give her away; alarm the household, yet determined to risk it.

In a moment she had you in her arms, her hot blistering kisses raining on your lips; her writhing body warm against yours, her rich beautiful hair all over your face, and the sweet smell of her breath in your nostrils. You could hardly speak or cry out even if you had wanted to, so much was her lips upon your own. Your hands were everywhere, but mostly trying to push her away, though all the time you wanted to embrace her. But now you had no wish to escape and you could feel the warm shape of her in the darkness; a sweet blindness that dug your fingers into her warm flesh, thrusting your body against hers. Now she had you in her power,

burning with a passion that was rising within you. In a moment
you would be hers, far stronger than she imagined; a man on the
instant that would surge upon her in uncontrollable lust . . .

But the fall of Bathia's stick on the floor sobered you in a
moment. It fell with a crack and a clatter that was like a tree
breaking in the wind; a loud snap that wakened Lena and stirred
the household. Bathia let go of you at the sound and old Hosey's
door creaked open at the head of the stairs.

"Oh aye, Lena is a' richt noo. We'll be back tae bed in a meenit
or twa. Nae need for ye tae come doon. We'll manage fine!"
Bathia spoke calmly, deliberately, restraining her words in her
heavy breathing and a pounding heart.

Lena whimpered a little but soon fell asleep again. You picked
up Bathia's stick and placed it in her hand. Once again she kissed
you: gently this time, softly; like a kiss of goodbye, touching your
lips with a warmth and sweetness that blotted out your boyhood.
Then she hirpled towards her door, a crippling vision in the darkness, while you tip-toed up the stairs.

Soon you was back in bed again with Chae, careful not to waken
him, though now you was cold and glad of his warmth. But you
never slept a wink till morning, dreaming about Bathia. Day by
day she was becoming more beautiful for you, more desirable;
but she was a woman and you was only a loon.

But at last Rowena was back from the toon and you was almost
disappointed at the sight of her. Bathia was much more exciting;
younger by far and much more beautiful, and the fact that she
was a cripple never bothered you, or that she was your master's
wife. In such a world as yours anything could happen; even
miracles, and maybe you could learn to be a doctor and cure
her . . .

How had you got on in her absence? Rowena had asked,
handing you a small present, a pipe or something. Oh just grand
you said, and nothing gave you any trouble at all.

Soon you was back in the parks with Chae, a drab scene compared with Bathia's charms; her sweet soothing kisses and her
lithe body that was smooth and warm against your own. But now
it was hairst and Chae in the swing of the scythe, slashing the ripe

corn into a swath, while you gathered and bound it into sheaves And Chae cursed you for falling behind, your thoughts far away —obsessed with an impossible dream. Now you was sulky and moody and disliked Rowena. You hated her for coming back and spoiling the most beautiful thing in your life. Nothing would ever be the same any more; discontent and desire wracking your wild thoughts. You had tasted of Eve's apple and wanted another bite. Now you knew what all that stite was about in the bible. Bathia's lips had been the apple, your apple; her arm the serpent, and you wished she had stung you more.

Rowena still dished out the food at mealtimes, licking the spoon between each plateful, perhaps as good as a kiss for any of you, but a poor substitute for Bathia's warm breath. Rowena was a likeable old spinster to say the least of her; a Friar Tuck of a woman who coddled Chae and the bairns. But for you Bathia was Queen of Sheba; Queen of all your little world, where she had launched a thousand sighs. But the best that you could wish for now was that next summer Rowena would take another long holiday . . .

MOONLIGHT FLITTING

AS a married chiel it was never easy to get a cottar job on the Buchan fairms at the November or 'Martinmas' Term. It was never easy at any time to get decent wark but doubly so if you were looking for it in winter time. Married men always fee'd at the May or 'Whitsun' Term, once a year, but a single chiel could change his job at November if he wished. But as a single billie you had only your kist to move, whereas a married bloke had to shift all his bits of furniture, mostly on to horse carts fitted with harvest frames, wife and bairns and chaff beds, crockery and dishes, pots and pans and the baking girdle, cat or dog and the loons' rabbits, and maybe even a jar of tadpoles that the quines wouldn't leave on the window sill. Sometimes the cats took scare at flitting time and were nowhere to be found on the Term morning, so it was best to fasten them into a box the night before, just as you cooped the hens, for it always broke some bairn's heart to leave a pet cat behind. And you had to be careful to put the wife's pot flowers into the wash tubs on the back of the second cart, for if you placed them on the first cart the horse beast coming behind would maybe eat them down, especially if he had a fancy for gereniums, despite the bit between his teeth. Bicycles, prams and clothes props were another problem and the worst you'd seen was a pair of breeks on the back of the second cart and the man's braces trailing on the road. Of course you had been packing your stuff into boxes for weeks, and all that remained on the eve of the Term were a few cups and teaspoons, a jar of treacle, a half-loaf, milk and sugar and the tea-pot; even the beds had been dismantled and you had a 'shakie doon' on the fleer, lying on a chaff mattress and the curtains down from the windows, waiting for the cock crow and the early sound of horse carts on the Term morning.

Most cottars were on the road at the May Term, moving from place to place, seeking pastures new, maybe a bit more money or just a change of job; from driving a pair of horses to sorting nowt, or the other way round. Maybe you didn't like the neighbours or your growing bairns had too far to walk to school, or you just couldn't get on with the fairmer chiel and he had never asked you to bide on for another year and you just had to leave. But the smallest excuse was good enough reason to be on the road with your flitting, rain or shine, but if it was a fine day folk said the sun always shines on the righteous, or that the deil was kind to his ain, so you could make of it what you liked, depending on your views on religion. But heaven help you if it was a slashing day of rain and your chaff beds sodden and your bairns like drookit rats sitting on the carts among the wet furniture, or walking behind to keep them warm, an old jacket over their heads, and your poor wife with the smallest child in her oxter, the rain drops from her hair falling on its cheeks, chilled and blue with the cold. Folks that weren't moving would be watching you from the comfort of their cottage doors, and the wisest of them would say among themselves that maybe in changing your job you would get a change of a deevil but it would still be the same hell, a hell that got sadder as you grew older and less able to cope, for though you were rid of the bairns you still had a living to make and jobs were scarcer for an older body, now frail and sair from the long years of toil and wet and rheumatism.

But God bless you or Devil curse you, wet or dry, young or old, some folk accepted the May flitting in holiday spirit, even as an adventure; the fond memories of leaving an old home, some sweet some sad, depending how long you had lived there, and the excitement and thrill of entering a new one—all the labour of scrubbing out your old house and the bother of papering a new one. Of course your wife always wanted to leave her old hoose as clean and tidy as possible, brushing down the roofs and walls, even to placing newspapers on the floor for the bairns running out and in, and then you'd go to a new place and the paper all torn off the walls and not a flower or a berry bush left in the gairden, mostly done out of spite by a leaving tenant for some grudge against the farmer. But the worst you'd heard of was the farmer chiel who so disliked his cottar who was leaving that he fired a shotgun over the horses' heads and they bolted with the loaded carts and smashed all the lad's furniture. But for all its set-backs it was still fun to be a cottar; especially for the bairns, the only real holiday they ever knew, a change of scene and school and play-mates, despite the slippery stone they say that lies at every doorstep.

But by the time you came of age to be a cottar things were changing a bit for the better, and instead of sending horse carts to flit you farmers were paying for a motor lorry or a steam-wagon to move your furniture, with cover and ropes for wind and rain, and your wife and the bairns got a seat beside the driver while you could ride on the wagon, waving to the lads in the parks, though there weren't many at work on a Term day, except those that were staying on at their places; maybe the odd grieve with a turnip-seed barrow, or a horseman with a 'bone-davie,' scattering manure on the drills.

Ach but you were tired of the bothies and the chaumer life and thought you would like to set up home yourself. It was almost instinct that you had to become a cottar, just as your father had done, and the food that you got on some of the fairmtoons, or the want of it, was beginning to give you sore bellies, so that the only decent dinner you got was from your mither at the week-end (who could least afford it) when you went home on your bike to change your dirty sark. You were supposed to be working in a land of plenty: a land flowing with milk and honey, beef corn and tatties, producing the nation's essential diet, yet you were sometimes treated like the Prodigal Son at the swine's trough, eating husks and offal. Rather than thole it some lads joined the army at the feeing markets, where the brass buttoned recruiting sergeant was waiting to offer them the King's shilling, which some preferred to the arles, or bargaining money, offered by the farmers, and with a good chance of better conditions, so they rallied round the big drum and the pipe bands that were always at the fairs. Some of the best soldiers in our Highland Regiments were recruited at these slave markets, where the harshness of the fields and the strictness of farm life had bred them well for discipline; men who could endure in all weathers and march on empty stomachs and blistered feet as they had done behind the harrows—men who had seen the blood on nature's claw, and would bury a dead comrade as he would a beast of the field. Yet mony a weeping mither prigged sair with her sons not to join the army on market days: widows who remembered the fathers who had bled to death in the trenches of Flanders.

But you had no hankering for the kilt or the khaki, or the barracks for the chaumer, for at least on the grun your mind had the freedom of the birds of the sky or the wild creatures of the field, and regimentation or conformity was something that you remembered and hated from your schooldays. So maybe a bit wife that could cook a decent diet and having a hoose o' yer ain was the better answer to your problem. But you had never been a lad for the quines really; never went to dances or concerts where you could meet them, so you found it a bit difficult in finding a lass that would suit you. Oh you had been tempted once or twice and had met a quine or two at the meal-and-ale or Harvest Home festivities, but it never came to much and they jilted you or you deserted them and that was the end of it. So you took to the pictures, for you were a great admirer of the film stars, especially the quines among them, and you had their photographs plastered all over the walls of your chaumer and inside the lid of your kist, where other lads usually hung their ties or their harness ribbons, rosettes or martingales to decorate their horses. And when the mistress or the kitchiedeem came to make up the chaumer beds they were fair amazed at your gallery of glamour girls, maybe a bit envious that they couldn't compare with your taste for beauty, thinking that you was ill to please, and that you would find it hard to get a wife to compare with those for looks. But those were your dream girls and you were determined to have one just as bonny.

You lived in a world by yourself a bit with your dreams and books and film stars; never taking a dram with the other lads or having a bit hooch of a dance, a bit of a radical you was with a different view of everything from anybody else, though you never got yourself into trouble over it, just thinking deeply, poet like, though you didn't realise it at the time. So the other lads in the chaumer got used to your reading and your picture-going and left you to your own wiles and fair admired your pin-up quines. But sometimes for their amusement you stuck up a quine with not much on, for you were far ahead of your time on the fairms, where a bra or a bikini had never been seen or heard of in those days. But it riled the farmer's wife when she came to make the beds, and she ordered that those "painted, brazen hussies" should be taken down. But the chaumer billies wouldn't hear of it and she got used to the pin-ups eventually, though not without protest, and probably regarding you as a protogè of the devil for introducing them, until she discovered that you sometimes went to the kirk on Sundays, which was more than the other lads did, and then she forgave you completely, perhaps remembering that even Solomon and David had their sins and that you was no worse than them. You even joined as a member of the kirk to please her, drinking the blood of Christ and eating of his flesh at Communion time, cannibal like, until the elder came round collecting for the kirk funds, when you was that hard up you gave him only eightpence, which he said would never get you over the Jordan, though maybe he meant the Red Sea, so you told him to remember the Widow's Mite, and the other billies fair got a laugh at you and your kirk going.

But while you still kept looking for this quine of your dreams, and the other billies came and went at the Term times, and though the food got worse and worse, you stayed on for nearly two years at Slabsteen, maybe because you had an easy kind of job, when lo and behold at the May Term comes the lass you had been waiting for all these years, the new kitchiedeem. She was quiet and bashful for a time and wouldn't speak to any of the lads and you could see at once that she was no ordinary quine. Here at last was your film star in the flesh; your dream become a reality, so that everything you looked upon was radiant with her beauty, arousing the poet that was in you, if only you had the pluck to tell her so, without being snubbed.

Of course you had your rivals at this game, but as none of the other chiels could get the quine to speak to them they gave her up as 'a sulky bitch,' bonnie though she was with her head in the air. The Third Horseman was the first to get a word out of the quine, and a bit of a smile as well, which made her even more desirable, and had its funny side to it. It was 'Knotty-Tams' for supper, brose made from oatmeal and mixed with boiling milk instead of water. But they were pretty solid, so that when the Third Horseman turned his bowl upside-down the brose never fell out but stuck to the bowl like cement, whereupon he asked the quine if 'He was good looking?' The quine stared at him in surprise and asked what he meant, or who the 'He' was? So the lad uprighted his bowl on the table and remarked: "Oh the lad ye was thinkin' on when ye made this brose!" The quine blushed and told him she was not to blame; that the mistress herself had made the brose, and that he'd better ask her. But it was all he could get out of the quine and she would hardly speak to him again for his impudence.

Now Francie Gatt, that was Third, was your best pal in the chaumer and you wouldn't have minded a bit though the quine had taken him on. He was the only one who really understood you and your flair for books and sometimes stuck up for you when the others would take the size of you. He was the only one who could swim in the mill dam and could take music out of a stone almost: could play on anything from a saw blade to the bagpipes, with fiddle, dulcimer, jews' harp, melodion and mouthorgan for bye; had even taught you how to vaump on the mouthorgan, and he had spent a whole fortnight mastering David Copperfield, a feat you admired in him more than anything he could do with a pair of horse in the ploo. You had worked with this lad for a whole year on another fairm and had moved together with your kists to Slabsteen; and you knew fine that Francie had a quine o' his ain and didna want yer lass, but ye thocht maybe that ye could confide in the chiel, seein' that he was yer best freen like, and had taken yer side in ither things, so after a bit tune together on the mouthorgans, sittin' on the edge o' yer bed, and him on his kist, ye told Gatt how ye felt aboot this quine and what he thocht ye should do about it. So Gatt said she already had a lad, and that the last Sunday he was toonkeeper this lad cam' tae see the kitchie quine, and got his denner in the fairm hoose, so that he must be gie far in with her and the fairm mistress and that ye hadna much chance; and besides, did ye no ken that the shepherd was after 'er, sneakin' in tae the chaumer here when the lassie was makin' the beds, feart that she wad ravel his Sunday breeks that he was pressin' under the mattress, but that it was only an excuse tae get a word wi' her, or even try something bolder, but that she told 'im off; that she didna want 'im, that she had a lad o' her ain withoot tripe like him. Oh maybe ye thocht she was quiet like but she could speak oot when she liked, and she might put ye in your place quick enough. All's fair in love and war Gatt said but that you were a bit slow with the quines and that unless you looked nippy aboot it ye would never manage tae ding oot this ither lad she had, and that Gertie Troup wad be married before ye got started.

Now it just so happened that about this time your old grandfather died and in a week or two your mither asked if ye would put a bit flower on his grave; that maybe the farm wife would give you a bunch from the farm gairden, and that ye could put it on when you went in bye to the kirk. So bein' a kirky body like hersel ye had nae bother gettin' a bit flower from the farm wife, and what was better she sent Gertie with you to pluck them. And a fair picture she was with an oxter of flowers, and the sweet smile of her when she handed them over, fond like, as if she was loth to part with them, but didn't mind seeing it was you, the quiet one who never took her on much. And was it true that you wrote poetry? Folk said that you was clever and wrote things to the papers, all about your film stars that were hanging on the chaumer walls. Would you write a poem for her? My but you must be awfully proud of your old grandfather to put flowers on his grave. Not many lads would bother to do that. But how could she be sure that you wasn't giving them away to some quine that went to the pictures with you in the toon? Seein' it was Saturday night you didn't deny this was possible, and the farm wife wasn't at the kirk every Sunday to see what you did with them. You were that damned shy you hardly knew what to say, but after a time or two at the flower gathering you plucked up courage to tell the blushing quine that a flower like herself didn't need a flower: that she herself was the loveliest flower you had ever seen in nature's garden; and a lot of other things you told her, and she looked at you so sweetly and said that no lad had ever said things to her like that before, that surely you must be a poet, like the ones she had read about in her school books. So you told her that you wouldn't be wanting any more flowers for your quine in the toon, or whatever she thought you did with them, and that if she waited up for you the next Saturday night in the back kitchen you would bring a flower for her, and maybe the bit poem she had asked for.

So you spent the next week with the muses, mostly in secret, writing a bit poem for the quine in the kitchen, and on the Saturday night you went away on your bike as usual like the other lads, maybe to the pictures they thocht, but you returned in the gloamin', when the farm folks were in bed, and you crept into the back gairden and plucked the loveliest rose you could find, scented fresh from heaven's pharmacy, sun-kissed with colour and tipped with dew, and you tapped on the back kitchen window, where the quine had been knitting in the twylight, waiting for you, just as she had promised, and when she took the snib from its catch, and you pushed the sash half up, ever so quietly, not to waken the farm folk, you handed her this one single beautiful rose and a box of chocolates you had bought at the Bog shop. She placed the dewy rose against her lips and smelt its fragrance, and with the flower against her face she seemed an angel in the mirk, the shadow of your dream come true.

And you had to stand on a backet from the peat stack to reach your quine at the open window. Oh aye you could call her Gertie and you gave her the poem you'd promised her and she said she'd read it in bed by candlelight because she couldn't wait till daybreak to see what you had written. So you whispered to each other till long after midnight, in the smoked-glass light of a midsummer morning, when it is never really dark, while the leaves rustled in the quiet sigh of the wind that was rich with the smell of dewy bud and the tang of earth, soft and sweet and warm as the lips of your quine that you touched with your own ere you parted. Syne you jumped on your bike and dreamed your way home in the colder flush of dawn, while the birds and the cattle beasts were still asleep in the deep green of the fields, and the world quiet about you, and you knew in your heart that something wonderful and mystifying was awakening in your young life. And you wanted to tell your mither about this new quine you had met at the fairm, but when mornin' came you thought better of it, because you knew she didn't like you to be goin' out with quines, though she didn't object to your film stars on the walls, because they couldn't do you any harm, neither break your heart nor ruin you.

But bye and bye you were spending nearly an hour with Gertie in the back scullery when you was supposed to be shaving and washing your face, taking care you was last for the wash basin, so's you wouldn't be molested, while the other lads were in the chaumer, playing cards or the gramophone; and by the time you went round to supper your horse of a winter evening they were sometimes in bed. But with Francie Gatt on your side they didn't bother you much about the quine, except to say that you were a lucky bugger, and that if ever you married the sulky bitch they'd blacken the pair of you from head to foot. Sometimes you got your tea from the farmwife, you and the servant quine, with home-baked scones and honey, mostly from ben the hoose, for she spoiled the pair of you and the lad that used to come on a Sunday had fair got the go by. And whiles you'd cycle down to the Bog shop for an ounce of tobacco and Mollie Kane that kept the place would measure out a length of black twist from a roll and cut it on the edge of the counter, and when she put it on the scales she was never far out. So you'd buy a pucklie sweeties for your lass and Mollie would coup the pan from the weighing machine into a paper whirl she had twisted at one end like a cone, and she'd tell you that you had the bonniest quine in the whole of the Bogside, as her mither was afore her day, for fine she minded when she cam' tae the shop hersel' as a young deem. So you'd make an errand back to the fairmhoose with the sweeties, where you'd find Gertie in the scullery, and you told her what the shoppie wife said about her mither and gave her the poke of sweets. And if the farmwife appeared you'd ask for a book to read and Gertie would hide her sweeties under the mou' of a pot where they lay up-side-down on the skelves. So the farm wife brought you **The Last of the Mohicans,** because you had just finished **Deerslayer,** and she knew you was fair daft on this Fennimore Cooper lad that wrote about the backwoods of America.

So Gertie liked your poem fine, and she wrote you a bit letter back to say she had always wanted a lad like you, and you read it all by yourself in the chaumer and fair thocht yourself King of the Castle. And so the summer wore on, hyow, hay, peats and hairst, and sometimes at the shim with your odd beast you would be caught in your sark sleeves in a thunder pelt, but then the sun came out in a blaze of heat and by the time you'd reached the other end of the neep drills you was dry again, thinking all the time about the beauty of your quine and the wonder of the world and not a real care in your young heart. Even on the longest warm sunny days you'd never weary, and you'd jump on your mare's back and drag hay coles from the hill fields down to the stackyard, where the grieve and the farmer chiel would be building and trampling the rucks, with two three billies on the forks, one on a ladder as the stacks got higher, pitching the scented forkfulls to the builders, while the hayseed went down the back of his neck. But you'd kinch up your rope and hang it on your hames and trot away back for another cole, maybe a bit further afield this time to give the lads time to top their stack, and you'd meet the second billie on the way, with two bairns riding on his cole, and when your quine appeared with the piece basket they fair made a picnic of it. Then there was the wark in the moss, with a flaggon loaf saps or sago for your dinner; cutting, barrowing, spreading, rickling and driving home the peat, a job that sometimes lasted the whole summer, depending on the weather and when you could get at it, and you'd have your harness polished and your clear hames and chains glittering in the sun, while back at home the peat stack got bigger and bigger, the grieve building it and a lad throwing up the peats to him, for you just couped your loads and away back for another dracht, and when the stack was finished they topped it with dross to keep it dry, though some folks had a shed to stack their peats in.

Syne the hairst, clearing roads for the binder, swinging the scythe and gathering sheaves and setting them against the dykes, the golden ears of ripe corn rustling in the sun. Then long golden days stooking behind the binders, rows and rows of upright stooks, setting them north and south to catch the sun, tidy as you could make them. And maybe you'd get a glimpse of your quine on her bicycle, when her mistress had sent her with a ball of twine for a binder that had run out of yarn, and the horses standing idle in the hairst park. But soon she would be back with the piece basket, and when she got you by yourself in the lithe of a stook she whispered that you had gone too far with her lately in your 'Garden of Eden,' as you called it, the high walled gairden ahin the fairmhoose, with its rustic arbour, summer-house and lily pond, where you had made your trysts with her in the gloamin', and that maybe you would be a father before you expected it. But she was smiling all the time and bonnier than ever and you knew she was happy about it and trusting in your love. Nor was you unhappy about it either, for you had always wanted a place of your ain and a quine that you liked whatever came of it. But you would have to tell your mither for God knows you had little enough to get married on and you'd need her blessing and whatever else she could give you by way of a little money and some bits of furniture she could spare. But you told Gertie not to worry, that you would stand by her whatever happened, and she said she knew that and gave you the sort of smile that comes from an angel's heart, cheering you on the hairst rigs with a song on your lips. You usually drove a horse cart at the leading-in, 'cause they wouldn't trust you with building a ruck yet, lest you watered and spoiled it, much as you wished to try it, so you had to be content with building your carts and driving them home to the stackyard, where you forked your sheaves to the builder. Then came the thatching and the tattie-lifting and as Martinmas drew nigh you knew you would have to look for a cottar job and a hoose o' yer ain for your wife and bairn.

But married jobs were ill to come by at the November Term, and though you bicycled far and near to answer adverts in the papers someone had always been there before you and you were turned away, though some farmers did earnestly thank you for looking in by. By now the cottar wives at Slabsteen were beginning to claik among themselves about the loon and the quine that were getting married at the Term: "Still waters run deep," they said, "for you would hardly have thought by the pair of them that they would be at it already; and the quine with the mark of the school-bag hardly off her back, and the lad only a haflin with nothing saved up for a rainy day—and the quine expectin' at her age— Gweed sake! What was the warld comin' till?"

So you dressed yourself in your best serge suit and took the train to the feein' market for single men at Maud, for there was just the chance that some odd farmer billie might be looking for a cottar. But na na, there was nothing for you there but the blether of wark and the swagger of the heavies and the lads that got drunk on their arles, and while you stood there with the bite of the wind in your Sunday clothes not one farmer asked your price for a six months' Term. Dinner was out of the question, you just couldn't afford it so near the Term, for it was nearly six months since you got any wages, and unless you got a fee and some farmer chiel offered you a dram you had to be content with a cup of tea at Morrison's bakery, and then you lit your pipe and made for the station platform to wait for the train. Going back on the Buchan train the face of your quine haunted you; though not unpleasantly, but smiling at you from a mother-of-pearl sky, playing hide-and-seek with you from the pine woods on the hill-sides; even as you thought of her the watery sun dried his wintry tears and burnished the autumn gold at the feet of the stricken beeches, filling you with hope that together you had nothing to fear, though you envied the lads at the ploo or pulling turnips, confident and content in their sense of security.

On your way home from the station you got off your bike at the smiddy and told the blacksmith of your plight. But he never stopped tugging at his bellows handle and twirling with a tongs at a red-hot horse shoe in the glowing forge, chewing tobacco and spitting the juice into the tiny flames. "Ach man," says he, "ye'll get a place a' richt, and ye could aye go intae Rascal Friday in Aeberdeen. Ye're hardly startet yet and ye're baith young; a' the warld afore ye and a hirst o' geets, ye'll be feart tae throw a steen in owre a skweel dyke for fear o' hittin' ane o' yer ain!" This nearly tore the arse out of your breeks so to speak and made you rise from the anvil and make for the smiddy door. And the blacksmith's parting words rang in your lugs like a kirk bell: "Man, if ye're willin' tae work ye'll never want for a job!"

Maybe he was right for you got a cottar place little more than a week before the term, a dairy job, which you had never done in your life before, but you'd have to learn it, now that you was taking a wife. So this new farmer chiel that was called Lowrie took you into his parlour at the Blackstob farm and offered you a £1 a week plus house and perquisites for second dairy stockman on the place. You a dairyman, you that had never milked a cow in your whole life—but before you could make up your mind the 'phone rang and Mr. Lowrie went ben the lobby to answer it. When he came back he said that was another chiel applyin' for the job and would you be willin' to take it on for something less than a £1 a week, seeing this man was experienced and you would have to be learned to milk with the new machines. But na na, you stuck to the figure he promised and said you wouldn't do it for less: after all maybe it was only a trick because you couldn't hear who was on the other end of the 'phone; maybe it was only so-and-so asking Lowrie for an extra pint of milk on delivery. So you settled for a £1 a week and came away from the Blackstob farm feeling a rich man, because it was more money than you had ever made in your life before, and just wait till you told Gertie.

Gertie was delighted, but the folk at Slabsteen were determined to have your feet washed before you left at the Term, both the pair of you, but what with all you'd been through already you got roused at this and threatened to strike the first one to lay hands on you or your quine. This marriage business was beginning to make a man of you and putting some spunk in your veins. Just let them try it and you'd land the first one in the horse troch if you got the chance. You wasn't worried about yourself but what they'd do to Gertie; maybe not thinking about the condition she was in and the harm it could do. But Gertie tamed you down and humoured you to go through with it for her sake, because she didn't want any fighting, and that they'd never lay a hand on her because the mistress was against it and would protect her. So you bought a bottle of whisky and allowed the devils to wash your feet and blacken you from head to foot, even taking your boots off yourself not to hinder them, though you never missed a chance to give as well as you got, until you hardly knew one from the other, and it took you nearly half the night in the back kitchen to wash yourself clean again. But they never got hold of your quine, for the mistress had been as good as her word and kept her inside, even to milking the kye herself until it had all blown past at the Term. But maybe the cottar wives had some influence on their menfolk in this respect, for they were sure it must be a 'forced marriage,' or how else would you be getting married at the Martinmass Term. But they drank all your whisky and gave Gertie a small present, and when you left at the Term the farm wife threw a horse shoe after you down the avenue, wishing luck to the pair of you in your new venture.

You wasn't getting married for a week after you went to the Blackstob farm, so you'd work as a single man and board next door with the McPhee's, while Gertie stayed with her parents at the Bogside. But you'd never forget the first night that you and your quine approached the Blackstob place. It was in the gloamin' of early winter that you went up the avenue on your bicycles, but had to get off when you met the foreman and the second horseman coming out of a dubby field with four tremendous loads of marrow-stem kale; such enormous loads as you had never seen at Slabsteen, and such dubs and stern chiels you thought this must surely be a hard place to work on, and that you had certainly jumped out of the frying-pan into the fire.

But you both liked the little harled three-roomed house down the back road from the farm, with a fine big garden and hen-run and plenty of room for Gertie to hang her clothes line. You had your kist and some bits of furniture gathered together that you had gotten from your parents: an iron bedstead with brass knobs, blankets, sheet and pillows, table and chairs and washstand and an old second-hand dresser that was little better than a hen-coop, besides some pots and pans, kettle, tea-pot, dishes and spoons; some curtain material for the windows, rugs for the floor and roll of linoleum, and you'd pick up some other things in the sale rooms bye and bye. There were no blinds on the windows but you lit the paraffin lamp and set it on the table to let you see to put some messages you had brought into the wall presses, which were fitted with shelves, scrubbed and clean, though Gertie placed a sheet of newspaper on each shelf before she used it. This done, and Gertie getting the tea ready, the first you'd ever had in your own house, when the door opens without warning and a wash tub is thrown into the little kitchen. Four men stared in at you and your quine from the open door, their faces dimly visible in the light from the paraffin lamp. Two of them you had seen with their loads of kale, now both grinning with mischief in their eyes; the third was McPhee from next door, who would be your boss in the byre, at first glance a proper ruffian, strong and sturdy as a nowt beast. Standing in front of the other three, tallest of the lot and evidently their ringleader was Jock Herd, gaffer at the Blackstob for mony a year, his eyes agleam with mirth and his white teeth shining in his dirty face. All four had flaggons in their hands, brimming with warm milk, which they had no intention of pouring into the tub, so that any visions you had of being treated like Cleopatra were soon dispelled. Na na, water will do the job they said, cold water at that, and Herd ordered you and your bride to get your boots and stockings off so that they could wash your dirty feet. But your birse began to rise at this and you told them that your feet had already been washed at the last place, your quine as well, for you had to tell a lie to protect her, thinking she would fair be in for it this time. But Jock Herd was dubious: "Expect us tae believe that?" he cried, "a likely story. Fill 'er up lads and we'll wash the pair o' them!" All four left their flaggons outside and went in search of pails and water. Gertie was almost in tears and you was mortally terrified at the uncouth brutes. Surely they would have some sense or pity seeing you was just newly moved into the hoose and everything in an uproar. Jock Herd came back with the first pailful of icy water and poured it into the tub, threatening to wash you stockings an' all if you didn't get a move on, and to clart you with axle grease and harness blacking. He hadna time to scutter he said for he was hungry and needin' his supper. Then the other three appeared and tipped their pails of water into the tub. That would be enough Jock said and waited to see what you was going to do, solemn like, looking at your scared faces, and then all four burst out laughing. "Did ye really think that we wad bother tae wash yer feet?" Jock asked. "Na na, we wis only haverin', and we'll tak' yer word for't that ye had them washed afore!" So you told them that you was beginning to wonder if they were in earnest and you gave them each a bottle of stout that you had in your kist and they departed in great glee, taking the tub with them. It was a relief to see them gone but Gertie said she felt sure they wouldn't manhandle us; that Jock Herd looked so like her own caperin' father and had quines o' his ain and she could see by his face that he was only in fun. So you had your tea in peace after all, and a bit cuddle after the light was out, though it wouldn't do for the two of you to sleep together, not just yet anyway, so you lit your gas lamps and got on your bicycles and you saw Gertie home to the Bogside.

So you wouldn't be seeing Gertie for a whole week, and by then you was fair convinced you had taken the wrong turning with a dairy job at the Blackstob: but as the saying goes 'when you've made your bed you've got to lie in it," trouble was the damn the very lang did you get to lie—up at half-past three for the milking, and you had bought a new alarm clock to make sure you could manage it. Back at Slabsteen you had lain in your bed till six and didn't know how well off you was till now. McPhee wasn't all that sharp himself but he caught up with you in the avenue, his pockets bulging with empty milk bottles and his fag a red spot in his mouth. But you was still in a daze of sleep, the stars winking down at you, the moon grinning low in the violet blue of the west, while you stole a glance at it with your bleary eyes. But the warm stink of the crowded byre, the cold water you was throwing about, the hard work feeding and mucking out, the struggle with the new-fangled milking machines and kicking cows soon had you out of your daydreams.

McPhee's wife made porridge for your breakfast, rich with cream that McPhee had skimmed from a can in the dairy, and no sooner was the spoon out of your mouth than you was fast asleep on their couch. McPhee was used to it and after a short nap he sat and smoked and played with the bairns while his wife rigged them out for school. Faith but they were a rough and

ready crowd, the worst you'd ever seen but good at heart, though
the house was a mess of dirt and stank with casten sarks to be
washed and had a bairns' footpath from the door to the fireside,
sair needing to be scraped, never mind scrubbing, and empty milk
bottles standing everywhere, even in the window sills, where one
or two had a bit flower in them. Faith but the woman wasn't all
that to be blamed, for she worked hard in the dairy for about a
shilling a day, washing cans and bottles, and all that McPhee did
to help was to light the boiler fire for her. And what with all that
geets and a man like McPhee always on top of her, and always
in debt, 'cause he spent so much on fags and booze; and sometimes she was so far behind with the grocer that when she saw
his van coming up the back road she went away up the whundyke
with the bairns that weren't at school, because she hadn't a copper
in the house, living on meal milk and tatties, besides an egg from
her hens and what McPhee could steal—and when the vanman
had gone (hoping to get his money the next week) she'd come
away home again with a birn of sticks on her back, pretending to
be in search of kindlers. Syne in the evenin' McPhee would be
fair cravin' for a smoke and he'd send a bairn to the shop for
fags on tick, and if the bairn wadna go it got a skelpin. But for
all that McPhee and the wife were a lovin' pair and you never
heard an ill werd between them, and she forgave him everything,
even a rough-and-tumble on the straw in the barn with the scullery
maid, or a bit cuddle at her in the sly, thinkin' maybe it was
something to be proud of to have a man that other women wanted,
for she fair adored the brute.

On the night of your marriage Jock Herd and McPhee put a
sod on your lum, spiced your bed and slackened the screws that
held it together, while all the time you had the key of the door
in your pocket and never knew how they got into your cottage.
You had a piper at your wedding and thought yourself gie braw
and came home cock of the walk after midnight in a motor taxi.
Oh you fair did it in style and even gave the driver a tip and he
carried all your presents into the house from the back of the car.
When he had gone you picks Gertie up in your arms and carries
her over the threshold into the little dark kitchen, like you'd seen

them doing at the movies, right through to the bedroom, where you sets her down and lights the lamp, while she hangs a bit blanket over the window. The pair of you were a bit bashful getting your clothes off together for the first time and Gertie was that shy in her nakedness that she had you screw down the lamp or she got settled at the back of the bed. But the weight of her didn't dislodge it, not until you put your knee on the edge of the bed to get in beside her when the whole damned thing collapsed in a heap, both ends coming together and giving you a nasty crack on the head. Oh it was well contrived and the disturbance set the spice going and the pair of you started sneezing like you would never stop, while all the time through the partition you could hear McPhee and his wife skirling with laughter. So you both gets up again and tries to put the bed together, but when you couldn't find the key for it you lost your patience and threw one of your boots at the wall, thinking to quieten McPhee between your sneezes, for by now you was in a tearing rage, fair bloody mad and threatening to go round and kill the bastard. But Gertie was wiser than you for she knew they just wanted to have you roused and managed to quieten you down before you made a shambles. When the sneezing stopped you managed to get back to speaking in whispers again, setting the ends of the bed aside and lying down together on the mattress on the floor, your arms round each other's necks, your lips together and the blankets over your heads, not caring a damn for anyone. But no bloody honeymoon because you had promised old Lowrie you would be at the milking in the morning, 'cause there was a man off work and nobody to replace you and he would give you a day off later on.

So you only had about two hours in bed the first night of your marriage, lying on the floor at that, but in the morning you never let dab to McPhee about the racket you'd had with the bed; you was quite calmed down by then and wasn't going to give him the satisfaction of making a fool of you, though you knew damned fine it was to make up for being denied the fun of washing your feet, and McPhee would soon be whispering to Jock Herd about the fun they'd got when the sneezin' started, and how you had been fair roused and swearing like hell at the lot of them.

43

But that wasn't all, for there was this bloody sod on your chimney, and when you got home to breakfast for the first time in your own home, sair chauved in the byre, your kitchen was full of smoke and your wife standing at the door hoasting for want of breath and her eyes watering. You couldn't see a stime in the place for the reek, and had to run outside again for breath, thinking that your house was on fire, and you ran round to McPhee to ask for help. So he had another bloody good laugh at you, and his wife fair giggling, while McPhee pointed to the turf sticking on your lum. It was damned provoking, especially on a teem belly, but you was that relieved the house wasn't on fire you was beginning to see the funny side of it yourself, though it was all at your expense. McPhee gave you a ladder he had taken from the farm to let you up on the slates, and when you stood up on the coping to get hold of the chimney pot the confounded thing came away in your oxter and you nearly lost your balance. Can and sod went crashing to the ground while you held on to the stonework. But it stopped the laughter and while you came slithering down the slates McPhee held the ladder for you, a bit white faced and scared lest you should fall. Back at the farm you told Lowrie that you would need a new chimney, but he looked stern like and said "Damn the fit, ye'll replace it yersel', or I'll keep it aff yer wages!" But you saw him winking to McPhee and you knew that he was only joking, for he was as bad as the rest of them with his pranks on newly married folk.

But it wasn't long before a slater lad was clambering on your roof fixing your new chimney pot and you got a ton of coal as your first perquisite. A wagon load of coal was shunted off at Binkie Station for the Blackstob and Jock Herd sent the horsemen with their carts to drive it home to the cottars. It was Scotch coal because English was considered too expensive; but it was a whole ton of coal to yourselves, more than you had ever possessed in the world before, and even though you were come of cottar folk, both the pair of you, it was a bit of a thrill having it couped at your own shed door. Gertie was that excited about it that she gave you a hand to shovel it into the shed, happy you were the pair of you at it, by the light of a cycle lamp in the evening, and all your other set-backs were soon forgotten. Next day you got three bolls and a fillet of oat-meal, which is about 4 cwt, and the foreman carried the bags into the kitchen and set them on chairs, where you left them until the grocer came to buy the meal off your hands or take it in exchange for provisions over a period. Of course you had ordered a girnal to hold your meal, a fairly big one with a desk lid and lined with zinc to keep out the mice, but the joiner hadn't finished making it yet, so you kept a bag to store in it for your own use. Then you got ten sacks of tatties, which you buried in an earth-pit, to protect them from the frost, but again the grocer relieved you of half of them. It wasn't until you had a big family that you needed all that stuff, and you got another supply in six months time, so in the meantime you sold as much as you could to buy the bits of furniture you needed to set up house in earnest. Besides all this you got three pints of milk a day and £4 a month in money, with the balance at the Terms, less £1 in six months for Insurance, so you considered you was much better off now than you had been in a chaumer, and with a quine all to yourself for company and to keep you warm at nights.

About six weeks after your wedding old Lowrie decided to give you a day off for your honeymoon, the first whole day you'd had to yourself since you came to the place, so you fair looked forward to your holiday. You were that excited you didn't even take a long lie and got up about an hour after you heard McPhee leave for the milking. He had been sleeping-in lately and you usually gave him a bang on the wall to make sure he was up, but today being your honeymoon you didn't bother, and you couldn't have cared less though he had slept till dinner time.

It was a fine mild morning for mid-January, with a dark dreamy sky outside the window and a star winking here and there and the cottars' cocks crowing to each other with all the promise of a beautiful day. So you dressed yourselves in great excitement and had your brose and cocoa and set sail in the dark on your bicycles for Binkie Station to catch the first train for Aberdeen. At the station you blew out your gas lamps and left your bicycles in the waiting room and bought your return tickets and waited on the platform for the train. The signal was at green so you didn't have long to wait, and when you got on the train it was all lit up and not many folks in it so you got a whole compartment to yourselves with fine red plush cushions and pictures under the luggage racks. Gertie had never been in a train before so you knew you was giving her a real treat, so you just sat and smiled across at each other as if you were the richest and happiest pair of creatures in the world. Outside in the dark you could see the lights on the passing farms and you knew that folks would be at work in their byres and stables; but this was your day of adventure, your day of days, your's and Gertie's, and you were going to make the best of it.

It took the train nearly two hours to reach the black tunnels in Aberdeen and by then it was daylight and the lights all out in the carriages and a great bustle of folk when you got off at the station. By now you was hungry, so the first thing you did was to get your tea in a restaurant, not too posh because you couldn't afford it, and then the two of you went linking down Union Street, hand in hand, on a shopping spree. Gertie had you inside 'Raggie Morrison's,' at the corner of St. Nicholas Street, where she told you she had bought her wedding frock for £1 when she was in the city with her mither and one of her sisters at the Term. Now she wanted some hanks of wool to knit something for the coming bairn. Then to 'Cockie Hunter's' place at the head of the Castlegate, which used to be the old Sick Children's Hospital, but now so crammed with everything that you could hardly get up the stairs. Cockie used to boast that he could sell you anything 'from a needle to an anchor,' or could get it for you if you wanted one, but you settled for a second-hand dressing table for your bedroom, which cost you a fiver, and overmantle for your kitchen fireplace, with a mirror in the centre and a picture by Constable on either side, which you had for about three shillings, besides a roll of linoleum and a huge hand-painted flower pot at 10/- that Gertie fancied for her front window nearest the road. And when you paid Mr. Hunter for these things he promised to send them out with the carrier that passed your way once a week.

MOONLIGHT FLITTING

In the New Market you was a bit shy to go upstairs because of the quines, but maybe with Gertie with you they mightn't be so bad. When you was a single chiel they used to torment you at the Term time to buy a broach or a pair of stockings for your lass, when they knew you had the money, and unless you snubbed them proper or just clean ignored them they had you into their shabby booths by the arm or the tail of your jacket and you was glad to buy something to get rid of the bitches. They just sat at their stalls like a spider at a web, waiting for the unwary fly that might come in by, mostly farmers and country chiels that were a bit canned and careless with their money; but some of them offered to buy the stockings if the quines would bare a leg to let them try them on, which usually quietened the limmers, and if some of the chiels took hold of them they were glad to leave the lads alone. But you wanted to get to Low's bookstall, which was at the other end of the building, and though the quines pestered you a bit it wasn't nearly so bad with Gertie by the hand, and you being such a lad to read you got plenty to choose from at Low's, where the books were piled to the roof and cheap enough for your purse.

Then you'd go along to WOOLWORTH'S 3d. & 6d. STORES, where nothing was dearer than a sixpence, including gramophone records labelled 'Victory' and 'Eclipse,' and the hit of the moment was 'Little Grey Home In The West,' sung by Wilfred Eaton, a boy with the sweetest voice you ever heard this side of heaven, and having a special appeal for you at this time you just had to buy one. There were plenty of places where you could have your dinner, even in the New Market, but you remembered a place in King Street that was plain and cheap, where you had gone as a loon with your parents, Stephen's Restaurant, so you went there with Gertie and had a grand dinner of mince and tatties, plum-duff or trifle, tea and cakes, and a blow at a fag to finish it off, though Gertie never smoked. But she waited while you looked through the books you had bought, and then you daundered up Union Street again, dodging the trams and the horse dung, and the lorries that clattered over the causeway stones, up to Stead & Simpsons, where Gertie bought a pair of shoes and you stood her a black leather handbag. Back on the streets the tram-cars were whining and grinding to and fro on the rails, double-deckers powered along by a steel finger on their roofs attached to an overhead cable slung between the houses across Union Street, while here and there a Rover or Bydand bus, even folks on bicycles, threading their way among the motor traffic and the cars of the gentry, though they were few in those days. So you went back to St. Nicholas Street, just behind Queen Victoria's statue, to have a look at the suits in the windows of 'The Fifty-Shilling Tailors,' which was the price of their suits; comparing them with those at Claude Alexander's, Hepworths and Montague Burton's, an area which you had always regarded as Jews' Corner, and many a day in the driech of the neep park or the trauchle of the byres you were cheered by their enterprises, for you had read in the **Picture Post** that the Jews had made the desert blossom, growing fruit and oranges where once was sand and scrub, and you being a young lad still full of dreams and ambitions you wondered if some day you could match their enthusiasm, or perhaps become an H. Samuel and fill your lighted windows with golden rings and watches.

Having but one short winter day in the city you couldn't venture far from Union Street in case you lost yourself, or couldn't find your way back to the railway station, where the last train left at seven, but you went along George Street as far as Jerome's to have your pictures taken, especially as you didn't have a wedding photo. Gertie said that when her brothers came to the town at the Term they always went to the scenic railway or to see Harry Gordon at the Beach Pavilion, but you hadn't time for this after all that shopping, so you took her to the pictures, which she had never seen before, up at the old La Scala in Union Street, where they were showing the new 'Talking Pictures,' and your quine was fair mystified, especially when they sang and danced "Way Down Upon the Swanee River,' and it was a fine rest after walking so long on the hard pavements, you being accustomed to the soft grun or the sharn midden. When you came out of the darkened picture house the streets were all lit up cheerfully and as you walked to the station down Bridge Street with your parcels you had a cup of coffee as a final treat and then made for the train. Back at Binkie Station you lit your gas lamps and cycled home with your parcels in one hand and steering with the other, tired but happy, the pair of you, after your honeymoon, and you'd have to be up for the byre again in a few hours' time.

In about a week's time your dressing-table, overmantle, flowerpot and bit of linoleum arrived with the carrier, so Gertie paid the chiel and he gave her a hand to carry them into the house. What with the curtains that your wife had made and the rugs she had clicked on a frame from old coloured rags in a pattern of her own, the papering she had done on the walls, the pictures she had framed, your varnishing of chairs and table and the old dresser, and your lino laid down, your house was almost furnished, even with a chiming clock for your mantleshelf, which Gertie had bought at a sale in the toon. She was getting big with her bairn but bonnier than ever, and sometimes in the dead of night she would take your hand and place it on her naked midriff, where you could feel the child turning inside her and bulging the skin, like a little Jonah in the whale's belly, so you kissed her fondly and turned on the other side and fell asleep, for morning and another anxious day was soon upon you.

Sometimes a cow calved during the night and being head cattleman McPhee had to get up in the small hours to deliver her calf, and although he never got anything extra for this he never came home empty-handed, and you'd be wakened from your sleep with a big thump on the floor that you heard next door through the wall and it was a huge lump of shining English coal that McPhee had pinched out of the farm coalshed, and when you tackled him about it next day he told you bloody plainly that he wasn't going to rise to their cow calvings for nothing, and before long he had you so much in his confidence that in the dark mornings you'd take one end of a railway sleeper on your strong young shoulder and McPhee would take the other, down the road to your coalshed, 'cause it was nearest, and in the evening you'd get a cross-cut saw and share it between you. You'd been a born cottar but never in all your days had you seen such thieving as went on at the Blackstob. Had you been soft enough McPhee would have had you into the hen arks for a dozen pullets coming on to the lay, but here you put your foot down and refused to join him. And he told you how he and the man before you had been locked into a field henhouse by the kitchiedeem, she not knowing they were there, and how they had to burst the door open after dark or stay and be caught in the morning.

But nowadays you had to waken McPhee every morning, banging on your bedroom wall with your fist until he answered you that he was up, depending on you entirely as a sort of alarm clock. Jock Herd said you should let the bugger lie and sort your own side of the byre, but you had been so much obliged to McPhee for showing you how to work the milking machines that you didn't want to offend him; and he shirked enough as it was, capering with the kitchie quines and newsing to folk out-bye, expecting you to do more than your share of the wark, quite enough without having to help him out after a sleep-in, which would have happened in the end, being the sort of lad you was, so you shielded the brute from getting the sack and thought it better to get him out of bed for a start to save trouble. And after all McPhee was your neighbour and Jock Herd would have liked fine to see trouble between you, so you had to be tolerant and use some diplomacy to keep the peace, though you felt all the time that you was being taken advantage of by force of circumstances.

But McPhee had a better idea and got both of you an extra while in bed in spite of everybody. The diesel engine was supposed to be going about a quarter-to-five for the milking, driving the pulso-pump, after you'd fed the kye with draff and bruised corn and mucked out their stalls, but McPhee didn't get up till half-past four and started up the engine as soon as he reached the steading, so that old Lowrie would think that everything was going normal when he heard the engine purring. So McPhee hid his empty milk bottles by the dairy door and started milking immediately, while you went before him with your draff hurlie feeding the beasts, and when finished with this you started mucking out behind him, while he worked all the machines himself and carried the milk to dairy and watched that the cans under the cooler didn't overflow.

MOONLIGHT FLITTING

He certainly had a full-time job and you wasn't sure but that he had the worst of it: in fact you thought it was an excellent idea because you were doing two jobs at the same time, and you had finished mucking the byre or he was half-through milking, thus giving him a hand to finish and feed the calves. But Lowrie of the Blackstob had just gone in for tuberculine tested milk, first in the district, him being an enterprising kind of farmer, and it gave him a half-penny a pint more than his neighbours on the retail side of the business, though a lot of his cows failed in the test and he had to spend a lot of money replacing them with accredited stock. Cows that failed went to the outfarm and their milk went to the pool at the usual price. But when Lowrie was short of tuberculine free milk he dispatched a lorry to the outfarm for a couple of cans of diseased milk and bottled it up with T.T. milk at the higher price for his customers. Now you were supposed to be much more particular with the production of this new germ free milk; wearing white coats and caps and wellington boots, washing the udders more thoroughly and stripping off each cow for dermatitis, making sure there were no curds in the strainer before you put the milking cups on the teats. But Lowrie got up earlier one morning to see what was happening (or maybe Jock Herd had told him) and he was waiting in the darkness of the byre when McPhee switched on the lights, fortunately hiding his empty milk bottles before doing so, but a good half-hour late as usual. So Lowrie had fair caught you this time and he ranted and raved at McPhee about how things were being done to deceive him, starting up that damned engine to make him think you was on the job as usual, while all the time you were cheating him and mixing muck with milk in a certified T.T. herd. And what would happen if the Inspector called and you without your white coats and caps? Surely you had to think of that and you fair thought that McPhee was going to get the sack on the spot. And Lowrie took you aside and asked how long this had been going on, but you wouldn't tell on McPhee, and when Lowrie saw that he couldn't get anything out of you he said he knew you could rise in the morning and that you should come up at the proper time and let the tink lie, and then he'd know how to deal with him.

STRAW INTO GOLD

But McPhee was too smart for Lowrie and comes up to him and says he could produce clean milk though the beasts were on a sharn midden, which was no worse than mixing rotten milk with good, and Mr. James Lowrie being a councillor he knew fine what McPhee was hinting at and left the byre in a sulk, so that everything went on much as before, except that it stopped the sale of infected milk to innocent customers.

But you never forgave McPhee after you saw him killing a premature calf with a hammer, smashing in its forehead until it died, for he had little patience with them if they wouldn't take a bottle teat or sup their milk from a bucket. Two or three days he hungered them and if this failed he splashed the milk in their faces and killed them. You had never seen such cruelty and was fair shocked though it did save you a lot of time scuttering with the ill-nourished creatures, lacking the instinct to suck the teat, which nature would have given them had they remained the normal time in their mother's bellies, nine months with the umbilical cord instead of the seven or eight caused by abortion. And Lowrie wouldn't have thanked you for 'phoning the knackery cart for a wee calf that had died, and as you didn't have much time to dig a hole you toppled it into the dung court from your barrow and covered it with sharn, thus spreading the disease where in-calf heifers were wintered in the building, besides angering Jock Herd and his horsemen when they came upon the stinking carcase with their graips while loading their carts in the springtime. And much as Lowrie wanted you to keep the mother in milk McPhee did his best to put her dry; turning off her water supply and cutting down her share of turnips, even rubbing her udder with vinegar, and in his ignorance was preventing the spread of Brucellosis, which was little understood in those days and known in humans as Undulent Fever. But as the beast wasn't isolated it wasn't long before you had another abortion, unless you used plenty of Jeyes Fluid, which did something to prevent it. Indeed it was a long time before the agricultural colleges got on to the scourge in dairy herds, though you suspected all the time what was causing it but didn't know the cure, except that your old grandfather kept a billygoat in the byre to save his cows from

'casting their calves!' Eventually, when the veterinary lads came
round in their white coats and wellington boots with needles to
inject your heifers against abortion before serving you discovered
they were trying out a vaccine from the goat, so maybe your old
grandad had been right after all, but merely using the breath and
discharge of the goat in his old-fashioned way among the few cows
that he kept, until the disease went rampant as the dairy herds
got bigger and more commercialised. But just think what might
have happened if you had taken this disease home to your poor
Gertie that was expecting her bairn shortly.

But for all his faults McPhee never teased you about your wife
expecting a bairn, whereas Jock Herd in his crude way never
missed a chance of comparing beast with body, and how the first
calving was always the worst, until he had you nearly out of your
sleep with worry, especially after that case when he'd had to help
you with the ropes and fencing tackle to relieve a young heifer
of her calf, four or five of you pulling with all your might, and
another holding the arse of the beast that was chained by the
neck to her forestall, lest you should haul her on to the greep,
while she lay on her side panting and foaming at the mouth and
bellowing in agony. And you pulled so hard that the fore legs of
the calf came away in your hands, and you had to tie the rope
around its neck and strangle it in delivery to save the life of its
mither. What with these experiences and Jock Herd's taunting you
became feared for your wife and wished you had never caused her
such trouble, and next day McPhee would halter a cow that was
in season and take her round to the bull, trying to make fun of
it, while you began to understand the blind instinct and cruelty
in the life force and survival of nature. And some of the cottars
would tell you that most of their bairns were mistakes, or that
they could hardly shake their breeks in front of their wives and
they were nicked. But for all his taunting Jock Herd would give
a bit hach of a spit in the wind and say it wasn't so bad as all
that for some. Ach these were really bad cases and his wife would
look after Gertie for you, seeing there was no district nurse; that
she was damned good at that sort of thing, being a midwife like,
having had a few herself, though she was past it now poor bitch.

And there wouldn't be much to worry about with yon Dr. Craw, 'cause he left most things to nature and used chloryform at the end to make things easier kind for the creature that was having the bairn.

Of course you never mentioned any of these things to poor Gertie, who got bigger and bigger as the weeks dragged on, and the bigger she got the more you pittied her sitting there knitting by the fire while you tried to settle your mind to a book. But books didn't seem all that important nowadays since you had been in contact with another human being and caused her a great hurt which you was going to have to answer for. The thought of it nearly made you sick, and you wondered how poor Gertie could smile in your callous face so patiently, so sweetly, while she held up the garments she was weaving for the bairn, which you now regarded as a sort of demon you had created within her. But after all she was herself one of ten bairns that her mither had suffered with, all born at home in the box-bed, and all brocht into the world by the same doctor, yon fat cloart of a chiel they called 'Whistling Rufus,' because he sat on a chair and whistled all the time the woman was in her pains; but right clever he was too, for he had cured one of the bairns that had St. Vitus' Dance, by making it sit on the sunny doorstep for days on end twirling its little thumbs between its knees until the rest of its body stopped twitching. And when another of the bairns swallowed a safety-pin he wouldn't let them give it a drop of liquid, but had them feed it on nothing but dry meal for three days, until the pin came right through the creature harmlessly. But surely Gertie must have seen or heard her own mither in the throes of this hideous thing—yet she never mentioned it and you were afraid to ask. Maybe she could laugh your fears to scorn, you silly chiel that had only one sister and had lived in a dream world with your books and film stars all your innocent life. But after all the things you had seen in the dairy byres you just couldn't forget the savagery of nature. You had always worked on the beef producing farms, where they kept only two or three old pet cows that calved easily, and you'd sometimes helped with the ewe lambing; but with heifers it was different, heifers were young cows with their first calves, and Gertie was a heifer, a virgin before you'd touched her.

MOONLIGHT FLITTING

There had been a fluffert of snow in March and you had to sweep and shovel the snow from the drills to get at the turnips, your feet freezing and your hands numb with the cold. And when the storm cleared McPhee went away to a wedding all by himself and was that drunk he spent a week's wages and left the wedding present on the train. You had to lend the poor devil some money to buy fags because they couldn't get any more credit at the shop. His wife had taken to the whindykes again when the butcher or the baker called, sitting out there in the snow, and the poor woman was that much in debt that Gertie shared with her what she could spare, for she had confided in Gertie of their poverty. Yet she wouldn't hear an ill word of her man though he spent every penny, and from what you could hear of them in their beds through the wall they were a loving pair, though sometimes she protested loudly that he was going too far with his foolery, and that she didn't want any more bairns when they were so much in debt. And sometimes old Lowrie took McPhee's bairns home from the school in his car and his wife gave them tea in the fairmhoose, almost made a party of it. But McPhee didn't like this sort of charity and it sobered him up for a while, trying to make ends meet.

But somehow you dreaded that a day of reckoning was coming for McPhee, when he would have to settle these debts that were hanging about his neck like a millstone, tightening the noose with a creditors' list that would drive them to plundering his household in a bill of sale, by warrant of sheriff, for the little it was worth, as you can't take the breeks off a Highlander, as they say, when he wears a kilt.

But now the knife-edge winds of a late spring were blowing on the budding trees, but with little heat in the sun to nourish their growth; a dry, cold withering blast that swept across the frost-bitten fields with a pittiless hand, where the sprouting grain struggled to keep alive in such a heartless world. A haze of dust rose behind the dancing harrow and the hungry gulls sailed aimlessly in the wind, placquered against a chill blue sky of broken, fleeting cloud. Sometimes a lark went darting into the cold sunlight, chirping out his hearty song that was carried away in the wind. Out bye you could hear the earie wheeble of the teuchats, 'peezie-weep, peezie-weep,' over their broken nests, angry with the horsemen that were disturbing their peace, darting down in defiance of the ceaseless furrow, skimming low over the heads of the horses straining at the yoke, and the chiel hirpling between the stilts, steering by the coulter buckled to the beam of his plough, and the reins from the horse bridles twisted round his wrists. Aye it was cold out there where Gertie hung your sark and your drawers to dry in the wind, but inside it was warm with the sun at the windows, where you might put your finger in a flower pot to feel the warmth of the earth and the green smell of the plant.

You knew in the cold grey of morning that you were likely to be a father before nightfall. You could feel the sword thrust in Gertie's back and you could see the anguish in her whitened face, so at breakfast time you went down to Jock Herd's wife and told her what you thought, so she ran up to your Gertie and you 'phoned the doctor from the parlour at the Blackstob, not caring a damn for your muddy boots on the carpet. The doctor's car was at your gable by nine o'clock, where you saw it from the turnip shed, and it was still there at noon when you had your dinner in McPhee's kitchen, not to disturb your wife. You wanted to go inside at yoking time, but the doctor being there you were shy, so you denied her the little comfort that even the sight of you might have given her.

Even at milking time the big black car was still at your gable. My God! What were they doing to Gertie all that time? You could hardly settle to the milking and fell behind McPhee, for you kept running to the door of the turnip shed, where you were sure you heard the screams of your wife on the wind. But you could stand it no longer so you took your jacket from a nail on the wall and left McPhee to the milking and ran down the road to the little white house where all your world existed. Shame or guilt or fear had no power over you now, for you must see at once what was happening to your Gertie.

But when you reached the door there was silence, not a scream, nor even a whisper, while you stood there listening, the whip of the wind in your ears. But you opened the door and walked inside just the same, cap in hand, now knowing what to expect, though you had every right to know. Your wife was almost naked on the bed, a lifeless crucifix of mortal agony, her nightdress rolled above her navel and her knees apart, the doctor between them with his bare arms, one foot on the floor and a knee on the bed, a gentle but powerful man, pulling at the bairn with brute strength, while Herd's wife had both arms under Gertie's oxters, her knees against the bed, holding with all her weight against the strength of the man lest he pull your wife to the floor, a tug of war between life and death, and your loving Gertie the awful sacrifice. She lay athwart the bed, her sleeping body writhing in the grapple of pain that seized her, her bosom heaving quickly with her breathing, her rich black hair ravelled over her sweating face, her mouth convulsed in speechless motion, her white feeble hands still clinging to the iron bedrails as she had sunk into the chloroform. Dr. Craw glanced at you over his shoulder; merely glanced and ignored you, while Herd's wife shook her head and glowered at you with big frightened eyes full of concern.

Then you heard the first faint cry of the infant, its crimson head cupped in bloody irons in the doctor's hands, pulling it forth in a flush of blood and water. The doctor cut and tied the ends of the umbilical cord, while Herd's wife relaxed her hold on your still unconscious Gertie. She poured a bath tub of lukewarm water by the fireside, then took the bleeding bairn from the doctor and held it in the water, all the time skelping life into the creature until it began to move and breathe and cry. "You've got a loon!" she cried gladly, looking at your scared face. But you was watching the doctor, while he hid your wife's blood-stained hips with the blankets. He untwisted her death grasp from the bedrails and slapped her cheeks through her ravelled hair, flexing her arms and speaking to her until she opened her eyes, half smiling at you standing there like an overgrown schoolboy. Then Dr. Craw got a needle and cat gut out of his bag and said bluntly that he would have to stitch your Gertie. But you had seen enough to scare you for a lifetime and you dashed out of the house, never even looking at your skirling infant—back to the Blackstob and the milking, but with a strange new gladness in your heart, the first young pride of being a father.

STRAW INTO GOLD

You had your supper at McPhee's again and then went round to see your wife, the house smelling strongly of lysol and baby powder. The doctor had gone and Herd's wife left when you entered, promising to be back after she had suppered her man. Gertie was peaceful now, lying with your bairn beside her and her black hair laced over the white pillow. It was a loon she told you and you said you knew and looked at his puckered crimson face in your wife's oxter; and then you kissed her sweetly and fondly, holding her gently in your young strong arms. But your quine was possessed with a great gnawing hunger she said, and had a great craving for corn flakes, so you got on your bike and went to the shop for corn flakes, the first time you had ever seen the stuff, and you shook out a plateful from the carton, with sugar and cream, and fed your wife with a spoon, lovingly, until she was satisfied, and not allowing her to make any effort on her own behalf.

So you thought everything was fine, and the sun at your windows again, bringing forth the flower from the buds in the lovely carved bowl that Gertie loved so well on the sill, where she could see it from the bed, as the petals stretched forth their colours to the light. But on the second day of the doctor's absence a fever took your young wife that quickened her pulse and redened her cheeks and sent her into delirium. Dr. Craw came in the evening and injected Gertie with a serum which was supposed to arrest her fever, but it merely opened her closing eyes to the misery of your face, for even as you placed your rough loving hand on her burning forehead your tears landed on her cheeks—now hot now cold, but growing slowly colourless and feeling not the touch of your fingers in the creeping hush of death. Dr. Craw cursed himself and said he should have been sent for sooner. But it came upon your Gertie so quickly and Herd's wife said she had never seen it before, this child-bed fever that had sneaked up like a thief in the night, when the doctor's back was turned, and stole away your Gertie. Milk fever, child-bed fever, call it what they liked, but of all the terrors you had seen in the byres that this should kill your loving wife, her that should have been in a hospital ward, where they might have saved her. For had you not seen the vets inflate a cow's udder and tie her teats with tape, injecting her with glucose and calcium to save her life and managed it. Your Gertie had been a human being but was now a stiff corpse in your little bedroom. Up in the Bogside they had a district nurse for looking after the women, but not in this parish at the Blackstob.

So your mither took your wee son off your hands and you buried Gertie back in the Bogside, among her ain folk, where the kirk bell could be heard at Slabsteen, your Garden of Eden, the shrine of your betrothal, the Paradise you had lost. Your mither had also taken away the coloured things Gertie had knitted so fondly for her bairn, looking forward to its birth with such cheerfulness and patience, such bravery of soul, such confidence; and she had been right in her choice of blue, for she always said it would be a loon, but you couldn't stand the sight of them lying there on a chair, it brought a lump in your throat and a tear to your eye, though you'd have to get used to your son wearing them.

So you were back where you started at the Blackstob, but without your Gertie, living alone and sad in the little home you had built up between you; your 'Little Grey Home in the West' you had sung about so cheerfully in your courting, and Gertie smiling so sweetly at your boyishness as you pedalled along on your bicycles, thinking maybe that you would never grow up, this loon that she had married so hastily, so unavoidably. But now you'd grown up all right and your laughter had turned to tears.

But you still got a bite of meat from Mrs. McPhee, and the poor woman mothered you almost and sometimes turned her face away to hide the tear on her cheek. Life must go on but you had little interest in it and your care for your work seemed without purpose. And you were feart to look folk in the face lest you lose control and weep, folk like Jock Herd and his poor obliging wife who in her ignorance did all she could to help—except call the doctor in urgency, which might have saved your Gertie.

Then one morning in your sleeplessness you banged on the wall to waken McPhee and there was no reply. Maybe they had all died of food poisoning or something, and in your grief and bitterness of heart you didn't really care. But even in the midst of your returning sorrow you struggled into your working dungarees and grabbed your torch and went round and rapped on the door. But all was silent as you stood there in the cold loneliness of the morning, the full moon grinning down at you from an almost starless sky, when the full glow of his face dims their glory. His expression was mocking and mysterious and he only had to wink an eye to look the mischievous image of McPhee himself, lurking home with his lump of shining coal in the midnight hours. It was an expression that could tell it all: of what he had heard and seen in the silent midnight hours of your sleep, before your returning grief awoke you to tossing restlessness. So you shone your torch in at the black curtainless windows, shining on blank bare walls and a house devoid of its occupants. They had taken a 'Moonlight Flitting,' as folks called it, mostly flying from debt to God knows where, and local traders found it hard ever to trace them again. Folk like that got another job in secret, mostly by 'phone from the papers, even without references, maybe a hundred miles away, among strangers, where they could make a fresh start, and the contractors who flitted them were either bribed or sworn to secrecy.

But for a moment your sadness left you, lost in the thought of the plight of others, then suddenly it struck you that you were all alone at the little cottages, that no loving Gertie would come after you with a coat about her shoulders, her sweet kind face asking what ailed you; her soft tender fingers wiping away the tears that sprang in your bewildered eyes. Oh Gertrude! Even the thought of her ghost was a comfort that thrust all fear from your heart. No you wouldn't run like an excited bairn to tell Lowrie what had happened; you'd just walk quietly up the brae and knock loud and clear on the front door till Lowrie's light went on in his upstairs bedroom. For though you were numbed with grief, your manhood purged in youth, you must stumble on in your darkness of soul, and the memory of your Gertrude would be as a new star in the heaven of your heart.

SNOWFIRE!

THE river was frozen over to a depth of seven inches. You could see the ice encroaching from the banks as the days passed, closing in upon the flowing current, until only a trickle ran in the middle, and finally this disappeared and the water ran under the ice. And if you stuck a fork handle in the river at the Latch Farm you could barely touch the bottom. Snow blizzards came sweeping over the barren hills and whitened the fields and haughs in mounting drifts. Trees were exploding in the frost and turnips were bursting in the drills. And if you took hold of a wire to stride over a fence it stuck to your fingers and nearly tore the skin away. The old folks in Buchan couldn't remember the likes of it in their time; only once before could they mind on the river being frozen, away back in the 'eighties, when a fee-ed loon took a short cut over the ice, going home to his folks with his fule claes at the week-end, carried in a small bag over his back, what they called his 'chackie,' and on his way back to his place the loon fell through the ice at the Latch and was never seen again.

It was the winter of 1941-42 and the Russians were fighting for their lives in the siege of Leningrad. The folks in Buchan said they were getting the tail-end of the Russian winter, though others said it was blowing straight from the Arctic; but in either case it gave everybody a good idea of what the Russians were putting up with. Hitler was at the gates of Moscow, and you were damned glad he had turned on Stalin and saved your skin, so you thought about the Russian folk starving and dying in their fight for Leningrad and you tore at the neeps with a heartened will.

So you dug the snow from the turnip drills and tore at the frozen bulbs with a pick or an adze, and all you'd get for an afternoon's wark was enough to fill a horse cart, scarcely a starvation diet for all the beasts that were chained in the Latch byres, besides those loose in the courts. There was an ample store of bean and corn silage in the concrete tower, hay and straw in the barns, but as everything was frozen up and no water supply available these had to be balanced with the moisture giving turnip. The storm had caught Gerald Sansom of the Latch Farm with his breeks down, so to speak, without a store of fresh turnips in a clamp, and he neglected this because for so many years he had stored neeps and never required them, relying on silage in normal snowstorms to see him through. But already the beasts were getting hard in the dung and dry in the hair as the storm lengthened. You couldn't carry water in pails to all your beasts, about a hundred and twenty, including calves and the three milk cows for the cottars' milk, especially when everything was frozen up but the kitchen tap and the horse-trough, the latter supplying one of the courts. And those twenty-odd Irish heifers in the other court, which normally was supplied with rain water, in a trough from the roof—these were the biggest problem, and already howling in their thirst. Sansom had bought them just before the storm broke, and since they came off the boat he had been compelled to keep them in quarantine for three weeks as a precaution against transit fever or foot-and-mouth disease. He bought a batch every year and wintered them with the bull. Each one yielded a calf, and when the calf had been suckled and weaned he sold the mother fat at a profit. The calf in its turn added to his stock, which saved him buying so many store cattle at the marts as replacement when he sold his fat beasts. This year the ink was scarcely dry in his Record of Movement of Stock Book when the white inferno engulfed the turnip fields.

It was the hardest winter Gerald Sansom had known since he came to farm the Latch twenty years ago. The Sansoms were the landed gentry hereabouts, Gerald and his brothers, though he was the one that farmed the Latch, like his father before him, and you could walk from one end of the parish to the other and scarcely be off their land, except when you crossed the road, when likely as not you'd meet a Sansom with a flock of sheep or a drove of nowt, and you'd have to stand aside to let them pass, for they usually filled the road; and they would be off to eat some lad's grass who needed money badly or he wouldn't let a Sansom on to soil his parks, for they would eat it to the bone, till you could see the dung of the beasts like molehills, and the field as bare that you'd never loose sight of a mouse from one end of it to the other.

And maybe he'd have to wait a while for his cash the lad, for they were slack payers the Sansoms and liked to have you come begging for your money, like you was a tink or something, or a dog eating crusts from their table. The crofters said you was always better to go to the Latch when Sansom was off in his big car, for then you'd get his wife at the back kitchen door, when she would rant and rave at her man for his neglect and you'd get your money right quick after that, for she was a right decent body Mrs. Sansom they said, and it was a pity she had married that Sansom brute.

But the main grudge that the crofters had against the Sansoms was that their father had bought some of their holdings over their heads, land that was clay and the steadings were done, and no local laird to repair them, only a syndicate that had no interest in their affairs, so long as they paid their rents and asked nothing in return. When the Syndicate wound up and the places went up for sale the tenants got the first option. But some of the sitting tenants couldn't afford to buy their places, nor could anybody else for that matter, but the Sansoms had the money and they bought the crofters out. Some of them were glad to go, because they couldn't afford the horse or the oxen they'd lost in the driech darg of the clay, blue and dour in the turn of the plough, setting hard in their tracks, till the harrows barely scratched it, and they couldn't make a loam to take seed; iron hard or a squelch of myre, depending on the weather, and the crops were hanged in the baking clay or drowned in a spleiter of rain that spread out on the parks for weeks, because it couldn't get through the clay. By summer it had all drained away, leaving the land cracked and bare, so that the crofters had to cart water for their thirsting beasts, and the grass parks were seared and brown in the scorching sun.

And if a crofter ever looked back he'd see that the Sansoms had his place all in grass and crawling with sheep, after they'd waited a while and tilled in a season that would take seed, coming away fine on the clay that takes grass and clover better than free land, once it takes a hold, and will last longer. And the Sansoms had a shepherd in the old farmhouse and the steading in ruins, for the Sansoms had no use for a steading, all they needed was a few lambing pens and a dipping trough, and a fence round the place that even reindeers could hardly jump.

So if you was a Sansom you got yourself a bad name among folk, but God knows being a Sansom you knew you didn't deserve it. You couldn't let the places go to rashes and nettles just because nobody else wanted them, or hadn't the money to buy them, and sometimes you left a tenant in his farmhouse and gave him a job fencing the land or working at the Latch in a busy season—damnit, what more could they want?

But since the war started the Government had compelled Sansom to plough up some of the crofts again, and sent him big motor-ploughs that mastered the clay, growing flax on land that wouldn't take corn the first year, because of a weevil in the soil, and Sansom remembered how it had taken on the blue flower on the sweep of the hill, and the Government lads came back to harvest the stuff with plucking machines that bound it into sheaves like a binder. And Sansom only had to stook the stuff till it matured like rank heather, then build it into stacks until they were ready for it at the factory, but he got plenty of prisoner-of-war labour for that at a cheap rate, and the motor lorries drove it away. Sansom was on to a gold mine growing flax for the Government on land he had bought for a song, and the evicted crofters resented it and called him ill names for his better fortune.

But as much as they condemned Sansom and approved his wife the crofters didn't know all the outs and ins of the Sansom household. True enough Sansom was a bit tight-fisted among poorer folks, and maybe you wouldn't trust him with your school-going daughter, but for a long time there wasn't a man or a cottar woman about his place who would breathe a word against him, for they knew he wasn't so bad as he was painted, and that Mrs. Sansom had become a crack-pot who gave him a dog's life, and they wondered that the man had patience with the creature and didn't wring her dainty neck. She had grace Mrs. Sansom, Clara

as he called her, a cultured, sensitive, delicate woman, and she
moved about the farm mansion like a ballerina, sometimes singing
and throwing flowers about, or splashing water on the floor, just
for the sight of the maid on her knees drying it up, because one
day she had seen her man give the quine a playful skelp on the
hip in the bygoing, a daughter of one of the crofters who now
poisoned his name in the district.

Nowadays Sansom took to his bed by himself and his wife
hardly spoke civil to him. And she'd hold up his dirty sark with
a dainty thumb and fore-finger, as if it belonged to a tinker and
crawling with lice, and she'd drop it out from his upstairs bedroom
window, where it landed on the green, and the dog wiped his
paws on it, then carried it away in his big mouth and buried it
among the bushes, the earth flying on to the gravel path where
Sansom was dutch-hoeing in his shirt-sleeves, hat on the back of
his head, pipe in mouth, watching his wife at the window. And
Clara would skirl with laughter and then shut the window with a
clash, like a guillotine on a criminal's neck.

Sometimes in desperation Sansom took it out on his men,
just to prove his authority to somebody, and even among his own
cottars his name was beginning to stink, so that past kindnesses
were forgotten and they said among themselves that Sansom should
have his doup kicked, or that he should be tarred and feathered
and set fire to, or thrown in the river with a stone about his neck.
Fancy that, and you the farmer about the place, strutting about like
a bantam cock and everybody waiting a chance to wring your
neck. It was a sad state of affairs and you a big farmer among
the gentry and expecting to be looked up to in the parish.

It had been fine in the old days when the bairns were young,
before young Irvine died, and while Errol and his two sisters, Gail
and Muriel were still at school. These were happy days and Gerald
Sansom remembered them fondly, when they were all around the
log fire in the big bay sitting room on a winter's evening, the light
shining bright from the electric candleabra, glinting on Clara's
golden hair and her blue eyes laughing at the bairns, while they
tumbled on the big divan or rolled on the carpet, its lush depths
littered with their toys, while the red Setter lay by the fire, his

snout on his paws, with one eye watching the bairns, lest they sneak a ride on his back. Sometimes Clara would play the piano and they would all have a sing song, or she would read to the bairns till they all fell asleep in Wonderland, when she and the maid would carry them upstairs to bed, each hugging a big doll or Teddy Bear, and a deep silence fell upon the house. Then Clara would get out her easel, palette and brushes, daubing on the paint to form some sylvestral scene from her own lively imagination, while her finished works graced the walls in frames of figured gilt and ivoried wood.

On a summer evening Sansom would take them all for a run in the Chrysler and treat them to ice cream, and he'd drive them round the crofts and his shepherds, and Clara would get out of the car and visit them, like a queen among her subjects, and the shepherds' wives thought her a right genteel woman, whom they all loved and respected (whatever they thought of Sansom) though the sight of her jewellery dazzled their poorer eyes, and her perfume was not of their gardens. And Clara seemed so happy; a radiant, kindly, loving wife and mother, and Gerald Sansom thought himself blessed and fortunate in the arms of Providence.

But then the Gods withdrew their smiles from the Sansom household, and they smote their younger son with a long and withering illness that took the roses out of Clara's cheeks, yet left the trembling dewdrop, a transparent tear upon the pallid skin. Clara had never been quite the same since Irvine died, though it had given her joy to see their daughters married, Gail first and then Muriel, and now living abroad, while only Errol, their elder son remained, working on the Latch with his father.

And then Clara's smiling lips had gradually turned to snarl at Sansom, and the eyes that once caressed his soul now changed to beams of hate, her lilting voice more like the hiss of a snake. And Gerald Sansom searched his heart for any reason why he should deserve this, and he could find none to merit it, unless it were the slapping of a lassie's thigh, which was nothing to speak of, but you'd think to hear Clara that he had taken the poor quine to the barn.

SNOWFIRE!

Things had reached a pitch just before the war, and Sansom remembered the day they were going off in the car, Errol driving and his mother in the back seat, laughing and giggling at nothing, and just before leaving she nipped off Sansom's hat and threw it out at the window, and when he jumped out to pick it up, chasing his rolling hat across the windy lawn, Clara had Errol put the car in gear and drove off without him, leaving Sansom standing on the drive like an idiot, hat in hand and a strange curse on his lips. But he was puzzled about his wife's behaviour; she was so much changed from the Clara he once knew and loved. That the loss of their son had disturbed her was understandable; but it should have brought them closer together, not driven them apart. There was something sinister in her obsession about his familiarity with the housemaid, even to the extent of poisoning Errol against him, judging by the latest event in their relationship. Surely Clara had the whole thing out of proportion?

Then the war came and Errol was called up for the Militia. Gerald had tried to exempt his only surviving son from military service but it was refused him, and Errol had told his father he wouldn't accept it anyway. Errol had been captured at St. Valery and was now a prisoner-of-war in Germany, while Sansom was left with an estranged wife in a surly Arctic winter.

But while the snowdrop faded and the lily bloomed, as the crocus withered and the sunflower glowed, while the petal fell and gave way to fruit, while season followed seedtime into harvest and autumn into winter—in the passing of time Clara's illness crept upon her, revealing itself in a slight breathlessness; in her transparent, wilting beauty, in the lunar depths of her distant eyes, like dying stars where once the diamond sparkled. But when Sansom suggested a doctor Clara threw a vase at him, smashing it against the papered wall, scattering the fragments about his feet, and then she was seized by a fit of coughing and a lapse of consciousness. While she lay in a swoon the first big snowflakes came ogling across the lawn and melted on the panes of the great bay windows. During her revival they came thicker and faster, sticking to the glass and darkening the room. In her saner, more compassionate days, what Clara had always feared was beginning to materialise, for she had always dreaded someone taking ill in a snowstorm and all the roads blocked and no way of getting a doctor or an ambulance to take them to hospital, just in the same way as she always imagined a steading fire during a snow blizzard and no way of getting a fire-engine, quite normal fears and anxieties that Sansom always dismissed with a shrug and a smile, telling Clara that her imagination was running away with her better reason. But even as Clara opened her eyes the world was now engulfing her, closing in upon her with a soft white suffocation, and while Sansom pleaded for her permission to 'phone a doctor she cried out in protest against the rising blast. But Sansom rose from her trembling side and picked up the 'phone, Clara staggering behind him but unable to deter his stronger arm.

"It's a conspiracy," she cried, tearing at his shirt sleeve, "you just want me out of the way so that you can marry that girl!"

But now the doctor was at the front door, like a snowman from the wastes of nowhere. The maid took his snowy coat and hat and hung them on a peg in the hall, then conducted him to the bay room, while she herself retired to the kitchen. Doctor Crammond didn't know how he had reached the Latch in such a blizzard and was deeply concerned about getting back to town. "I don't need a doctor," Clara protested, "there's nothing wrong with me but a chest cold, and if you think you are going to get me into one of those horrid sanitorium sheds in the garden, like the one Irvine died in you are sorely mistaken. But I'll tell you something doctor, and maybe you won't believe it," and she walked over to Crammond and spoke almost in a whisper—"Mr. Sansom is taking up with the maid and wants me out of the way so that he can marry her!"

Doctor Crammond listened carefully, wiping the moistened snow from his glasses with his handkerchief, recalling to mind the good looking girl who had taken his hat and coat at the door. When he put on his glasses again Sansom almost winced under his suspicious stare. He then took Clara's arm and led her to the divan, where she sat down demurely, surprised it seemed that her story hadn't caused an outburst. Crammond then sat down beside her and spoke gently, reassuringly: "Mrs. Sansom," he said, "I have no intention of putting you into a sanitorium in the garden, least of all with a chest cold in weather like this—you'd starve to death woman. No no, we can't have that, but now that I'm here would you let me examine you? After all a chest cold should be attended to before it gets worse and a tonic might build you up a bit. Would you be such a good woman as to go upstairs to your bedroom and let me have a look at you. I should like to examine you pretty thoroughly or we see what this is all about."

"But you're not believing me about Gerald and the maid." And Clara looked at the doctor in a pleading, half puzzled sort of manner.

"We'll talk about that too, shall we? Upstairs then!"

So Clara was persuaded and went upstairs to her room, weak and short of breath, the doctor going up later, glancing at Sansom almost with a wink in his eye as he climbed the stairs. He examined Clara thoroughly, talked to her, gave her a sedative and left her lying quietly on the bed, then came down to Sansom in the living room. Sansom took the doctor into a side room for a wee dram to cheer him on his way, where they could talk freely out of Clara's hearing.

"Good God man," Crammond said, tippling his glass, "I should have been here years ago. The last time I saw your wife her general health gave me no cause for anxiety. But now this . . . and why the hell didn't you send for me sooner? You must have noticed that your wife's health was failing. Surely you don't want that on your conscience!"

Sansom stared at his doctor in great alarm. "Surely you know me better than that," he said, "and if only you knew what I have put up with all this time to save my conscience. All this nonsense about the housemaid . . ."

"You mean you could have harmed your wife?"

"Sometimes I was tempted, but as I say I spared my conscience. You don't believe that yarn do you? About the housemaid I mean."

"Of course not, but tell me about it."

"Well Crammond, you think you know me but you don't know Clara. She has given me hell lately about this quine and I should have sacked the poor bitch long ago for peace of mind. Clara could have done it herself for all I cared and I told her so, but she said it would hurt my feelings and used the quine as a weapon against me. Something went wrong after Irvine died and I couldn't understand it. I tried several times to send for you but Clara wouldn't hear of it; even now I 'phoned you against her will."

Both men eyed each other across the table and then Crammond spoke: "You know Sansom, I'm believing your innocence about the housemaid, and that your wife's accusations are false. But I'm a doctor, not a lawyer, and I'm going to tell you what I think."

"Yes."

"Your wife has tuberculosis of the lungs, well advanced, and I dare say that an X-ray would reveal them like a sponge. I'd need a specialist to confirm my further diagnosis Mr. Sansom, but I also suspect that your wife has tuberculosis of the brain; I'm not sure mind you but I think it accounts for her strange behaviour. It's an organic corruption of course, and what with her poor lungs and lack of proper oxygen to the brain I think she is deranged. In her condition that little familiarity you had with the housemaid would be enough to trigger off something of the kind in such a sensitive woman. Oh yes, she told me about that." And Crammond ventured a smile. "But it's nothing more than I've done myself in my time and got away with it!"

"But it's been a long time in doing her any real harm, this illness I mean!" Sansom ventured, sipping his whisky.

"Well there's been some spitting of blood or bowel discharge but we don't know what harm has been done; and I'll certainly need a second opinion Sansom. But most likely it will accelerate eventually: what is sometimes known as Galloping Consumption, and believe me it isn't called that for fun, but for its speedy end to the patient."

Crammond rose from his chair and walked to the window, hands behind his back, where he stood for a moment watching the snow-flakes whirling at the glass, coming ever faster in the rising wind, now howling in the chimney and moaning at the doors. Sansom sat with his elbows on his knees, rolling the whisky glass between his palms, a dry fear in his mouth, his eyes glazed with tears. "Doctor," he asked, "do you think she will last till Errol gets back?

SNOWFIRE!

I know she would like that. Maybe it's impossible to get the girls home just now but after the war it would be easier."

Crammond came back from the window, his face wrapped in thought. "Depends how long the war lasts, but I hardly think so; a month or two perhaps; maybe less, and she may go desperately mad . . . not the straight-jacket or the padded cell, she would be too weak for that, but insulin perhaps, and there's just the possibility that she may slip quietly away in a coma. Look Sansom, I'm terribly sorry about all this but when the end comes we could handle her better. Get Clara into hospital before the storm closes in completely; persuade her, tell her it's for an X-ray, anything, but get her there somehow, and the sedatives will help. I'll send an ambulance as soon as possible. I'll have to push off now while the roads are still passable; the wind is getting up and they could be blocked in a matter of hours. Tell you what: I'll 'phone an ambulance now, and I'll leave more sedatives. Tell your maid to get her mistress ready to leave!"

But the ambulance never reached Clara. Even while she was being prepared for hospital a howling blizzard enclosed the Latch, a white and furious holocaust that raged for three days and nights and had barely spent itself at the end of a week; then terrific frost and blowing snow that cut off the farm completely from the outside world. Sheep were buried everywhere and the shepherds on the crofts were digging them out at the risk of their own lives. For lack of turnips the cattle in the byres were bellowing for water, and those Irish heifers in the dry court were howling their heads off. The Latch farm was two miles from the main road; two miles of wind-packed snow, level with the hedges and still blowing. Sansom tried to 'phone Doctor Crammond but the wires were broken, borne down by a weight of ice that made them as thick as cables, snapping between the poles. So he got two of the cottar wives to look after Clara, because she resented the maid, and they took it in turns, day and night, looking after her, but intruding as little as possible, because she wouldn't hear of being an invalid. Sometimes in her sedation she cried out for Errol, thinking he was an angel, and would fly to her on wings of silver shining bright.

71

STRAW INTO GOLD

It was into the second week before the folk at the Latch could get about with their shovels, clearing paths from the cottar houses to the steading, to their wells and hen-runs, and all were short of food because there were no vans to supply them. There was no postman either, and no newspapers, though John Snagge and Alvar Lidell told them on the radio how the war was going; how the gallant Russians were still holding out at Leningrad, and how our convoys were still reaching them with supplies at Murmansk, despite attacks in the Arctic by German submarines, and the risk of pocket battleships. Though there was no meat for the dinner the cottars at the Latch boiled a frozen turnip and made neepbrose. Only on a Sunday would they kill a laying hen to make broth, for though it lasted a family for two or three days it was something of a sacrilege when you thought about the folks at Leningrad.

For the cottar bairns it was something of a holiday because they couldn't go to school. Nobody died in their little world and everybody lived to be terribly old. Sledges and toboggans were out in strength on the slopes and the snowballs were flying from every nook and cranny. Sansom had three horsemen and the grieve working on the road, heaving snow to a height of nearly eight feet, while it stuck to their shovels in the frost. But the powdered drifts still whipped across the fields and covered in their tracks again. Even the main roads were blocked, though Sansom didn't know it, with no hope of an ambulance reaching his wife. But he would have his men dig the two miles and take Clara by horse-sledge to the main road, where he hoped there would be motor-ploughs and a chance of reaching the town. Even the fields were over a foot deep in crusted snow, swept by choking powder drifts that filled the burns and piled against the dykes and hedges, impassable barriers for man and beast.

Meanwhile Sansom had to think of his stock, parched for want of water and without turnips, for they couldn't endure long on silage and dry fodder. The turnips in the sheds were for the byres, and even these were frozen. Kevin Porter, head stockman at the Latch was smashing the stone-hard swedes on the floor with a fencing hammer, because they wouldn't go through the slicer, and

72

when thrown in the feed troughs the animals thawed the pieces with their warm breath. Sansom told Kevin and his assistant, Geordie Thom to carry the old house bath into the dung court and water the crazed heifers with pails from the kitchen tap, the only one that was running, for he couldn't stand the noise of the brutes, and they were disturbing Clara. He had told her they were taking her away by horse-sledge for an X-ray, and she had cried about it and said she hated snowstorms. But the sedatives Doctor Crammond left were beginning to take effect, and Clara dried her eyes and seemed to be looking forward to her sleigh-ride; it would be so jolly she said, just like Christmas, with holly berries and tinkling bells, and Errol would be waiting for her at the end of her journey. Poor boy, he must be weary of waiting.

The horsemen still toiled on the road, never even taking time off to run their horses out on the snow, so that their legs were swelling for lack of exercise, standing idle in the stable, such a long time away from the plough. They would have to thresh a stack of grain shortly the grieve said, but while the straw still lasted in the barn the mistress came first. Neighbours came to help on the road and the small army of shovels managed about half-a-mile a day. The snow was freshening slightly, leaving their shovels cleaner. In three or four days they should break through.

But there was no satisfying the thirst-crazed heifers in the court. They drank water faster than the feeble tap would run, fighting to get at the trough, ripping each other open with their cruel horns. Even the horse trough for the store bullocks was licked dry and Kevin suggested letting all the animals out to eat snow, in spite of the quarantine. But Sansom thought he had a better idea, for he remembered Kevin smashing turnips with the fencing mallet, so he told him to take it and smash a hole in the ice at the river's edge, big enough for an animal to drink—to hell with restrictions, and he and Geordie would bring the heifers down to the haugh. It was the day the men reached the main road and at last an ambulance would be waiting there for Clara. The path cut by the men wasn't wide enough for motor traffic, but would take a single horse and sledge, so the men would be ready about an hour after dinner, once they got the sledge rigged out and a

73

horse harnessed. Sansom would take the beasts to water and be back to see Clara off; he wouldn't like her to leave the Latch and all that nowt howling, and he would like to kiss her goodbye, for if the storm came again it might be the last time . . . Even the frost had gone at mid-day and a dazzling sun shone upon the snow. Icicles were forming on the byre roofs, like glittering rows of sharpened spears, where the heat of the cattle had melted the snow. At night it would be brittle frost again, especially with a growing moon, but during the day it was a warm, blinding desert.

Kevin Porter shouldered the 14lb. hammer and struggled through the sun-flashed snow. The ice on the river was iron hard and he could only chip the surface with the rebounding hammer. It seemed that nothing short of a charge of dynamite or a German bomb could smash a hole in the steel-grey roof that covered the running water. Kevin swung the hammer until he was out of breath, but for all his labour he failed to crack the ice, merely smashing it into sugar in a slightly deepening bowl. But eventually he broke through and the hammer splashed in the water, now running under eight inches of ice, strong enough to carry a horse, Kevin thought, or even a herd of nowt, if anyone cared to risk it. Now it was easier and he hammered the ice to break the edges, to make a hole wide enough for a beast to drink.

He had barely finished when he heard the heifers come bellowing from the farm. Sansom hadn't wasted any time but had opened the doors of the court and let the cattle out, a snow-blinded, thirst-crazed, stampeding horde that floundered in the deep drifts and plunged towards the river haugh, Sansom and Geordie panting behind them, and the black Labrador that Sansom kept as a game dog sniffing at their heels, though he was little use among cattle beasts.

On they came, plunging through the snow wreaths, their broad mobile backs arched in a stifled gallop, their hot breath rising like steam, heading straight for the water hole, drawn by the scent of the water. Kevin did his best to head them off, swinging the hammer in their faces and over their heads, stopping them in their tracks, allowing only one animal at a time to the water hole. But the press was too great for Kevin to hold them and he cried

74

SNOWFIRE!

for Geordie. Kevin yelled and laid about him with the hammer, but it was a useless struggle, and for his own safety he had to step aside. Geordie couldn't get near him, and while one animal drank the others pushed her forward on to the ice, two and three for a start, now half-a-dozen, the dry sugary surface holding their hoofs, and several leapt on from the snowbank, skidding to a halt on their hurdies, landing on the ice with a sickening thud. Sansom kept shouting to hold what they had on the bank and tried to send the dog on the ice to turn the others back. But the dog merely broke their ranks and more and still more heifers sprang on to the ice. One got stuck in the water hole, tearing her legs on the sharp edges, while she struggled in vain to get out. Of the twenty-three heifers only two now remained on the snow, Kevin and Geordie holding them back, and no one would dare go on the ice for the others.

Sansom stood on the sunlit bank and cursed himself aloud as a fool; dreading every moment that the ice would break. If it did the Insurance Company wouldn't cover his loss, and he would be heavily fined for breaking the quarantine rules. Better that he had continued watering the beasts from the kitchen tap, slow as it was, but it was no use now crying over spilled milk. And then he remembered Clara, even now they would be wrapping her up on the horse-sledge and he would have to hurry back to say goodbye! Oh the folly of it! But how could he drag himself away from the dreaded spectacle before him? A score of Irish heifers sniffing about for water on a death-trap! While every moment he expected to hear the first deafening crack on the ice. Now he was in a fit of anguished indecision: whether to watch his heifers drown or hurry home to kiss his dying wife. By now she would be under way. Silly that he thought he heard the noise of sleigh-bells, mingled with the mooing of the cattle.

Kevin was first to see the 'plane, a great black bird that came shining out of the westering sun, with the sign of the swastika under its wings, flying low over the snowy landscape, spattering the steading with rapid gunfire. Next moment it was roaring over the river, spurting hot bullets into the ice, stampeding the cattle, the rear-gunner's dome-shaped turret glistening in the sun, its twin stings swivelling downwards and spitting bullets at the running heifers, strafing them with deadly fire, a staccato that ricocheted far up the quiet valley, while the great stinging wasp sped on, a black shadow on the snow, an angel of death spattering gunfire on the distant farmsteads.

"Great God!" Sansom cried, but even as he spoke the first crack in the ice was like a gunshot. Several cattle lay dying in their own blood and the others burst into panic, scared by the noise of the plane and the gunfire they charged at each other in frantic bellowing fear, horns goring deep in hide. There was another succession of cracks, clear and sharp in the winter sunlight, and visible splinters appeared on the ice. The next moment the river split open and half-a-dozen heifers disappeared. Great sheets of ice slid apart and toppled the roaring animals into the blood-stained water. They pawed and scraped at the toppling edges as huge chunks of ice gave way. Animals were swimming desperately in circles while others vanished helplessly under the ice. Up and down the river where the cattle ran the ice gave way, and the crackling of ice and the lowing of nowt went far up the silent haugh, the swift black current sweeping the animals under the ice-roof, while some few sprang to the banks and safety. Only the dead now floated, blood seeping from their bullet wounds, and Sansom could look no longer. He turned wearily towards the Latch, his stick going deep in the snow, the black Labrador behind him, while Kevin and Geordie brought back the six surviving heifers, tamed with fear, shaking their wet hides and trembling in the cold.

Sansom had just missed Clara, the horse and sledge a mere pencil point between the distant snowbanks, where the white arch of the world met the china blue of the skyline. He met one of the cottar wives in the close. "The mistress has gone, Mr. Sansom," she said. "We had her on the sledge, all wrapped up in blankets and two hot-water bottles for her hands and feet; then that terrible 'plane came over, a German it was, shooting at the steading, and it frightened the horse till it bolted with the sledge, but my man held on to the reins and it didn't get very far in the deep snow. Your wife got a terrible fright Mr. Sansom and she cried out for you. But she came to no harm poor soul, and now she will be gone on the ambulance on the main road. It's the second time the Germans have gunned up everything hereabouts. Remember the last time when they nearly got one of my bairns going to school?"

"I remember, Mrs. Burr," Sansom said calmly, "I remember. And I thank you sincerely for your great kindness."

"Poor man, you've endured a lot lately," the woman ventured kindly.

"Aye, and besides that I've drowned nearly all my Irish heifers in the river. These that you see with Kevin and Geordie are all that survived, the others fell through the ice."

"Oh dear!"

That night all the lights failed at the Latch farm and Sansom said the turbine wheel must be frozen to the wall of the water-shed. Next day the men set to with hammers and chisels, chipping at the ice on the water-wheel, frozen at the spokes to the stone wall. But their efforts were in vain, because the buckets were solid in ice, a mere trickle of water coming from the chute, freezing like candle-grease as it dripped over the wheel. The bucket-wheel drove a generator that supplied the farm with light, though not the cottar houses, and up till now it had never failed, day or night, except perhaps when there was a spate, which floundered the wheel in water, and the light would rise and fall with the speed of the wheel, because it was direct current and no storage batteries. It was a cheap and fairly reliable source of power, diverted from the river, where once had been a meal-mill, even driving the turnip slicer on a three-phase system, and Sansom had never bothered to instal accumulators or an engine in case of break-downs.

Before the war the Latch Farm was all lit up at night and folk passing with their bicycles in the dark thought it was a great sight. They could see the road for half-a-mile on either side of the farm without their gas-lamps, and for miles around you could see the Latch lights twinkling on the river, a little Venice in the night. Sansom was proud of his illuminations, and that was why some folk called him the Bantam Cock, because he wasn't a big man physically, rather short and stocky, so maybe it was because the folk out by had to be content with stable lanterns that they called him names.

Of course the war and the black-out had ended the illuminations at the Latch, but the wheel had never stopped until the present freeze-up. Now it had failed Sansom in his hour of greatest need, and he didn't have a single lantern to light his farmhouse, nor even a hurricane lamp for his steading, nothing but a bundle of candles, which he handed out at nightfall to his workers; for stable, barn, courts and byres, and told them to be careful in case of fire, and he would see to it that such a thing would never happen again.

So Kevin and Geordie stuck a lighted candle on some of the travis posts along the double byre, two or three on pillars in the courts, and one in the barn, though not above the straw. At supper time they collected all their candles and put them safely away until morning, when they were lit again for the usual routine of feeding and mucking out the fattening steers. During the day they still carried water to some of the beasts or struggled in the neep park with a pick and shovel, for the frost still persisted, especially at night, when the powdery blizzard swept the fields, while by day great mountains of snow cloud towered around the blue horizon. Sometimes a trio of spitfires would zoom overhead, veterans from the Battle of Britain, training young pilots from Tortoston fighter station. In the far meridian a thread of vapour might reveal a Flying Fortress, a mere speck in the blue, or you would hear the friendly purr of an Avro-Anson from Coastal Command watching the sea.

Folks were having to wade knee-deep in snow to the nearest shop for provisions, some waist-deep across the howes to Jake's Emporium, because the roads were still choked, and where the cottagers had cleared a path the snow was as high as the eaves. Some even took their shovels inside at night, because mostly they had to dig their way out in the morning, their windows battered with snow and their rooms in darkness. Kevin and Geordie went to the shop in the evenings because they hadn't time during the day, and Jake would give them their ration of fags and tobacco for the week, and maybe a box of matches if they didn't have flint and fleerish and saltpetre for a light. It was a sair trauchle after a day in the byres, but they didn't mind so much since all Home Guard duties had been suspended in the Bourie hall during the storm. Sansom yoked the foreman with the horses and sledge, to get provisions from the town, but the track was blown half full again and he had to turn back. So Sansom sent two men to Jake's during the day, each with a pillow-slip, and they brought something for everybody, including a tin of Three-Nuns tobacco for Sansom, his favourite blend.

A fortnight had passed with the candles at the Latch, Kevin lighting one from the other to save matches, when one evening he saw a fat stot swipe a burning candle from a travis post with his tail. Kevin searched carefully for the missing candle, turning over the straw among the feet of the animals and even their dung, but he never found it. It must have been thrown to the ceiling, concealed but still burning, perhaps against a cobweb or an electric cable, or dripping fiery tallow on to the straw in the cattle hakes on the walls, for by nine o'clock the Latch was ablaze, a perfect target for the German bombers that came over from Stavanger in Norway, only three hundred miles across the North Sea. Sansom had always wondered why the Germans had invaded Norway, but now he was beginning to understand, and the merchant seamen didn't call the Buchan coastline 'Hell's Corner' for nothing.

Kevin Porter and Geordie Thom were coming home from Jake's Emporium when they saw the Latch on fire, the skylights red in the darkness, and a tongue of flame on the roof, rising ever higher, licking the night sky. They started to run, but it was difficult with Wellington boots in the deep snow, and pillow-slips stuffed with groceries. As they approached the Latch they heard the moaning of cattle, deep in the byres and muffled in the snow. Kevin and Geordie ran breathless to tell their wives, dropping their pillow-slips at the doors, then to rouse the grieve and the horsemen, and finally Sansom, who had fallen asleep by candle-light in the big bay sitting room, the labrador at his feet, while the maid was visiting the cottar wives.

Sansom's first thought was the telephone. Then he remembered the wires were down, and the snow-ploughs hadn't yet come near the Latch. In war time it was all they could do to keep the main roads clear. There was an ample supply of water where Sansom had drowned his heifers, but no fire-engine to pump it; about six hundred yards to the river, too far to form a human chain, he would need half the parish with their own buckets to do it, and by the time they got to the Latch in the deep snow it would be burned down. These were impossible thoughts, like clutching at burning straws, but they flashed through Sansom's mind with the red fire at his windows, the nowt now screaming in his ears from the blazing byres. And there was always the risk of German bombers. A recent pub fire in the Broch had been a night target that had cost the town forty lives. And Sansom cursed the bombers. "Hell and damnation!" he cried, as he ran into the close. "Damn the war! Damn the snow!" He was usually a quiet man who took life in his stride. But his son a prisoner of war; his wife dying in hospital; his cattle drowned; his steading on fire and no fire-engine! Great God! Just how much could the man take?

But even as the Latch burned the frost was losing its grip. The stars disappeared and the sky grew darker, and a freshening wind sprang up from the south-west, fanning the roaring flames and lifting the smoke cloud that hung above the steading. The red glare of the fire lit up the white countryside, turning the snow to crimson, a throbbing glow in the darkness that brought neighbours in from miles around, struggling in the snow to reach the Latch.

Men folk were already in the hot byres unchaining the frantic nowt beasts, clambering over their backs as they pranced about in terror, fighting their neck chains that the men were trying to slacken. Once free the beasts charged to the far end of the byre and came back with their hides on fire, tiny flames licking along their spines as they rushed outside to the wind. Men struggled desperately in the heat to set them free, choking in the dense smoke and tugging at the chains with hot sticky fingers. They ran outside for breath and couldn't get in again for charging bullocks. What with the roaring of cattle, the neighing of horses, the squealing of pigs, the cackle of poultry, the yelling of humans, the crackling of flames and the sough of the wind it was hell let loose at the Latch. Fiery rafters caved in and trapped the chained beasts still in their stalls, roasting them alive till the boiling fat was running down the urine channels, yellow flames licking at the trickle. Falling slates came in a shower and bursting glass flew from the skylights. Heat and smoke overcame human effort. Men stood back aghast, their faces blistering hot, their eyes smarting from timber smoke, their mouths parched with fear and excitement. The inside byre walls glowed like an oven and there was a sickening smell of roasting flesh and burning hair. A cry went up that the roof was falling and the last daring men ran out from the turnip shed, chased by fire-maddened, careering stirks. A great arc of fire crashed down and smothered the dying animals in an avalanche of flame, while the wind took showers of sparks over the steading, floating like tiny stars till they died in the snow.

Freeing the horses had been easier because the flames hadn't yet reached the stables; only smoke, which was bad enough, but each man haltered his pair and led them out to a park, rearing and neighing at the sight and din of the fire. Once free they galloped about in the drifts, their nostrils wide and their eyes bright with fear, kicking at the squealing pigs that ran at their heels in the beaten snow. Men threw open the doors of the dung courts and chased out the cattle, herding them into nearby fields for the night. Hens were cackling from the tree-tops and ducks were quacking in the snow. Cockerels still safely on the roost behind the steading thought it must be morning and were crowing in the din. Out by on the brae you could hear the bleating of sheep, safe from the fire but huddled in the snow wreaths. Cats ran about with kittens in their mouths and rats and mice were leaping everywhere, running along the blackened rafters and falling into the fire.

Nothing could be done to save the steading. The straw in the barn was a blazing inferno, devouring the threshing mill with hungry tongues of flame, feeding on the greasy oil-bearings and licking at the paraffin tank in the engine room. Slates came clattering down and rone pipes came away from the hot walls. The barn roof blazed like a herring-bone bent in the middle, where the embered cross-trees gave way and crashed in a upsurge of flying sparks, the heat exploding the paraffin tank in a muffled bang, spewing liquid fire into the stackyard, but the rucks were wet with melting snow and the flames died on the thatch. The dung in the cattle courts was blazing like a peat moss, fanned by the wind from the open doors, the iron roofs sizzling hot, the latticed wooden trusses a scissors work of spreading fire. The granary floor collapsed with tons of smouldering seed corn, smothering the raging furnace in the stables below. Fire raced along the canvas corn belt and ravaged the hayloft, reddening the skylights and splintering the glass, while a spiral of smoke rose mockingly from the old bothy chimney. The men had pulled out the horse carts from the arched pends under the hayloft, and all the hand tools they could rescue. Most of the heavier implements: binders, mowers, drill-sower, manure distributors, ploughs, harrows and rollers, besides a Fordson tractor were all safe in a large shed behind the steading, near the tower silo, seventy feet of concrete that wasn't even hot from the fire. The mansion house was never in any danger, secure in its scarf of trees, and while the garage burned fiercely Sansom's car was pushed safely to the front drive.

It was long past midnight and the heat so unbearable that folk stood back in a ring round the steading, standing in slush from the melted snow, their faces aglow in the firelight, while the wind still carried sparks and smoke far across the snow-lit fields, dotted with cattle and wandering pigs. "It's been a quick thaw!" somebody joked, and a ripple of quiet laughter went round the spectators. But the conflagration was dying and Gerald Sansom looked around at the many faces who had come through the snow to his aid. Some of them were evicted crofters of his father's day, now old men with bent backs and sharp piercing eyes: had they honestly come to help or to gloat over his misfortune? Others were neighbours of long acquaintance and some were folk he had never seen before, so that he couldn't tell farmers from cottars, master from man. But to Sansom that sad night all were friends; more than he had ever hoped to share in the days of his triumph, and the thought of it warmed his breaking heart and moistened his eyes with tears.

He invited everybody into the farmhouse for a dram or a cup of tea, something even he could ill afford in these days of rationing. But Clara's cupboards were amply stocked and everyone got a share, while the maid and the cottar wives served them at table or on chairs in the candle-light.

Then somebody cried out 'Fire-engine!' And sure enough, when everyone ran outside a fire-engine stood in the close, white with snow and clustered with helmeted men. Folk in the toon had seen the red glow in the sky and told the police. A snow-plough had been dispatched to open the road and they had struggled through, alas too late to save the steading. But the firemaster had a message for Mr. Sansom; a last minute telegram from the hospital in Aberdeen, sent to the police, and they had asked the firemen to deliver it. Sansom took the small pink envelope from the fireman with a trembling hand, and as he split it open and read its contents his great heart broke at last. So Clara had not lived to see her dear Errol home from the war. It had been his earnest wish but even this had been denied him. Gerald Sansom turned his broad back upon his friends and walked slowly through the slush to the farmhouse. He didn't want them to see him cry, to see his body heaving in the great sobbing that soon would overtake him, to watch the hot bitter tears that would spring from his eyes; these were for the black Labrador only and the quiet of his ain fireside.

"Water!" cried the fire-crew, "where can we get water?" "To the river," someone shouted, "this way to the river!" Aye it had been the tail-end of a harsh Russian winter. The folk in Buchan were sure of it, and while the storm lasted eight people had been suffocated in her barren fields. But for Gerald Sansom, this little Napoleon of the Buchan farmlands it had been something of a retreat in the snow from the flaming gates of Moscow. Even as he sobbed quietly in the great bay sitting room the firemen were snaking their hoses towards the broken ice on the river, where bloated cattle still floated, pouring loss upon loss to quench the last embers of a dying snowfire.

THE SECRET OF TORMUNDIE!

The Old Laird Wouldn't Allow Anyone To Alter The Steading, And People Wondered Why?

THERE was a new laird in Tormundie House, you could tell by the alterations they made to the steading, especially in the barn wing, 'cause that was a part of the buildings the old laird wouldn't allow them to touch, him or his mistress, while they were alive. Of course it didn't matter at all in the old days, but what with all this mechanisation, tractors and machinery, combine-harvesters and such like, steadings had to be altered to suit the new conditions. Some folks were even knocking their steadings down flat and rebuilding from scratch, and what with drying kilns, tower silos, Dutch Barns, milking parlours, self-feed cattle courts and sludge-pits, the new steel and concrete structures look more like rural factories than fairm toons.

While the old laird and his lady were alive the manager and the factor had worked round the barn wing, not daring to touch it, but changing this and that in a hap-hazard sort of way, for even then there was a crying need for labour-saving development. Heaven knows what would have happened nowadays had they still been as thrawn to change anything: what with the urgent need for a corn-drier and storage bins the barn wing would have been a must for conversion, and when the new laird took over it was one of the first things he started on . . .

So from what you had heard of Tormundie you had never expected to see the old mill thrown out of the barn, but there she was in the close, her great wooden hulk lying where the tractors had left it, for it had taken two of them all their might to wrest her from her trestles and drag her up the steep slope to the road. The scrap merchant had robbed her of her fine brass bushes, roller-bearings and steel stripper-drum, while all her leather belting, elevators and riddles had yet to be disposed of, and maybe a bonfire was the quickest way for that. The great length of chain elevator for the straw had been taken down from the rafters and fitted up on wheels, which would be a great help in lifting bales of hay and straw in the new Dutch Barns, saving labour in years to come. The only thing they'd forgotten was the 'shackin' spoot' for taking the corn along the loft, where it was still suspended on its lath sticks from the rafters, perhaps a memorial to puzzle future students of an agricultural heritage.

There had been a threshing mill at Tormundie since the days of the flail, driven first by a team of horses on the revolving spars, what is known as the 'mill course,' or tread-mill, which rotated a steel shaft connected to the workings of the mill. You could still see the hole in the wall where the shaft went through, though the spars and pinion-wheels have long since disappeared. Tormundie was a hill farm, where it was impossible to irrigate water in sufficient volume to drive a threshing mill, so there was never a mill-dam or a water-wheel on the place, and wind-mills were never popular in Scotland for this purpose. But you could still see the covered opening in the blackened roof of the engine-hoose where the brick lum stood in the days of steam, and the old rusted cinder brander still lay in the stackyard. "Oh aye," they would brag in the old days, "Tormundie was a gie toon, she had a stem staak and a styag aboot 'er!" meaning of course a smoke stack and a stallion, a prestige that could only apply to a farm of considerable size, and with the resources to support it.

Then came the internal-combustion oil-fired engine and you can still see the concrete base where this monster stood, chugging away with his great fly-wheels and tireless piston. In our own time this was replaced with electricity and press-button threshing, which was a long way from the flail and proved to be the ultimate in barn threshing when the combine-harvesters appeared. But the old mill had been through it all, and though she had given you mony a 'het sark' a body never thought to see the day she would lie stripped naked in the farm close. But there she lay in her cobwebs, a relic of the bye-gone days of farming, and many a time in your sweat you could have wished to see her in smithereens, though you never expected it to become a reality.

STRAW INTO GOLD

And they've just had the close concreted at Tormundie and the farm road tarred, not a dub about the place or a weed to be seen, nae mair scrapin' dubs or howkin' weeds roon the steadin', they canna pay you for that nowadays, and what with that glass roof over the place you would think you was working in a railway station, were it not for the stink of the silage. All this self-feed and slatted floors, sludge-pits and tanker sprays they're just hauling the craps home from the parks and putting it through the nowts' bellies and spraying it back on the grun again, with hardly a teeth mark on it, and the stink of the stuff is enough to drive you to the drink. This is modern farming and you've just got to accept it, though you rather fancied the smell of the old dung cart and the sharn midden, which was a healthy smell compared with this sludge stuff.

But never a load of muck to drive out nowadays or a load of neeps to bring home in the gloamin'; never the knack of a wooden cartwheel in this age of machines, nor the neigh of a horse or the whistle of a ploughman, now drowned in the jangle of transistor radios in their tractor cabs, and they've even got them in the dairy byres, where the kye are chewing the cud to the tempo of the Top Ten and letting down their milk to the Beatles and the twang of electric guitars.

But the new laird hadn't demolished the barn, for he had left the walls standing and repaired the roof before he installed a corn-drier and storage bins for the corn and barley that would come off the combines next harvest. The barn wing also contained the corn loft with the cartshed pends underneath, key-stoned arches of dressed stone that rested on enormous square pillars of stone and lime, a lasting credit to their builders. These he had blocked up with bricks and cement between the pillars, which still preserved the original appearance, so that you could point out to a stranger where the horse carts were penned in the old days. But the loft floor had been removed, and with it the hatch over a pend where the horsemen used to back their carts to load corn, dropping the sacks through the opened hatch into their carts. This was the part of the steading that really mattered to the old Laird and Lady Margaret; the arched pend that went under the hatch in the loft floor to the old dung court, a very old octagonal building with a pagoda like thing on the roof, as if its builder or designer had spent his life in the Orient. Nobody had dared to touch this part of the steading while the old laird was alive, or his lady after him; they wanted it left just as it was, and they had bought the whole estate to keep it that way.

Now you may ask what the old laird and his lady could be wanting with a draughty hole of a cartshed pend when they lived in a mansion fit for a prince, not at Tormundie of course, but up at Kingowrie yonder where they had built a palace so grand that common folk were feared to go near it, unless you were employed on the estate. Great dykes had been built round it with stone lions at the gates, and when you shone a light on them at night their eyes glittered like diamonds. Folk said the laird had spent all his money on this 'White Elephant,' and that he couldn't afford to repair Tormundie, which they said he had bought for sentimental reasons, to please the Lady Margaret, who had once worked there as a kitchiedeem, as he himself had done, as a stonemason.

But when you hear folk say that so-and-so was "born in a cartshed" they usually mean that so-and-so always left all the doors open and nearly starved you to death, because there are no doors on a cartshed pend and so-and-so had never got into the proper habit of closing them. But the laird wasn't born in the cartshed pend, nor his lady either, for folk would tell you he was a barfit loon out of Pitarrow yonder, where he had served his time as a stonemason, and when he was sent to big up the dykes at Tormundie, where the Lady Margaret had worked as kitchiedeem, her father, who was grieve on the place, fell through the hatch in the cartshed pend and broke his neck. He was looking over the place at night, without a lantern, up in the loft where he fell through the hatch, where the horsemen had been loading corn during the day and left the lid off.

When the old grieve died and his widow left Tormundie the kitchiedeem got a job as nursemaid with the local dominie, looking after the bairns for his wife. But then the dominie goes and does a most extraordinary thing, for he gives up his job as schoolmaster, sells off all his furniture, packs up the rest of his belongings and sets sail for that Bolivia place in South America yonder, where all the tin was being mined, and people were getting rich quick, and the dominie takes his wife with him, and the bairns, and what was more important—the serving quine to look after them.

Och but there was a great hue-and-cry about the tin that was being dug up in that Bolivia place, and also about the gold and diamonds that were being mined in South Africa, so that people went mad with a sudden lust for money, and a lot of them clamouring to go abroad. Quite ordinary folk, who had always been content with a bite and sup, and somewhere to sleep, now had a frantic desire to get rich quick, and they just up and off from their daily darg like a dry leaf in the wind of fortune, which they hoped would fill their laps with gold. Even our stonemason got caught up in it, for ach he was fed-up with Tormundie and his dykes for all he got for it, so he gets a few of his cronies together, and they decide to have a go at the diamonds, which they thought would be richer than tin, working their passage as deck hands on a boat to South Africa. But just about the time they landed at the Cape the Boers started a war with the British, more likely as not about the gold and diamond mines which they said was theirs in the first place, since they were Dutch settlers and had been there before the British, and the lads were likely to be involved, which was not their intention at all, because there was no money to be made fighting the Boers, and maybe get killed in the process, so they gets on a cattle boat and works their way across the wide Atlantic ocean to this Bolivia place, where the dominie and his wife had gone, and the little kitchiedeem from Tormundie.

So they all gets dug in at the tin, each man to his claim, employing cheap local labour and making a lot of money in a short space of time. And folks said they didn't treat the natives any too well, paying them little more than pocket money for a hantle of work in bringing up the tin from the mines, lashing about them with whips and cursing at the creatures till they gave themselves a bad name and some of the natives threatened to shoot them in revenge. So they just got out in time with bulging pockets before the tin boom went bang and they had to sail for home, but not before the stonemason had met up with the dominie's nursemaid again and got married because they knew each other at Tormundie. But now they were a wealthy pair, and a son was born to them out there in Bolivia, who was nearly ready for school when they returned to Scotland. But they had to have somewhere to live, somewhere splendid, now that they could afford it, and they made up their minds it would be awfully nice to buy Tormundie, that grand mansion where they had first met, for the quine had loved bidin' there and she had been loth to leave it when her father died; surely it would be the thrill of their lives to own a place like that, where they could be lord and lady where they had once been servants, a dream to be realised now they had the money. The only snag was that Tormundie was not in the market, nor could the resident laird be tempted out of it with money, so they would just have to wait, and maybe some day . . .

In the meantime they bought the estate of Kingowrie, which was miles from their beloved Tormundie, but they had no choice, and here the stonemason built a huge mansion, one of the most beautiful homes you ever saw, and planted the grounds with trees and shrubs and flowers and made an artificial lake where the white swans floated gracefully in delightful settings. But even in the midst of all this grandeur and luxury the laird and lady of Kingowrie still sighed for Tormundie and its fond associations with the past.

But before the new laird of Kingowrie built his mansion house he and the Lady Margaret travelled extensively in Europe, where the laird studied the classical ruins of Greece and Rome; he became a great scholar and studied the works of John Ruskin on 'The Seven Lamps of Architecture,' and together the laird and lady of Kingowrie visited a great many of 'The Stately Homes of England,' the great country mansions built by the Smiths and the Adams brothers, and other famous architects. Kingowrie was modelled on what the laird had learned in study and travel, a classical structure of mixed design, something in the nature of a

Grecian Temple, supported on a double colonnade of Corinthian, Doric and Roman pillars, with a flight of marble steps leading up to the front entrance, and a glass observatory on the roof where you could look at the stars through a giant telescope. The stonemason cared nothing for tin, but for what he could do with the money it brought him, and while his interests abroad still flourished he threw it about him with a lavish hand. His only regret was that it had not been spent on Tormundie.

But after a year or two even this aversion was overcome and Kingowrie began to gain some affection in the hearts of its creators, and but for a terrible tragedy might have earned their love and Tormundie would have died in the past, forgotten in the joys of raising their young son to inherit the fruits of their labours on the new estate. But their short-lived joy became a lasting sorrow which turned them against Kingowrie for ever, for their only son was killed in a riding accident, thrown from his pony against a tree in Kingowrie woods, which broke his back and killed him instantly, so they took him down to Tormundie and buried him in the local cemetery, as near their old home as possible, and folk thought it was a queer thing to do with their only bairn.

But now they were without an heir, so there wasn't much point in adding to their estates, and to minimise death duties the laird declared his assets as a private liability company, under his own chairmanship, with a factor in direct contact with his tenants and the farms he worked himself.

And so the years passed, and by the time Tormundie came on the market the laird of Kingowrie was an old and disenchanted man, crusty with the rigours of life, and his lady but a withering leaf of her former self. But they had their chauffeur drive them down in the Rolls to Tormundie, the old man with a staff, a rug on their knees, and they drove round the estate and looked at their old home from the road. They swung in at the lodge gates, smooth and silent, and up the drive, now ablaze with rhododendron flowers, mauve, white and purple, and the sun flashed down on the shining black Rolls through the tall beech trees that lined the avenue. Finally they stopped at the big house where the chauffeur got out and opened the car doors to assist his master and mistress on to the gravel path. But so eager were they in sight of a great fulfilment that hardly any assistance was necessary, and they met the estate agent at the front door with broad smiles, and with footsteps that were lightened with the memories of youth. The agent took them into the great drawing rooms, still richly furnished, where they hadn't dared to set foot as youngsters, the laird not at all, and his lady only on a special errand for her lord or mistress.

But it was a disappointing dream: a dream realised too late in life and the laird almost wished he had never seen the place again. What he had lavished on Kingowrie he should have spent here. In his watery eye was reflected the palace he would have made of this fading mansion, for he still had a notion for masonry; for the classical moulding and the chiselled stone, and his eye for landscape gardening had not dimmed with the years.

When the old couple left the mansion house the laird told the chauffeur to drive slowly round the steading, and to stop at the arches over the cartshed pends, where the Lady Margaret's father had been killed, and they peered forward to look at the old cottage in the woods where she had played as a girl. But for these circumstances they would never have been laird and lady of Kingowrie, perhaps never even lovers, or at best only a pair of ordinary cottar folks you'd never have heard a cheep of again. It was indeed a day of nostalgia for the ageing couple as they drove back to Kingowrie, half happy and half sad with the memories and prospects their journey had aroused.

So they bought Tormundie, which, besides its several farms, also included a smithy, a joinery shop, a meal mill and property in the village; a self-contained estate, and the purchase price ruled out any intention of restoring the mansion house to the glory they had already made of Kingowrie, whereupon the laird and Lady Margaret decided that Tormundie should remain in their day exactly as it had been in their youth, stone upon stone, which in time was to prove a great stumbling block when the age of machines burst upon the land, and but for the farsightedness and dogged persistence of the resident manager would have left Tormundie as much out of touch with the present as a Highland croft of last century.

The factor now ran the two estates, comprising perhaps a dozen farms between them, large and small, and a resident manager was appointed to each Home Farm, one for Kingowrie and one for Tormundie, run as independent units and both responsible to the factor. The factor stayed at Kingowrie, but you could easily tell when he was visiting at Tormundie, about once a fortnight, when you could see his big posh car parked in the drive in front of the mansion house, where the manager lived with his young wife and family. Most likely they would go over the books together, the factor and the manager, and then, after tea on the lawn, if it was a fine day, you'd see the pair of them taking a stroll across the fields, or motoring round to one of the farms on the estate, where some alterations might be taking shape. And what you might ask could the factor creature know about farming? Him that used to be a barfit loon selling newspapers at the street corners down in Glasgow yonder, for the lad had fair gotten up in the world, starting as a clerk for old Kingowrie and now running the show himself, or so you would have thought, but as far as farming was concerned the managers kept him right, though they couldn't match him at counting up figures.

And so the years wore on and the laird became a dottard and endured stroke upon stroke like hammer blows which slurred his speech and crippled his limbs until he was eventually confined to a wheel-chair. He was now in his seventies and taking little interest in what they did at Tormundie, which perhaps was a good thing, because agriculture was in the throes of the new mechanical age and alterations to the steading were an absolute necessity if the place was to survive economically. The manager made his suggestions to the factor, who conveyed them to his mistress at Kingowrie, who, in her common sense, consented to everything except any interference with the barn wing; this she insisted must be left intact, as she and her husband had agreed upon before his senility, for she wouldn't break her trust with the dying laird.

The old stonemason was now confined to one of his grandest rooms in Kingowrie mansion, where the purple walls were hung from ceiling to floor with silk and wool embroidery, damask tapestries in richly coloured scenes from myth and legend: battles, flowers, saints and landscapes, peopled with incidents from history seemingly still alive in their transparency and brilliance, fine art treasures bought in the salons of Europe and Asia Minor at incredible price. Heavy velvet curtains, likewise emblazoned shrouded the mullioned windows, while marble statues graced every corner of the room, with busts of great men in the alcoves. The ceiling was carved in polished wood without a nail that would rust, and painted with oil periodically to make it everlasting, while suspended from the centre on a golden chain was a chandelier of purest shining crystal. The floor was also inlaid in wood and scattered with the skins of lions and tigers, still with their heads on and showing their teeth, and eyes that glittered in ambient life. The furniture was carved as from ebony, inlaid with brass, stolid and elaborate, and adorned with ornaments of priceless value, amethyst, ivory, pewter and bronze.

Here the old laird of Kingowrie and Tormundie spent the whole day in his chair tearing up old newspapers, tearing them into strips until the heap was as high as his knees, when he would fall asleep by the marble fireplace and the blazing logs. A watchful maid would then tip-toe into the silent room and remove the heap of torn newspapers and replace it with the latest editions from the city, for the laird in his own way was still following the share markets and dabbling in high finance. The maid would then tidy the room, moving in elf-like silence on the animal skins, add a few more logs to the fire, replace the safety-guard and then retire into obscurity. When the laird woke up he began tearing the pile of newsprint into strips again, and if you had given him pound notes he wouldn't have known the difference.

Day after day this went on, week after week, month upon weary month, year upon year, while the ageing Lady Margaret watched over her husband with pitying gaze, reflecting on the tragedy that a man so gifted and resourceful should come to this: the pros-pector, empire builder, business magnate, classical mason, land scape gardener; the architect of great mansions like Kingowrie, now like a child in a nursery, depending on her and her servants for his every bite, for his every want.

Then one day suddenly the rustle of paper ceased. The listening maid thought the laird had fallen asleep again, or maybe he was dead, for he sat so still in his wicker wheel-chair. She tip-toed into the quiet room as usual to remove the customary heap of torn newsprint, and while she knelt to pick it up the laird spoke to her. The quine got such a fright she nearly screamed, almost ran from his presence, for she had never heard him say a word before. But she composed herself and stared at the old man, waiting and listening. He wasn't looking at her but staring at the fire. Then he habbered something and she bent closer to hear him. In a jumble of hesitant words she thought she managed to make out "Take me to Tormundie!" She was sure that was what he had said, and she repeated it herself to see if it made sense "Take me to Tormundie!" The old man was silent now, not even nodding his head, but the maid dropped the paper rags and ran to tell her mistress.

The Lady Margaret came into the room in great haste, bent and crippled though she was, eager to catch the laird in one of his lucid moments, which were few and far between. He was still awake with his palsied hands on the arm rests of the chair, peering vacantly at the glowing fire. She knelt down in front of him, listening hopefully, but all she heard was his hoarse breath coming and going gently and moving his frail body with each little spasm. She looked at his wan face in the firelight. His eyes were strangely blue and clear but vacant and far away, seeing not what was presented to him but that which his contorted mind reflected, as in a broken mirror, far in the past. She knelt there till she was nearly cramped, waiting and listening, watching his shrivelled frame rise and fall gently with his steady, mechanical breathing. Surely the maid couldn't be mistaken. Perhaps it would be too late to make sure. She touched his cold quivering hand on the arm rest and eventually it crept over hers. He never looked at her but his parched lips were moving again, mumbling something that brought froth to his chin, a mutter of broken syllables that sounded like ". . . back to Tormundie!" But the Lady Margaret understood, and she knew what she must do, and she fell up on his breast and wept.

94

THE SECRET OF TORMUNDIE!

The 'phone rang at Tormundie House and the manager's wife was told to prepare one of the best rooms for the laird, to have beds in it and to air them, to light a fire and fill a box with newspapers, and next day at noon, when it was warmest they wrapped the laird in a plaid, with a hot-water bottle at his feet and drove him in his smoothest Rolls to where he wished to die . . .

The Lady Margaret did not long survive the laird, and the great mansion of Kingowrie has been stripped of its finery and its empty rooms are used as a store for fertiliser and animal feeding stuff, its beautiful oak ceilings still resplendent but its peeling walls a stark reminder of its former glory. The farms on the estate were sold to their tenants and the only semblance left of the old laird are to be found in the neglected but still beautiful policies which still surround the mansion house. But you will search these grounds in vain for a gravestone or memorial to its former owners, nor will you find them in the local churchyard, and you may ask—"where then did they bury the Laird and Lady of Kingowrie?"

Perhaps you could ask the new laird of Tormundie, where the cartshed pillars have been blocked up but not obliterated, where above the old pends you can still perceive the strength and perfection of the great key-stone arches, and there, as sure as you may find a Pharoah in the heart of a Pyramid, or a living martyr built into the walls of a monastery, there in these bricked-up cartshed pends you will find the Secret of Tormundie, you will find it in the shape of a silver casket, containing the ashes, and maybe the spirits of its former owners.

RIG TWO

ESSAYS ON AGRICULTURE

STRAW INTO GOLD

" SEEDTIME and Harvest shall not fail!" Thus saith the Holy Scripture, and the cynics reply: "But there has to be a first time!"

This time, in this Year of Grace 1966, it has happened! Harvest has failed in the North of Scotland, and particularly for the oat-grower.

Barley growers were a little more fortunate, with an earlier crop and a blink of sun at the start of the season. But the oat-growing farmer had to wait longer for the grain to ripen, and while he waited the windows of heaven opened and the rain poured forth upon his crop, which was cast down—and some of it not yet harvested even now, late in December.

Admittedly the barley grower endured the 'big shak'' at the opening of harvest, when the heads of barley were lashed from the stalk and after the combines had finished could be scooped up in bushelfuls from the stubble. This was a frightful loss and may not be indemnified by the shrinking deficiency payment scheme.

What is wanted here is a suction-type machine on the lines of a vacuum-cleaner, broad and light, with a grill to filter out stones, to sweep the stubble fields immediately the straw has been removed. The nearest we have to this is a type of forage-harvester which is much too heavy and too restricted in present use.

And what about the straw? This winter there hasn't even been a chance to burn it. For those who did manage to salvage their straw, and can afford to sell it, the opportunity to turn it into gold now awaits them, to the tune of £10 to £12 a ton, or roughly 3/- to 3/6 a bale. Straw may be worth more than the poor samples of grain being offered for sale, and may compensate a little for the shaken barley.

Farmers have been forced to sell their cattle prematurely for lack of fodder and grain-feed still lying out in the sodden fields. They have been forced to sell in a falling market because so many others were doing the same thing for similar reasons.

Because of the Credit Squeeze and bouncing cheques, some of these farmers were forced to take their cattle back again, paying double transport charges, besides buying fodder and cereals at exorbitant prices from those few still in the lap of fortune.

And all the time the rain still poured down and the corn sprouted on the flattened stalks, and the rusting combines waited and lost money for their hirer-owner contractors.

Now, since the first mention of combine-harvesters there has always been a minority who maintain that this mode of harvesting will never be a success in the North of Scotland.

The cynics argue that our climate is too liable to extremes of rain and fog for the successful operation of combine harvesting. And since in this scientific era we cannot even yet change wind direction or move mountains the cynics are having the laugh of a lifetime.

Never mind who the cynics are. He could be your next door neighbour, or your best friend out of hearing—or he could even be a barley grower who has been forced reluctantly through adverse circumstances to adopt combine harvesting, in which case you would never suspect him. The important thing is to prove that the cynics are wrong—or figure out what to do if they are right.

The fact is that progressive farming in the North of Scotland has reached the point of no return. Banking reserves have been sunk on new plant and reconstruction of buildings and disbanding of labour to meet present economic farming necessity—and in this burning of boats and bridges any hope of returning to traditional harvesting methods has gone for ever.

This of course is in relation to the rest of the country, except that, according to all accounts and statistics, they have had a bumper harvest and record yields.

Could it be that the introduction of combine-harvesting to Northern Scotland has coincided with an adverse weather cycle of wet autumns? We haven't really had an autumn suitable for profitable combine-harvesting since 1959, a ratio of one in seven in favour, or one golden harvest for six black ones—a depressing majority with which to endorse the cheques for new drying plant and bins, combines and balers that are either out of date or in dire need of repair or replacement before they have even begun to recover initial costs of installation and acquirement.

And, of course, there were the zealots who urged that the combine machine was the answer to our bad-weather harvests. They predicted that a blitzkrieg in the harvest fields would catch the weather man in his sun-bonnet, while this year in particular he has never been rid of his oil-skin suit.

Mass growing of early barley to catch an end-of-summer harvest offers a glimmer of salvation, accompanied by fairly heavy fertiliser to lodge the crop against the stripping wind—and devil take the hindmost with a glutted market.

After all, our distillers have never looked favourably on Scottish barley and prospects couldn't be much worse in this respect. And since the barley-beef incentive in cattle feeding seems to be on the way out another door has been slammed in the face of the barley-grower. And of course it doesn't take much imagination to realise what would happen if we all buried our heads in the sand and started growing barley for seed.

As a last resort, even at the risk of throwing pearls in front of swine, in an evident resurgence of the pig-fattening industry we could hope to supply the proverbial offal in the shape of home-grown barley. At the very least it would give us a chance to salvage the straw which is yearly becoming too precious to burn, much too scarce and expensive to be regarded as a necessary evil.

When the combines first started up here the night sky was aglow with bonfires, farmers burning their "surplus" straw for cheap and easy disposal. But intensified cattle feeding in open courts has changed all that and most of us need all the straw we can get. The longer stubble left by the combines compared with the old binders has made things worse, creating a still greater shortage of straw, and farmers are beginning to realise where they have gone wrong. No doubt adjustments will be made to meet requirements but in the meantime it has made a gold mine of the straw market.

Mind you, if the oat-grower had resorted to the traditional methods of harvesting last year he would probably have had the last laugh. While he languished in indolence awaiting his crop to ripen sufficiently for combine threshing, he could have cut with a shade of green and matured it in the stook. The chances are he may even have got the entire crop stacked before the autumn rains came. Some of the smaller places and family farms managed it, and there was a noticeable panic at this stage to buy old binders, some of which were selling at the marts at three-figure prices.

But if a man has scrapped his threshing mill, sold his binders and sacked his labour he has no choice but to wait on providence.

In the present sludge and soft state of the ground keen frost provides the only opportunities for operating a heavy baling machine. Temporary removal of the packer plates from the baling chamber makes lighter going and saves a lot of breakages in gudgeon pins. You may expend a little more expensive twine, but as less moisture is compressed with the straw the bales are lighter, easier to handle, and may dry out quicker in storage.

Some farmers, in desperation, are pushing the straw aside with tractor-sweeps and buckrakes to get their dung carted out on the stubble. Others will chew and scatter their straw with forage-harvesters when the land dries for ploughing—for by then the straw will be as 'fooshinless,' brittle and lacking in substance as the stubble gathered by the Children of Israel when Pharoah denied them straw to make brick.

Necessity is indeed the mother of progress and you never know what new process might emerge from the present dilemma.

But the biggest heartbreak of all is the many thousands of acres yet to harvest. Even last Spring when the snow cleared there were isolated cases of harvest and sowing in simultaneous operation. Indications are that in 1967 such a spectacle will be widespread, from the Mearns to the Black Isle, and the middle Highlands, where livestock are already in poverty. Great loads of straw are already in motion in that direction from the sunnier south.

Unless the weather dries up soon the real fodder famine will be felt by the end of January. By then the grain has perished in the ravages of winter, but with any prospect of a second chance to harvest the bleached straw, in the disillusioned gaze of an impoverished farmer it suddenly turns to strands of twisted gold in the Spring sunshine.

THE VANISHING CORNYARDS

W HEN you go for a run in the car this autumn you may notice the absence of cornstacks around the farmsteads. Ever since John Constable painted his famous English landscapes we have been accustomed to cornstacks at the farm. Now they are fast disappearing and we are bound to note their absence. It is like a harbour without boats, or a railway yard without trucks, but whereas these omissions usually denote dereliction the opposite is the case in farming: here it is a sign of progress, of mechanisation—a manifestation of the factory farm in operation, where everything is processed and stored on the farm, mostly under a roof, and cornstacks are no longer necessary.

The first question a townsman must ask himself is—what was the use of a cornstack anyway? What was it for? And of course the answer leads to the other question—why has it almost disappeared?

A cornstack is a sort of silo—a temporary storing of grain and straw until it can be conveniently threshed for oatmeal, porridge-oats or cattle feed, or for sale as seed in a rising market. But such an answer to the townsman's question is not so elementary as it may sound. A cornstack must be built watertight, otherwise it becomes an unmanageable mountain of germination. Moisture germinates corn and sprouting must be avoided at all times. The only time a farmer likes to see his barley sprouting is when it is on the malting floor at the distillery, and that is for a different reason, as all partakers of John Barleycorn can vouch for.

Few people realise the importance of good stack-building. No matter how good the crop is, or what pains or expense have been expended on it in the fields, an incompetent or careless stacker can ruin the lot, so much depends on his skill. I have seen a whole stackyard spoiled by such a man, and his employer brought almost to bankruptcy, because the entire crop was unfit for threshing and sprouting in the stacks.

A stackbuilder is really a sort of architect—he must have a geometrical instinct for poise and balance, an eye for the aplomb and a straight line, and a head for heights, otherwise he will never get off the ground. He should also be an artist who takes a pride in his work, because in the course of construction a stack resembles a drawing on an easel. It has to be viewed from a distance. It is no use standing at the base of a rick watching it grow against the sky; you must stand well back from your work to see whether it is veering north, south, east or west, and if you are a good stacker you will know what to do when this happens, without so mis-shaping the stack that it cannot resist the weather. Remember that a great many stacks have to stand throughout the winter, in sleet and hail and wind and rain, until such time as they are required in barns and lofts, and must in themselves be made watertight and waterproof, without tarpaulins, slates or asbestos. Thatching of course is a help, especially in snow, but will not guarantee the preservation of a stack; that depends entirely on the builder.

But at the same time a stack of corn, wheat or barley must be allowed to breathe; it must swing in the wind so that dry air penetrates to the core of the rick, or very nearly so. The centre must be kept hard and well packed and higher always than the rest of the stack, so that all the sheaves slope downwards to the outer circle, which should be built loosely, and so round and round until you have a hard core of grain in the centre, with the stubble end of the sheaf always facing outwards. Stackbuilding is like a bad dream, because you are crawling on a slope in an endless circle, higher and higher, and every minute likely to topple over the edge, and when your ladder disappears from sight your nerves are really on a see-saw.

When you have reached the eave or shoulder of your stack you must then start slating your sheaves by pulling them in slightly on each round, until a cone is formed and you finish up like a weather-cock on a forlorn church steeple, until someone throws you several 'rapes' or ropes to hold it in place, and fetches the 'long ladder' to let you down. Then you can have a look at your stack, and set a 'staff' in it where you think it is required, when most likely it will settle down to your satisfaction.

THE VANISHING CORNYARDS

After a week of crawling you will find that your knees are so numb you can hardly walk, and your wife will have to sew pads on your trouser legs before they wear out. And if there are thistles in the sheaves you will find your fingers so tender you can scarcely handle a spoon at mealtimes, or fasten your bootlaces in the morning, all the more reason why you should wear a pin in your cap, for thorn extraction in your few spare moments. After a fortnight on the bigger farms you may be getting used to the discomfort, which may provide some consolation for your weariness.

A cornstack gets smaller with age, mostly owing to the drying up of moisture during the year of its normal life, so do not let the smaller stature of some stacks deceive you, because in their new state, fresh from the succulent fields they are much higher, or as high as you dare to build them, without letting them become top-heavy Towers of Piza, lop-sided and leaning on crutches, tiresome monuments to your inefficiency that will earn you plenty of taunts and very little credit from your associates.

And why then, the townsman may ask, if cornstacks are so important, has it been so easy or necessary to dispose of them? The answer of course is necessity, due to rising costs, scarcity of skilled labour and mechanisation. Compared with the old method of cutting and handling each sheaf of corn individually, nursing and fondling it with care, all the time from the field to the threshing mill, the combine-harvester can cut and thresh corn and deliver straw and chaff simultaneously, thus slashing time and labour costs by about 75 per cent.

Consider a sheaf of corn, a bundle of corn stalks held together by a piece of string, and count the number of times it had to be handled from the moment it was bound until someone slit the string and threw it into the mill. It was lifted from the stubble to be stooked, forked on to a cart, built on a cart, forked from the cart on to a stack, placed in position by the stacker; pitched off the stack again, rebuilt on a wagon, carted to the barn, pitchforked from the wagon on to the mill bench, where the man with the knife picks it up for the last time—nine times that sheaf has been handled in autobiography, and if you allow for the stooks being blown down at least twice—and the old-fashioned method of filling the barn prior to threshing, you can count another three times to the total—twelve times in all, a prodigous waste of time and effort when you consider that the combine-harvester doesn't even trouble to make a sheaf. And remember there were many thousands of sheaves on the average binder-cut farm.

Of course the binder was a great innovation in its day—a vast improvement on the sickle or scythe or the mechanical reaper (which isn't a binder), just as the threshing mill was a wonderful replacement for the flail, but in the combine-harvester we have them all combined in one unit, with one man doing the work of ten or twelve.

I remember in the old days my grandfather used to cut his corn crop with a back-delivery reaper, while the whole family were employed behind him for days on end trussing and binding the sheaves, all of which had to be stooked, forked, stacked and threshed afterwards. Nowadays with a combine that crop could be harvested and threshed in something less than one single sunny afternoon. Of course the grain has to be stored for the drier and the straw has to be baled and built into barns or ramps, but even so it is a mere trifle compared with the old system of harvesting.

Of course if you really go to town with combine harvesting you have the initial costs of installing a corn drier plant and storage bins, plus the purchase or hire of a combine and baler machines, but even so these overheads are not exorbitant compared with the expense of present day manual labour on overtime over a number of years.

The factory farm has come to stay, the cereals are in the storage bins and the straw is in the Dutch Barns, that is why there are very few cornstacks around the farmsteads nowadays. Oh yes there are still a few who stick to the older methods, especially on the family farms, where operating costs may be lower, and stacks go up much as usual, and these are the ones you must watch when you are out for an autumn drive in the car—because they are providing you with your last chances of watching a harvest being tackled in traditional style, stacks and all.

And even Constable would have to alter his landscapes considerably were he to set up his easel again in the smiling English countryside

STRIP-TEASE

I DON'T suppose there are many women in Buchan (or anywhere else for that matter) who could hand-milk a cow nowadays, which isn't surprising when you consider that the milking machines have been with us now for forty years or so. Perhaps this is a good thing, for the women I mean, because I have known women who have been injured or practically disabled for life by temperamental cows; and when it came to milking heifers for the first time it was hardly a job for a woman. I've been kicked in the face myself in my time and gone about with a bull-dog look for a week until the swelling went down.

It isn't a pleasant experience for a newly married cattleman to see his sweet young bride prostrated behind a high-spirited cow, her overall ripped from bib to hemline (and the distance was further than it is nowadays), her hair and clothing soaked with the contents of the milk bucket, which had been kicked over her head when she fell. Such was my experience with Jane a week after our marriage and I could scarcely get her to sit down to a cow again. The poor quine was in tears and trembling with fear.

Jane had hand-milked before, two or three petted old cows for domestic use on the family farms; but stripping after the milking machines were taken off in a commercialised dairy herd was a different undertaking. Machine trained heifers were averse to having their teats stretched by hand, just as hand-milked cows behaved badly in the old days when they felt the new machines draining their udders; and yet the machine method of milking is the most natural, almost like the sucking of a calf (without the head butting) and much more gentle than the squeeze of nail-tipped fingers.

Even today there are heifers who are afraid of the milking machine, whether it be the noise of the pulsation or the suction of the cups on their inflamed udders, tender and swollen with the flush of milk, and as kicking is the natural instinct of defence in bovine psychology you have to prepare for the worst; but once the cups are on you are much less at the mercy of a frightened animal than you were on a stool with a bucket of milk between your knees. And over the years dairymen have learned a method of yoga or ju-jitsu by which a frantic animal can be subdued or partially paralysed until the machine has done its work, and gradually, by relaxing the tension on nostril, back or tail, whichever system is used, the beast gets used to its tormentors, especially as the udder softens, and your most ferocious beast may eventually end up as the pet of the herd. It is fear rather than aggressiveness which dominates the lives of the byre inhabitants, while patience and kindness rather than brutal retaliation usually tames them. Really hopeless cases are sometimes given the chance to suckle a calf or two, which, if successful, may prolong her life until they are weaned; but if through her mother-hate relationship she denies even them she is dried out and given over to the butcher's knife. Just as in the theatre, in spite of stage fright the show must go on—and so with the milking, whether it be strip-tease or mechanisation.

Jane was employed in the byre with me as a stripper, and she went around squeezing the teats into a pail after the milking cups had been taken off, an expedient which science and experience has now proved to be unnecessary, despite the belief that this end product of the milking contained most of the butter-fat. Of course Jane had to seat herself on a stool in the usual manner, with a pail between her knees, her head in the cow's flank, a proper target for a vicious side-kick, when Jane, stool and bucket would land on the greep, for no doubt the cow considered her a tantalising nuisance, since she had already been relieved of her milk by suction.

This form of 'strip-tease' had an entirely different meaning from that to which we generally refer, and yet it was not uncommon to see an advertisement in the paper which might run something like this: 'Dairy Cattleman wanted, wife to 'strip' when required,' and you could make of it what you liked. It was futile in the old days to say that 'stripping' was no job for a woman, because farmers insisted upon the job being done, and if you hadn't the time for it yourself your wife had to lend a hand, or two hands rather (and often unpaid) or you were out of work and home, because there were always plenty of cottar lads who were quite willing to let their wives 'strip.'

In the old days of hand-milking the cows were milked three times a day, for it was feared by the older folks that twice milking would put them dry. Machine milking has proved them wrong (except perhaps for a newly calved beast—and even that has gone now) but the suspicion persisted that unless a cow was milked or 'dribbled' completely dry at least twice a day she would still go off her milk. Here of course they differed from nature in the wild, never dreaming that a Highland calf stopped sucking when his belly was full, regardless whether or not his mother's udder was empty; or if it occurred at all to the old folks maybe they thought they were bringing order out of nature's carelessness, yet nature's calves lived at winter's teat while their own died of the scour at the summer cogie.

Of course the old folks were hoodwinked or deceived in spite of their caution but the kye were kept in milk. Some of the bailies (stockmen) were cute enough to carry a stool and pail along the greep with them while they changed the machines from cow to cow, pouring a little milk into the pail on the stool in the bye going, and if the farmer chiel came in from the cold for a crack or a smoke and saw the suppie milk in the pail he was satisfied. But sometimes the chiel would overstay his welcome in the cosy warmth of the byre, taking a stroll up and down the greep, and the bailie lad would take the pail and stool from under his eyes and sit down to the quietest beast he knew, pulling away gently at her flabby teats until the mannie disappeared, back to his bottling of ice-cold milk in the draughty dairy, or whatever hell he was supposed to be doing

But I was never very good at this form of deception and sometimes Jane had to suffer for my honesty; which may be another way of saying that the deil is aye kind to his ain, or that God helps those who help themselves and that deceit is the author of progress.

The labour market was glutted with able-bodied men at £1 a week, with the wife at a shilling a day for washing utensils. Before the machines came in the cottar wives were paid sixpence a milking for ten cows each, which meant a shilling a day for two milkings, seven shillings a week, and if your wife could milk it gave you a better chance of finding a job, even though you were yourself a horseman. And sometimes you'd cycle for miles to a place and stand for hours in a queue among other lads who had done the same thing—all waiting for the same job. And you'd stand about in the farm close or sit on the stone dyke for hours after a hard day's wark in the parks or byre, waiting till the farmer chiel took you all inside one by one to ask your price, then pick the cheapest worker, sometimes as little as £46 to £48 for a whole year driving a pair of horses, usually the second pair as you got a bit more for foreman, £52 to £54, with £2 off for Insurance, which came in handy if you took pneumonia or rheumatic fever from working in the wet, when you'd get your doctor free and about a guinea a week instead of your wages, and if the farmer wasn't all that bad maybe he'd fill your milk flagon each day with the others while you were off work, and what with meal in your girnal and tatties in your earth-pit, coal for your fire and a free house, and your dozen hens or so cackling off an egg apiece each day, and the cock crowing every morning and the cat licking himself on the sunny doorstep you was just dying on your feet to get back to work. You was well protected but nothing for your wife and bairns, not unless she had another one, when you got about £2 maternity benefit to pay the doctor's bill. But your wife having a bairn was a bad thing, because it stopped her from the milking, so you had to be very careful about these things, and you learned about birth control all on your own.

The hours for a dairy bailie were usually from 4 o'clock in the morning to 6.15 p.m., or thereabouts, with one hour off for breakfast and two for dinner, with no half-day off for Saturdays and Sundays made little difference; a hiring day for the fee-ing market, two Term days (one in May and one at November) with New Year's Day at a pinch were all the holidays allowed, and even then a body sometimes had to sort and milk the kye before you got away. These hours did not apply to the women folk, who were employed solely for the milking, which took about four hours a day.

Of course you had to work long hours but everybody else did the same and it never gave you a thought. You were up before four in the morning but the stable lanterns were lit at five, only an hour later, and while you were finished in the byres round about six in the evening the horsemen had to go back at eight to 'supper' their horses. So it didn't matter much what you did: it was just that some lads hated the kye and the skitter of the byre and loved brawly to whistle behind a pair of horses on the lea rig; but here again you were exposed to all the rigours of surly winter, while the byres provided shelter and warmth from the cold. Sunday was a bit of a drag because the horsemen had the day to themselves, apart from their week-end on stable duty, and so you were alone at work. But with youth on your side and all the world before you tiredness never bothered you. And a £1 a week was more than I had ever earned in my life before, besides the usual perquisites. We were paid £4 a month with the balance at the Term. Being newly married we managed on £3 a month and saved £12 over the year. And no wonder when I could get an ounce of bogie-roll for eightpence and twenty fags for a bob; a gramophone record for a shilling (a tanner in Woolies)— though you paid half-a-crown anywhere for a 'Cornkister' on Beltona Records. Forbyes this you could get a seat at the pictures for sixpence or ninepence and a fish supper for sixpence when you came out; all the riches in the world wouldn't have made me any happier. And Jane and I had each other in this great new adventure of marriage, so what more could we want?

But the milking machines, whether parlour or bucket plant had made the cottar wives redundant. Perhaps a pity because it gave you a cosy sort of feeling to see them about the place in the cold mornings. They were sharing something with you that seemed to make it easier, and when they had gone for ever from the byres you missed their banter and their flirting and even some of them for their looks. On the other hand there were those who said they hadn't gone before time, because on some places they used to splash each other with milk and tear each other's hair out, all like spitting cats because the boss had spoken more favourably to one husband than to another, or because their kids had been fighting. But the farmer, poor devil, was almost afraid to open his mouth about his own steading, lest he offend someone, for jealousy sat in every eye, and sometimes he was at his wits' end about who to sack because of whom. In fact you could say that in many cases the cottar wives were a problem, what with having their bairns and their men coming and going maybe the milking machines came as a Godsend in the hour of need. Nowadays the milking plant can be managed by one family; a father and his sons, with wife or daughter to wash utensils, and there is usually more harmony in the byres.

And even though it was more expensive initially to instal milking plant than it was to pay the cottar wives the more enterprising of the dairy farmers persisted with this new scientific aid to end their milking squabbles. But at this stage some risk was involved: Were the new machines reliable, efficient and clean? At least the cottar wives were efficient, and in their white caps and overalls they were certainly clean. Yet more and more byres were piped and fitted out for the new machines, with concrete channel floors and tubular stalls to meet the new regulations in sanitation and hygiene. Gradually the new machines were recognised to be consistent in all that the cottar wives had been; even moreso, because they had no fear of a kicking cow; they could not be hurt and if damaged spare parts could be provided; in fact they were the first Daleks we had ever seen, the first robots at work in agriculture, providing the first step towards mechanisation and the factory farm, even before the horse had gone, and while very few tractors were yet to be seen on the land.

The milking machine provided mankind with one of his most difficult inventions and it took nearly thirty years to perfect a working model. Even before 1900 Messrs. Lawrence and Kennedy were experimenting with pulsation, while an inventor named Murchland tried out a machine with continuous suction. A marriage of the two methods solved their problems and provided a prototype of the milking machine as we know it today, for even pipe-line milking or the herring-bone parlour has not altered its basic principles, or the function for which it was intended—except that the cottar wives of forty years ago can hardly believe they are living in the same world.

But those wives of yesteryear had a knowledge of the bovine world that our modern women can never share. For now behold

the sad fate of the cow: Her pregnancies are never accidental—
they are compulsory! In other words she has to be kept in milk
to pay her board and leave a margin of profit. Her continual
lactation is her only chance of survival; from the day of her birth
she has no other choice in life. In giving birth to her calves her
pains in labour are by no means relieved, except by brute force
(should she require it) after nature has had its way; and if this
fails her, to the extent of endangering her future usefulness, she
has a pistol at her ear, because a Caesarean operation on a cow
would hardly be feasible, although it has been done in exceptional
cases, where the pedigree of the mother is of commercial value.

Of all domesticated animals surely mother cow is the saddest,
for except in a breeding herd she is not even allowed the satisfaction of bringing up her own children. Except for a few fond licks
at calving, baby cow (or bull) is snatched away to the nursery
and mother seldom sets eyes on her offspring again. The calf may
survive as a heifer, or as a steer for fattening, depending on the
breed of the parents, but as an undesirable bull calf it may be
slaughtered for veal within weeks of birth. And don't imagine
that these partings don't give mother cow a pang, because her
mother instinct is just as strong as it is in most other mammals.

The sheep family are more fortunate in that the mother is
allowed to coddle her lambs until the weaning, a period of five to
six months, and even the pigs and broody hens have their bairns
around them. In the old days of the horses a mare enjoyed the
company of her foal for a whole summer, except perhaps for a
yoking at the shim, when she was taken from the pasture and her
foal was shut into the loose-box, mostly for an afternoon only,
and when her work was done at eventide you stripped off some
milk from the mother, just let it run through your fingers to the
cobblestones in the stable, a teat at a time in the palm of your
hand, and as the mare has only two teats it did'nt take you long.
This was the only time you had to strip-tease a mare, because the
farmer said that 'heftet melk wasna good for the foal,' whatever
that meant, or perhaps folks were afraid that the foal would take
too much of his mother's milk after an absence, more than was
good for him. While you were about it, milking the mare, she

4

would 'nicker' impatiently to her foal, anxious for you to finish, and then you led her from the stable to the loose-box, where you opened the door and the long-legged foal came cantering out, making at once for his mother's teats, but you led off the mare while he followed, never giving him a chance to suck or you had returned both mother and son (or daughter) to the grass park and shut the gate.

But with all her miseries mother cow is more fortunate than most other members of the bovine family: her life in fact is a blessing compared with the fattened steer, who enjoys a couple of years at most on the fat of the land, only to be prepared for the butcher's slab. Compared with his short existence a healthy cow may see old age, which could be ten or twelve years in a thriving herd, or even twenty years as a crofter's pet.

But mother cow is never allowed to become a widow or an old maid, and a spinster cow is unheard of in commercial farming. The birth-control 'Pill' is also forbidden but she may indulge the promiscuity of artificial insemination. She lives a precarious existence, because a trampled teat or the loss of her teeth, or any injury that might endanger her calving routine can prove her undoing. Dehorning has played a big part in reducing this sort of risk, though she is still exposed to the infection of tuberculosis and brucellosis and all the other ailments that beset the flesh of beast and human body.

But with her four stomachs mother cow has one supreme consolation which is never enjoyed by her human counterparts: she can make two diets out of one, with equal relish, by chewing the cud, and she doesn't give a snort for her statistics, but may eat till she is bursting at the seams. In India she is a sacred beast, immune from slaughter, and her precious dung is used as household fuel.

Such is man's power over the animal kingdom that he is indeed a god, holding their lives in the palm of his hand. But as our vet says: "Where there are cows or women there is always trouble!" Perhaps not of their own choosing but by the power of nature over their lives.

STRIP-TEASE

As for the father bull—surely he is the most polygamus creature in the animal society; more fortunate in his love affairs than any man under the sun, and his concubines are amorous to the point of licking his face or jumping on his back or lying down at his hoofs. He is lord of the harem and can enjoy his numerous wives without having to endure them; living as he does in splendid isolation, pampered and admired by all and sundry from the day of his birth. His only worries are old age and sterility, and lacking the intelligence and sensitivity of man he is spared even the knowledge of this perplexing problem.

Mother cow enjoys intercourse but once a year (if all goes well) and she has her teats pulled twice a day: indeed they say that this is why she has such a long face. How now, brown cow!

SOCIAL HISTORY

CLARKIE'S AND AUBREY'S

I SUPPOSE there are some people in Peterhead and elsewhere who still remember James Clark the ironmonger who used to run the Palace Theatre in Hanover Street. 'Clarkie,' as he was popularly known, was one of the most colourful personalities in the history of the town. Churchillian almost, in appearance, he was what we might nowadays call a small town tycoon; a cigar-chewing, sartorial dandy with an American flair for showmanship and a bright eye for the cash register.

Some have said he was hard and mean, an old skin-flint, but unknown to many he had a charitable side, and there was many an old-age pensioner who got five-shillings slipped into his pocket on the sly. Because he was ostentatious in business and clandestine in beneficence his associates were encouraged to form a rather biased and unfair opinion of Clarkie's real nature.

Actually he was a kind-hearted family man with a contented mind and almost incapable of invective. Although he shunned the social crowd he had a pleasant disposition and always wanted to be on the best of terms with everyone. But because of this ostrichism he was often ignored by his business associates and civic heads of the town, a factor which never worried Clarkie, but perhaps it was the main reason why most people in his own sect never really got to know him.

But Clarkie studied the share market as others might permutate their football coupons. It was his favourite hobby, and while others went the social round Clarkie would sit late at night with a computer brain on the stock-exchange charts. A magician with figures, he had an intuition for the gamble which usually hit the jackpot, earning rewards which enabled him to become a landlord, to own a motor car (before anyone else), and to spend his holidays abroad, mostly on the continent, where he spent his time and money on wholesale purchases for his ironmongery business at cut-throat prices.

He was a man of sudden decisions and sometimes his family got little warning of his departures, and as Mrs. Clark had no desire for travel he went mostly alone, almost overnight, when he would be away in France or Germany for weeks on end and return as suddenly with some new enterprise which was supposed to set the town on fire.

Mr. Clark was a native of Peterhead but he began his business life in Fraserburgh, where he carried on an ironmongery trade for twelve years. Around 1900 he returned to Peterhead and opened a shop in Marischal Street. Shortly afterwards he bought the old cattle mart near the railway station and turned it into a roller-skating rink, then a music hall and finally a cinema, an enterprise which rewarded him well while it lasted. It was first called the Electric Theatre, then the Palace, as a great many people may still remember it, writing in 1964.

When the craze for roller-skating faded and the fans returned to Music Hall Clarkie was obliged to turn the Skating Rink into a Palace of Varieties, with an occasional film show between the acts. Names like Harry Gordon, Dr. Walford Bodie and Dan Williams appeared on the Palace playbills, interspersed with travelling film shows, currently being popularised in Aberdeen, and other Scottish cities by men like Robert Calder, William Walker and Dove Patterson.

But Clarkie was an astute business man: he foresaw that moving pictures were to become more than just a novelty to be shown between variety acts, so he installed two projectors and draped a screen over his back-drop on the stage—all set for the pictures that moved and mystified and made fortunes in those days.

Now in contrast to Clarkie's Palace the Picture House was a real posh place upstairs in the old Music Hall buildings, part of the Townhouse in the main square, and was named after Mr. James Aubrey, who held it in lease from the municipal authorities. Aubrey's had been the town's main Music Hall but when moving pictures became more popular they also went over to films. They renovated the hall and discarded the stage in favour of more seating. The stage space was now occupied by the manager's office, the projection room and an entrance corridor. But while Aubrey's went over to pictures completely Clarkie still put on a short variety act between the films, a decision which proved most profitable and popular with the townsfolk. "Have ye seen the Turnie at Clarkie's this week?" the fishwives would ask each other over the herring barrels. "It's affa good!" So the 'Turnie' became a regular feature of Clarkie's programmes and proved Aubrey's wrong in giving up Music Hall fun completely.

My first visits to 'Clarkie's' Palace was as chaperon for the girl next door with the milk boy. We lived three miles out of town. Sometimes we walked, or went by horse bus, usually on a Saturday night, but on every occasion all my expenses were grudgingly paid by the milk boy, a condition insisted upon by the girl's mother, regardless of his feelings in the matter. I was about thirteen at the time and no more to be trusted with the girl than was the milk boy, except that he was four years older.

One of the first films we saw at Clarkie's was Marguerite de la Motte and Lionel Barrymore in THE GIRL WOULDN'T WORK, which I thought was a jibe at the girl next door, because she didn't work either. Other showing included Aileen Pringle in WILDFIRE, which provided my first glimpse of a race track; Tom Mix in THE CIRCUS ACE, which included an early parachute jump; BLOW YOUR OWN HORN, WELCOME STRANGER, and so on. Then we went to Aubrey's for a change.

Here the atmosphere was changed; women in fur coats, men in hats, flowers in the vestibule. Here I got my first big look at Greta Garbo, Rudolph Valentino, Vilma Banky, Buster Keaton, Larry Semon, Harry Langdon, Fatty Arbuckle, and I got a ringside seat for one of the greatest title fights of all time, the Jack Dempsey versus Gene Tunney World Heavyweight Championship —something like thirty years before television.

But Aubrey's showed mostly love pictures so I got off on my own and went back to Clarkie's for the Westerns and adventure thrillers like ROARING RAILS, with Frankie Darrow; Bert Lytell in STEELE OF THE ROYAL MOUNTED, Richard Talmadge in LAUGHING AT DANGER, William Fairbanks in SPEED MAD, Johnny Hines in THE LIVE WIRE, all real thick ear stuff, with a riot in the tuppenies when the spills came.

I was still a gaping schoolboy in short pants when I first clapped eyes on Mr. Clark. By that time he had made quite a fortune in the cinema business. At the age of seventy he was still running two business concerns when most men would have been glad to retire. To me he was the wonder of the age; this chubby-faced, laughing-eyed Punch and Judy man with the moustache and sweet smelling cigar, and the silver watch-chain across his waistcoat— for me, as for many others, he had brought nameless joys into the town, and had brightened our drab lives with a new magic that far surpassed Aladdin and his silly lamp.

Occasionally I was Clarkie's first customer, waiting anxiously on the pavement in Hanover Street until he opened the glass-panelled doors of the Palace, to me the Palace of Miracles. But the huge posters on the windows kept me in thrall while I waited. Lively coloured Herculean studies of SAMSON OF THE CIRCUS 'The World's Strongest Man,' which featured Bonomo & Louise Loraine, or a member of the Swiss Family Robinson stabbing a shark underwater in PERILS OF THE WILD, and I was almost biting my nails to see the current week's episode, which eventually led me to reading the book, the first instance, but by no means the last in which the cinema had introduced me to literature.

But of course Mr. Clark couldn't have been expected to share my enthusiasm for the movies. He and Mrs. Clark had worked all day in their ironmongery shop, trying to please all sorts of annoying customers, and the opening of the Palace doors was merely an extension of their working day.

Mr. Clark was a pioneer motorist, indeed he owned one of the very first cars to appear in Peterhead. Even as an octogenarian he was an impeccable driver. Motoring was another of his hobbies (besides the share market) and had been so for forty years, but you never saw his car at the Palace door. It was a single-cylinder Humber, with two huge brass paraffin headlamps. Clarkie was a born show-man but he was never ostentatious on the profits it brought him.

He was also one of the town's largest property owners but would discuss the merits of a local football match with anyone who shared his interests — whether he wore a bonnet or a hat made no difference to Clarkie. After supper he walked with his wife from their home at 19 Cairntrodlie to open the Palace. I could see them coming round the corner from King Street; Mr. Clark, an opulent, cheery figure in hat and greatcoat, smoking his inseparable cigar, and Mrs. Clark, somewhat dark and recumbent, clutching her hand bag, rather a big one to carry home the evening's money from the box-office.

It was still daylight in a long summer evening but I was pleased to get inside to the electric twylight of the Palace. I gave my six-pence to Mrs. Clark at the pay-box and took a seat on a hard-backed form at the front. One of the Miss Clarks was an usherette, and the other sometimes played the piano, but so far they hadn't arrived. The empty cinema had a musty smell of confection and stale fruit. Half-an-hour to wait so I read all the variously coloured advertisements on the stage curtain. Mr. Clark's shop was prominent in the centre while most of the town's leading merchants offered their wares around it. Indeed Mr. Clark's curtain was so exciting I could stare at it unwearied for thirty minutes while the theatre filled around me. The stage reminded me of our box-bed at home in coloured wallpaper: the side curtains tucked up with a red tasselled cord, the puckered apron under the footlights and the counterpane canopy.

From behind the stage I could feel the oil-engine pulsating the floor, chugging away quietly at the humming dynamos, charging the batteries for the evening's film show. There were no Hydro-Boards in those days and Clarkie and Aubrey had to generate their own power. You could hear this same sound up at Aubrey's Picture House, but softer, because it was a stronger building with thicker walls. Both shows began at eight o'clock with the ringing of the curfew in the Townhouse belfry, high above Aubrey's roof, except on Saturday nights when there were two houses.

The curfew in Peterhead was a legacy of the Keith Family, the Earl Marischals of Scotland, who owned the town and lived at nearby Inverugie Castle until they were disinherited for Jacobite activities. The curfew dated from the days of wooden houses and thatched roofs, when all lights and fires were to be extinguished by eight o'clock, but was discontinued at the start of World War Two, when the ringing of bells was to signify a German invasion. Ironically, a statue of the last Earl Marischal (a gift from the Emperor of Prussia) still stands before the Townhouse in the main square.

In return, the naming of Hanover Street (where the Palace stood) was Peterhead's acknowledgement to Frederick the Great for the statue, which gave both picture houses a link with the nation that was to end their curfew bells.

The Palace curtain was rolled up from the foot, revealing a broad white sheet of dazzling brightness, a mirror reflecting our adolescent eagerness.

The lights went out like a blink of your eyelid. Pandemonium broke out among the kids down front, yelling and screaming for action in the moment of darkness before the first flash of pictures on the silent screen.

Because of the curtain adverts. Clarkie didn't show slides. Mostly he started with an Our Gang, Thelma Todd or Charley Chase two-reel comedy to relax his audience. The Gaumont Graphic News brought them back to reality later in the programme, along with the serial and the vaudeville or 'Turnie,' and then the feature; but no trailers, Clarkie relied solely on his posters and his own reputation for the following week's audiences.

On Saturday matinees the feature film was shown first and the serial last. Clarkie knew it was the serial that the kids were waiting for and the cliff-hanger ending usually brought them back again the following Saturday, provided they weren't following one at Aubrey's. The programmes were changed Mondays and Thursdays, incuding the serial and newsreel.

This was a new projection of life: a new image of man as he had always wanted to see himself; a vain indulgence of his imagination which the new media had made possible. It was a new poetry with few words: a visual language that the poorest intelligence could follow, and each one identified himself with the action to the limits of his emotion and mentality.

STRAW INTO GOLD

He could swing on chandeliers, slide down bannisters, sword in hand, walk on train roofs, climb mountains, leap over rooftops, ski, swim, ride, drive or fly, shoot the villain of his life and flirt with the prettiest girls—all without reproach. It released the working classes from a millenium of boredom and they especially enjoyed it.

I have been a film fan for over forty years and if the cinema had never developed its latest dimensions I should still have been content with Clarkie's movies.

Dan Williams was on the stage and he overplayed his act by nearly half-an-hour. Everyone was delighted, except the projectionists, who were giving him the spotlight. Indeed they were that angry they ran the big film through so fast we could hardly read the sub-titles.

There was also in those days a great mystery about the movies. How was it done? How did they manage it? I must confess that for a long time I thought the whole thing was manipulated from behind the screen, rather than before it, like a puppet show, because the movies came before television and were the real miracle of the century.

Mr. Clark once admitted me to a children's matinee at the Palace for three-half-pence when the price of a seat was two-pence. He said he was acting against principle but that he didn't want to turn me away. I had been doing messages for mother and found myself a half-penny short three miles from home.

I did so much want to see the film that I approached Mr. Clark to let me in. The show had already started so I considered that the half-penny short didn't matter. Mr. Clark said it must never happen again because he would have to pay the half-penny himself to square accounts.

But mind you a half-penny was important in those days and a boy never forgets a kindness of this sort. In my day I have sold a dozen eggs to get to the pictures, or a number of jam jars, or even a stone of oat-meal; in married life I have been known to rob the children's bank, and if Mr. Clark had turned me away it is probable this short tribute to his memory would never have been attempted.

CLARKIE'S AND AUBREY'S

The name of the film was THE SHIELD OF SILENCE, but I think I have kept silent long enough and must now give credit to the man who first inspired my boyhood.

Clarkie's had the disadvantage of being out of bounds for the casual visitor to Peterhead. Aubrey's was bang in the busy centre of the town. To offset this disparity Clarkie stuck his playbills on the gable of a house at Drummer's Corner, facing Errol Street, the apex of a triangle formed by Marischal Street, Thistle Street and Albion Street. Coming into the town from the south or west, down Kirk Street, you couldn't miss Clarkie's hoarding at Drummer's Corner. Next to the 'Muckle Kirk' and Messrs. Jack's 'The Little Wonder' drapery arcade the posters caught your eye coming up Errol Street.

The site is now a car park. The old red-tiled house where Clarkie stuck his bills has long since been demolished, but often have I gazed enraptured at its glorified gable. It was there I first became aware of the seductiveness of the cinema poster. That was over forty years ago and they still excite me.

Bob Harvey's grocery shop was right opposite Drummer's Corner, at the top of Love Lane, and I called there every Saturday morning with my hand-cart for the week's messages. While Mr. Harvey made out my list I went over and stared at Clarkie's hoarding. It got thicker and thicker until the bill-poster stripped down to the plaster and started afresh. I used to try counting the edges to see how many bills the wad would hold before it fell down. I then went up the street to look at Aubrey's glossy stills, an extravagance Clarkie never indulged in.

Clarkie's posters were mostly larger than life, so you can imagine what Bebe Daniels looked like on a surf-board as THE PALM BEACH GIRL at Drummer's Corner, or Pauline Garron in briefs as THE CHORUS GIRL. Perhaps the magistrates of the day turned a blind eye to Clarkie's posters. They had certainly brightened Drummer's Corner and no amount of Nestle's Milk or Andrew's Liver Salt advertisements could replace them in glamour.

And up at Aubrey's you could see exotic stills of Patsy Ruth Miller in tattered sarong as LORRAINE OF THE LIONS. The **Buchan Observer** had even dared a double-column spread of Laura La

Plante in THE LOVE THRILL, half-hidden behind an arras, but peeping out as lissom and warm as life. Even today I doubt if the Buchanie would risk anything so daring for Aubrey's or anyone else.

Nowadays the cinema is merely a mirror of the times but in those days Hollywood set the fashion. There WAS a British Board of Film Censors but so far they HADN'T got the length of an X certificate. Anyone from nine to ninety could nip inside and stare gogo-eyed at Mademoiselle La Plante, or revel in the capers of Constance Talmadge in VENUS OF VENICE, a G-string romp that makes our modern Les Dors, Bardot, and Loren look like a trio of blushing schoolgirls.

Anyway, you could take your pick: SILK STOCKING SAL at Clarkie's or a peep behind LADY WINDERMERE'S FAN at Aubrey's; you could have the Can-Can in THE MOULIN ROUGE at Aubrey's or a farce called SHORT SKIRTS at the Palace, forty years before the mini-skirt.

We were in the middle of the saucy 'twenties. The girls shortened their skirts and bobbed their hair, danced the Charleston and stayed out late and I'm doubtful if Clarkie or Aubrey could be blamed for it. Talk about Pop Idols and the Twisters! They hadn't a patch on the Jiggerbuggers of the 'twenties.

When BEAU GESTE came to the Palace Drummer's Corner got a real plastering. As a Foreign Legionaire we had Ronald Colman all over the place. Clarkie ran a tie-up with the local booksellers and Johnny Miller's window was stacked full of newly pressed copies of the P. C. Wren masterpiece.

But if Clarkie's and Aubrey's were the Sodom and Gomorrah of Peterhead they were to suffer the fates of their namesakes. For not a stone of them is left standing to the eyes of men . . .

As I have already mentioned Aubrey's was a real posh place upstairs in the Townhouse, with tip-up cushioned chairs, a sloping floor, and the detergent rose up from the lush carpets like you was in a flower garden. They even had the usherettes spray scent on your shoulders, and with creatures like Helen Twelvetrees on the screen, or sunny-haired Marion Davies it was almost out of this world. The Palace smelled mostly of orange peel, Spearmint gum and Clarkie's cigar.

CLARKIE'S AND AUBREY'S

Aubrey's had framed posters on the stairs, coloured pictures of Rin-Tin-Tin (the wonderdog), Richard Dix, Antonio Moreno, Jackie Coogan or Pearl White, and these were changed with the film shows. The shuttered windows could be opened for kid matinees and there were hot-water radiators against the walls. The closing of the Picture House windows was like the lifting of Clarkie's curtain, yelling and screaming in the darkness, only it lasted longer because the attendants took their time about it.

When it was real quiet you could hear the film ticking over the sprockets in the projection room. Bobby Clark was Aubrey's chief projectionist. He was a son of James Clark (no relation to Clarkie) who had a carter business in Prince Street, next door to where Simpson's had their cartwright workshops, and now their garage.

They even had sound effects at Aubrey's: When BEN-HUR rowed in the galleys you could hear his wrist chains rattling over the gunwales; in pictures like MONS and THE SOMME you could hear the whine and crump of the bursting shells. Aubrey's had even shown a whaling film in colour, tailor-made for the town. It was called THE SEA BEST, from Herman Melville's novel 'Moby Dick,' and starred John Barrymore and lovely Helen Costello.

Mr. Clark had only a pianist to play accompaniment for the films. Aubrey's had a four-piece orchestra: piano and drums, fiddle and bass, and when they tuned their instruments before the show it put you in a dither. But what better atmosphere could you have for a Western than Clarkie's tinkling piano! There was great rivalry between the two cinemas, at least in the minds of their patrons, though I am doubtful if the proprietors paid much attention to it.

Clarkie's was sometimes called the Bug Palace. Folks said you sometimes got flechs at Clarkie's, and that you had to cast your sark when you got home and hold it over the fire. I must confess I never experienced this but perhaps I may be immune from the pin-prick of the flech, as some people are. Somebody said they had even seen a rat on Clarkie's rafters. You could certainly hear the rain or the hail on the corrugated iron roof and there was no heating system that I can remember.

But maybe Aubrey's had flechs too, especially with all that padded upholstery, warm with perspiring humanity; but maybe they were a more genteel species of flech, though just as long in the tooth.

In the autumn of 1926 Mr. Clark sold the Palace Theatre in Hanover Street. He retired from the cinema business and concentrated all his abilities on his ironmongery shop. Of course Clarkie deserved his retirement, but far-sighted business man that he was, he knew that the great days of the silent cinema were coming to an end, and that the public wouldn't long be content with his out-of-date Palace in Hanover Street. There was also a hint of talking pictures and huge new luxury cinemas were springing up in every town, so Clarkie sold his picture house for £2,000 to a Mr. Sterndale, an Edinburgh business man with a mind for the theatre.

Mr. Sterndale was a quiet, modest, friendly man, tasteful and cultured, but he had a fatal flair for bow-tie-and-tails, opera and posh musicians. 'Under New Management' appeared prominently on the Palace bills and he opend its door to his customers with a courteous smile. He spent another £1,000 on a 'face-lift' for the Palace. The smell of fresh paint and varnish replaced the aroma of Clarkie's cigar in the vestibule. Mr. Sterndale angled the floor and re-seated the Palace, with new chairs replacing the hard benches at the front. But before all this was complete fortune emptied her lap in his favour.

'It's an ill wind that blows nobody good!' as the saying goes, and as the new proprietor of the Palace Theatre Mr. Sterndale had good reason to believe it. Circumstances were contrived it seemed to enable him to take the town by storm, on the crest of the wave . . . .

In the winter of 1926-27 the Blue Toon was rocked by an earth tremor, lashed by a hurricane and threatened with a tidal wave. Buildings trembled, windows rattled, crockery was toppled from the dressers in the fishermen's houses. In the darkness of early morning the townsfolk were startled from their sleep. It was a Friday morning. 'The Deevil's Birthday,' folk said, and the wind rose before nightfall, rich with the smell of sea-weed.

CLARKIE'S AND AUBREY'S

The wind rose from the North-east and the Keith Inch was smothered in spray. You could hardly stand on the Smith Embankment and you could hear the gun-shot smack of the waves as they hit the breakwaters. Monstrous waves spiralled over the lighthouse and cascaded along the outer piers. Shipping dragged their anchors in the bay and their mast lights reeled like a drunk in the dark.

One of Jamie Reid's horse omnibuses was blown over near the Convict Prison, bound for Boddam. When the folk came out of Aubrey's Picture House they could hardly cross the road. The wind tore at their clothes and hurled them against the walls. Chimney pots and rone pipes littered the pavements. The hurricane ripped the slates from roof-tops and lashed the town with sea-spray.

The weather-cock on the Townhouse steeple was whirling like a spinning-top, its golden arms glinting in the lightning flashes, while the thunder now ricocheted above the gaslit streets. Just before midnight one terrific wind gust toppled the Townhouse steeple and sent it crashing through the roof of Aubrey's Picture House. The crowd who had just left were fortunate, and the resident caretaker and his family escaped with bruises.

Saturday dawned wet and surly. Folks gathered in Broad Street and gazed stupified at the topless steeple, sheered to the clock-tower, and the hole in Aubrey's roof. Some realised how fortunate they had been and swore they would never go to Aubrey's pictures again. "Clarkie for me!" they cried, waving their arms, "Clarkie's for me, every time!" Mr. Sterndale's 'New Management' meant nothing to the frightened townspeople; to them it was still 'Clarkie's,' and nothing he could do or say would change it.

The crowds came down Erroll Street to look at the red Gothic spire on the Muckle Kirk. A hand was missing from one of the clocks and the East face was bashed in; otherwise he was none the worse.

The wind had fallen but the cry of 'Tidal Wave!' seized the town with a panic. Wizened-faced fishermen of many weathers said it was most likely after an earthquake and a hurricane. There was talk of evacuation in Charlotte Street and along the harbour fronts. People in ground floors swore they wouldn't go to bed. Upper-storey folks were more confident and offered shelter for the night.

125

Buchanhaven and the Roanheads were late in hearing the news and they scoffed at the cry of 'Tidal Wave!' There were folks on the Keith Inch (owre the Queenie) in those days and they had more cause than any for alarm. Their small rocky island formed a bulwark for the town against the fiercest storms.

Meanwhile, up at the Palace in Hanover Street Mr. Sterndale had a rousing good matinee. Besides his own crowd he had all the kids from Aubrey's. They clambered into the dearest seats and the place was cheering full. Tidal wave or no tidal wave, people were going to the pictures, and there was nowhere else to go but 'Clarkie's.' Some were optimistic and said that a tidal wave wouldn't come the length of Clarkie's anyway. The first house of the evening was also packed out, nowhere even to stand, and it was a field-day for the sweetie shoppie next door. Clarkie never saw queues like this for they swarmed round the corner into King Street for the second house. Queue manners were bad in those days and you almost had to fight for your stance on the pavement. I was scared stiff but once inside I squeezed myself into one of the wooden benches at the front (so far Mr. Sterndale hadn't got the length of replacing them with tip-up chairs). People were paying to stand, blocking the exits if the tidal wave should come, and a great many were turned away.

Mr. Sterndale was running a boxing film called ONCE TO EVERY MAN, starring George O'Brien, a title which was pregnant with his own fate, but meantime a golden money-spinner.

And such a smashing show it was! All about a boxer defending his title with a broken wrist. I forgot all about the tidal wave and half expected the streets to be flooded when we came out. But no, for the tidal wave had subsided to a whispered ripple and the old town was quiet and sleepy.

Aubrey's was knocked out for a month and every seat was sold at the Palace.

Mr. Sterndale proceeded quietly with the renovation of the Palace Theatre. The transformation became more apparent as the months passed. Clarkie had films booked for six months in advance and Mr. Sterndale more or less rushed them through. He ran double-features and weekly festivals to get rid of them. We would have a Reginald Denny week, six Denny pictures, a different one for each day. I saw the last one on the Saturday night 'OH DOCTOR!' in June 1927, and I thought it was perfectly delightful. I fell completely in love with the heroine. I thought her the most charming creature I had ever seen in my fourteen summers, nothing quite like her among the kitchiedeems on the farms, or anywhere else for that matter, though I can't remember her name. I couldn't understand why Mr. Sterndale should be in such a hurry to be rid of films as charming as this one.

When Clarkie's film bookings were exhausted Mr. Sterndale brought in live shows, with specially selected films on alternate weeks, when live bookings were unobtainable. 'The Best in Revue, Drama, Pictures and Music' was written in letters of gold on a glass panel at the entrance, and the new proprietor did his best to live up to his promise. In redecorating the Palace he probably sought to attract a more elite audience, from the Queen Street, Landale Road and Prince Street areas, and from suburbia.

The celebrated Moss Players visited the Palace for a season, and their repertoire included BONNIE ANNIE LAURIE, MARIA MARTEN (The Red Barn Mystery), FORBIDDEN FRUIT, DAFT JAMIE, SWEENEY TODD, etc., and other companies followed with EAST LYNNE, JANE EYRE, MAIN'S WOOIN' and THE FARMER'S WIFE, all staged in beautiful settings and performed by competent artists. We even had Jack Radcliffe in a revue called SHAMROCKS AND HEATHER, another Scots comedian called Jack Tarbet, and Dan Williams was always a popular favourite.

Dr. Walford Bodie (The Electric Wizard) visited the Palace for the last time in November 1927. He was in an angry mood and from the stage he openly reproached Clarkie for leaving the theatre in such a state. He riled at the hard forms down at the front and hoped that by his next visit Mr. Sterndale would have them replaced with restful chairs for the working people. He also harangued the audience for their lack of support for their new proprietor (though the place was packed for him) and said they didn't know how lucky they were in having such a man in their midst. But Mr. Sterndale stayed out of sight, for he was far too modest a man to encourage such elation.

127

Dr. Bodie then asked for volunteers from the audience to come on stage to be hypnotized. I have a suspicion that this was pre-arranged, but in any case, three or four men ventured timidly forward and he soon had them out of their senses, running all over the stage shouting and singing 'Does your mother run a bike in the middle of the night, with your father on the handle-bars?' Bodie then had them strip to vest and underpants quite unconsciously and it nearly brought the house down. He galvanised a girl until she emitted sparks. Another he sent into a trance and suspended her horizontally in space. He lit cigarettes from his finger-tips and brought down fire from heaven. By the end of the performance people were actually frightened in their seats.

The chorus comprised a bevy of swinging, bare-hipped lovelies who danced and sang 'Down in the Quarry where the Bluebells Grow!' Quite the nicest thing we had seen at the Palace for a long time and made you forget all about your aching behind on the hard seats. Dr. Bodie was a Buckie man and since his day there has never been another magician to equal him. The great Houdini, with whom he was compared, died the previous year, in 1926.

Mr. Sterndale then brought Gilbert and Sullivan to Peterhead: THE YEOMEN OF THE GUARD, THE GONDOLIERS, H.M.S. PINAFORE, the lot, and he engaged the best singers and the most expensive musicians for a rendering of LA BOHEME, RIGOLETTO, CARMEN, THE STUDENT PRINCE, besides several other operatic ventures, and the resident conductor of the Palace orchestra was billed with F.R.C.S. and L.R.A.M. after his name.

But alas Mr. Sterndale was forced to raise his admission prices and audiences dwindled. They wouldn't pay even ninepence to watch opera. He really went to town with the classics, but in pandering to the more discerning patron he had lost the more regular customer. It was a fatal mistake. Perhaps the Palace was not the right place for high falsetto: it lacked atmosphere, there was no balcony, no chandeliers, no private boxes; it had a barrel-shaped roof supported by latticed wooden trusses, sadly lacking in the acoustic resonance of a vaulted ceiling.

CLARKIE'S AND AUBREY'S

Perhaps the artists were embarrassed by the circus tent environment, and the dressing and toilet facilities were cramped and inadequate. Dwindling audiences and lack of support may have affected their performances.

The workers took their wives and sweethearts to Aubrey's and thus deprived Mr. Sterndale of his main support. They turned up their noses at opera and wanted nothing better than good old-fashioned movies. Such high-falutin' material was poison to the teen-agers and they flocked to Aubrey's. And while Aubrey's queues lengthened Mr. Sterndale watched and listened to his beloved opera with a handful of the faithfuls, for you could hardly call them conneisseurs at the Palace.

When opera had been tried and proved unsuccessful Mr. Sterndale turned to vaudeville. Artists from the best Revues in the country came to shake a leg at the Palace, but I'm doubtful if it paid their train fares. Perhaps if it had come before the opera there might have been a chance; this way it was wrong and pantomime fared no better.

Mr. Sterndale began to book full picture programmes again and business began to revive. But it was a late and temporary recovery. It was 1929 and the 'Talkies' had reached Aberdeen. Jamie Sutherland was carting them into the city by the bus load to see (and hear) the wonder of the century, moving pictures that talked and sang songs. Hollywood went talkie mad and stopped making silent films. Even Aubrey's were finding it difficult to get suitable copy. Cinemas all over the country were being wired for sound. The future of the Palace became an enigma for Mr. Sterndale. He was already involved in debt and further outlay frightened him. The Palace was a doubtful venture for sound: acoustics would be poor with a tin roof, especially in a downpour of rain or hail; the public would certainly be looking for something better than that!

I saw my last films at the Palace in September, 1929, Gary Cooper in Zane Grey's NEVADA, and George K. Arthur and Karl Dane in BABY MINE, a programme that filled the hall on a Saturday night. Pictures stopped Mr. Sterndale's losses but didn't retrieve the money lost on live shows. He became a depressed and lonely man, faced with frustration and bankruptcy. For a few more months he suffered disillusionment and brooded over the loss of his life savings. Everything he had was sunk in a theatre without a future, gone beyond recovery, so he locked himself in his room and turned on the gas . . .

For nearly twenty years the Palace stood derelict and forgotten. Rust corroded its roof and grass grew in its gutters and around the doors. Vandals broke the windows and inside you could see the old stage curtains swinging in the draught, a sacriligious act that nearly broke my heart. And Clarkie's old Humber car still stood in a hot-bed of nettles round at the back, for he had given up motoring also.

And while the Palace died slowly Mr. Clark still plied his wares in ironmongery. He was eighty-two when I last talked to him in his shop in Broad Street. I spoke about his old days at the Palace and his eyes twinkled with memories. He rubbed his hands together and smiled gleefully, cherubic and cheerful as ever. He said he was accustomed to good crowds at the Palace, but when he saw me standing there alone on the pavement he decided to sell. "You were a bad omen," he said, "a symbol of things to come!" But of course he was only joking, and Mrs. Clark chirped over his shoulder that she had too much time for knitting in the box-office, and that was bad for business. They were clearing their stock for further retirement and managed to sell me a dozen spoons at cut price. Quite unconsciously this old couple had helped to frame the pattern and background of my thoughts for a lifetime.

Mr. Clark enjoyed two more years of bouncing, vigorous health and died quietly on January 3rd, 1940. His funeral was attended by a large following from 19 Cairntrodlie to the New Cemetery.

Clarkie was one of Peterhead's four Jamies who helped to shape the history of the town: the other three were Jamie Sutherland, Jamie Booth and Jamie Reid.

The Palace was eventually taken over by Messrs. Crosse & Blackwell after World War II, demolished and rebuilt as a warehouse. Take a quiet stroll along Hanover Street towards the public gardens and you would never know that Clarkie's Palace Theatre had ever existed. Yet for a decade it was everybody's dreamhouse, a miniature Broadway, gay with lights and noisy patrons, and perhaps yet alive in the minds of many of the older generation of filmgoers.

Early in 1929 I became acquainted with the late Mr. George Hylands, manager of Aubrey's Picture House for many years. I asked Mr. Hylands if he could bring back Rudolph Valentino's picture THE SON OF THE SHEIK, with Vilma Banky. He said he would try but the following week he informed me with regret that this couldn't be done, but to please me he would book Vilma Banky's picture THE AWAKENING in the very near future.

Now about this time I was fee-ed at Nether Kinmundy, near the 'Creeshie Raw' in the Parish of Longside, Poet Skinner and Jamie Fleeman country, about six miles out of Peterhead, and when Miss Banky's picture came to Aubrey's for three days I couldn't get in. Weather and circumstances conspired to prevent me making a tryst with my screen sweetheart. Mr. Hylands noted my absence and reprimanded me on my next visit. He had rented the picture especially for me and perhaps it hadn't done too well at the pay-box.

All the same this discomfiture proved to be 'The Awakening' of a friendship between Mr. Hylands and myself which lasted for several years. I used to visit his office regularly where he gave me many volumes of the old Bioscope Weekly and I learned the cinema business from A to Z or almost. Mr. Hylands took me upstairs to the projection room where Bobby Clark worked and I saw the films running through the projectors. I had the privilege of looking through the peep-holes at the audience below and I watched the light-beam playing on the screen far out in front.

Mr. Hylands gave me every encouragement to learn and I missed nothing, from re-winding films to change-overs, splicing broken films to threading the machines. For me this was far more interesting than pulling wet turnips or stooking sheaves on the weary stubble fields, so I asked Mr. Hylands for a job as spool-boy and he put my name down in the books. In the language of the cinema the spool-boy is the brat who rewinds and patches the films after or between the shows and gets them ready for the next performance. As a youth this sort of thing fascinated me and I would have left my jacket in the farmer's hands just to get it, perhaps even a month's pay, which didn't amount to much in those days. Pay was just as poor for a spool-boy, and digs would be a problem, but my enthusiasm would overcome all. But alas it was not to be, for Mr. Hylands left Aubrey's before my name came up and I lost my opportunity.

. . . But talkies were slow in coming to Peterhead. Aubrey's was now the only picture house in the town and they had the public on a string. During the summer of 1930, when the supply of orthodox silent films petered out Aubrey's resorted to showing films made as talkies but dubbed with sub-titles, and as the early talkies combined a minimum of action with a maximum of gab, most of them were nothing more than photographed stage plays with no spoken dialogue. The result was almost unbearable and picture-going in the town became merely a magic lantern reading session.

The COHENS AND KELLY series seems the most reminiscent of this arid period, when we had THE COHENS AND KELLYS IN SCOTLAND, THE COHENS AND KELLYS IN PARIS, and so forth, until the folks were almost glad to take the bus into Aberdeen to see a decent movie. It was not until the owners of Caledonian Associated Cinemas drew up their plans for the new Playhouse in Queen Street that Aubrey's shareholders began to think seriously of bringing talking pictures to Peterhead.

Meanwhile, since Mr. Hylands' absence Bobby Clark had been promoted as manager at Aubrey's. It was quite a change for Bobby to discard his greasy overalls for a starched shirt and evening dress, and to stand at the top of the stairs at Aubrey's, where he greeted his patrons with an embarrassed smile and proffered his oil-grained hand to nobility.

Bobby had worked all his life at Aubrey's. He started as spool-boy and ended up as manager. In between, as chief projectionist he used to nip home to Prince Street for a cuppa and a blow at a fag between shows on a Saturday night, because projectionists are not allowed to smoke on duty, for obvious reasons.

When we saw Bobby from the ninepennies coming back up the passage with his assistant we knew they had also been checking the oil-engine at the back of the building and it wouldn't be long

132

now or we had the slides and the Pathe Gazette. But the managerial post put an end to Bobby's hurried cuppa on a Saturday night because now he had to be on hand all the time. And besides, bow-tie-and-tails look most undignified in a hurry; these are meant to illustrate elegance, poise and a social dignity, not to be associated with an upstart rushing home to mama for a fly cup.

The younger generation can never fully appreciate the impact of the talking picture on a listening world. In these days of television, tape recorders, radio and transistors, sound and vision are taken for granted; they are there when we are born, we grow up with them, and they are as common as our daily bread. It is difficult to realise what it was like in the old days; certainly the gramophone record had enjoyed world wide popularity and the era of loudspeaker radio was available to those who could afford it; the moving picture was no longer a novelty but an accepted reality, a silent reality which many people enjoyed, indeed preferred them that way, but a picture that actually talked and laughed and sang, with all other relevant background noises—well it just seemed too much to expect from invention.

Aubrey's presented their first talking movie to the town on the last three days of 1930. They gave two performances nightly and the queues went down Marischal Street and through Fife and Duncan's Pend, almost as far as Threadneedle Street (where Jockie Birnie used to have a chip shop) and many were turned away. People stood in the street all through the first performance to be first in the queue for the second house.

But Peterhead's first talking picture was a heart-warming experience, like youth's first kiss or falling in love, sanctified by the presence of that wonderful creature Janet Gaynor. She was sweeter than sweet to most male hearts, and to hear her singing 'Sunny Side Up,' which was also the title of the film, and more especially 'If I Had A Talking Picture Of You' put my heart in a swingboat. I could think of nothing else for days and her beauty haunted me everywhere. For years later I remembered that film, and still do. It glorified our drab reality. Charles Farrell had the male lead, tall, handsome and manly-voiced, but I was all eyes and ears for the winsome, lovely, flower-like Janet Gaynor, who was to become the dream girl of millions for years to come.

In those days the average film show ran for two hours, and as SUNNY SIDE UP ran for about an hour-and-three-quarters the only support was the PATHE GAZETTE with a commentator (something quite new in newsreels) and the first Walt Disney cartoon with sound, THE DANCE OF THE SKELETONS, and such a rattling good experience it was that the audience responded almost as an individual.

THE DESERT SONG was Aubrey's second talkie, with John Boles as the Red Shadow, and Carlotta King, all in colour. This was followed by THE GOLD DIGGERS OF BROADWAY, JOURNEY'S END, ROOKERY NOOK (starring Ralph Lynne, Tom Walls, Winnifred Shotter, Robertson Hare and Yvonne Arnaud), Madeleine Carroll and Frank Lawton in YOUNG WOODLY, Marie Dressler and Wallace Beery in MIN AND BILL, Bessie Love in BROADWAY MELODY, and many more really wonderful films.

Everybody was singing 'Tip-toe Through The Tulips' and 'Painting The Clouds With Sunshine' and the gramophone industry got its first lift into the Pop Charts.

Some of the early talkies had a sound track, others merely sound on disc, synchronised with the projection of the film, a technicality which had many complications, which nobody minded, so long as they talked; lips moved and words were heard, songs were born and that was all that mattered.

The monopoly of the cinema trade by Aubrey's in Peterhead came to an end in July, 1931, when the new Playhouse opened with a sound track film called JUST IMAGINE. Here was super luxury modern cinema with the lid off and you can Just Imagine how it drew the crowds away from Aubrey's. However, there was scope for both cinemas in those days and they continued in friendly rivalry for nigh on six years.

Gracie Fields was the last great star ever to shine at Aubrey's. Her vibrant voice had scarcely died in the great hall when the place was ablaze from floor to ceiling. Perhaps the end is best described by the late Robert Neish in his book OLD PETER-HEAD: 'Came the early morning of Sunday, 15th December, 1936. Flames lit the sky! The Music Hall was ablaze! Dawn revealed its naked skeleton in the last phase of oblivion. The end of the Music Hall (and of Aubrey's cinema) meant more than the loss of a friendly landmark; it epitomised the end of an institution, a community of fellowship; an era in the happy life history of Peterhead which can never be replaced. Only memories remain.'

In the Spring of 1939 J. B. Milne Theatres Ltd. opened the chromium-plated glass doors of the new Regal Cinema in Marischal Street (directly opposite Drummer's Corner) with the late Sir Alexander Korda's film THE DRUM, introducing the late Sabu as a new boy star to the screen.

Now the Regal has gone over to Bingo and J. B. Milne has acquired the Playhouse as Peterhead's only cinema. Times change but I believe that if Clarkie had been alive in this age of television he would have gone one better, perhaps a discotheque or a bowling alley—or even an Ice-Rink! Clarkie was always just that little bit in front of anyone else—the bit that mattered.

THE LAST JOURNEY

Previously published in the BUCHAN OBSERVER, April 27th, 1965

S O the passenger service on the Buchan line is to end on May 1st!

In the middle 'twenties, when Jimmie Sutherland's buses first began seriously to affect passenger traffic on the line the directors of the London and North-Eastern Railway Company offered to buy him out.

The L.N.E.R. had just recently acquired control of the old Great North of Scotland Railway Company and they had wrought many changes and improvements on its northern branches. Engine colours had been changed from grimy black to bright green, with gold letters and numbering. Coaches were varnished in light brown instead of the old two-tone chocolate with cream windows, and corridor carriages on eight-wheel bogeys replaced some of the old four to six wheel-base vehicles. Stations were re-painted green and cream, with red buffers and white signal posts; stretches of new track were re-laid, new rolling stock introduced, signalling improved—business was booming—then it was time to approach the stocky, vigorous, red-faced Mr. Sutherland, proprietor of Victoria Stables, St. Peter Street, Peterhead, where the Union Jack fluttered gaily from the chimney stocks on the office gable, with gold lettering on the frosted glass of the windows.

Buy him out! Jimmie Sutherland was highly offended. The man who could yoke 250 horses in one day at the height of the herring season, the man who had a dozen motor buses on the Aberdeen run, and twice as many lorries, and giving as good a public service (and a cheaper one) than any railway in the country, fie man! And had he not built a railway himself, or helped to build it? Five miles of track for the old G.N.S.R. that ran from Longside station to Lenabo, and had he not helped to build the airship station there as well? Supplying the Air Ministry with traction-engines and wagons, horses and lorries, transport and labour,

136

driving stones from Cairngall quarries—buy him out! It was an insult that deserved a similar answer, so Jimmie Sutherland waved his cheque-book in the faces of the bemused directors of the giant L.N.E.R. and asked: "And what wad ye be needin' for yer ain bit linie?"

So what could you do with a man like that but leave him alone! But the gesture merely intensified Jimmie's endeavour. Maybe it is a pity that Dr. Beeching hadn't been around at the time. Perhaps he would have had more foresight and fixed a price, even a steep one, which would have given Jimmie Sutherland control of the Buchan branch line, with happier results than now faces it. And Jimmie Sutherland confided to his nearest associates that rather than let the L.N.E.R. run him into the ground he would take his passengers into Aberdeen and give them a cup of tea and bring them back again—for nothing! Maybe this was going a bit too far, but by subsidising his buses from his farming and contracting business he may have managed it, at least for a time, until he won public favour, for he was a shrewd man Jimmie Sutherland —and a determined one!

But let us go back a bit, to one fine Saturday morning in the Spring of 1923, when Jimmie Sutherland had one of his drivers take his first motor-bus out of the glass roofed garage at Victoria Stables and leave it across the road to await passengers for Aberdeen. Nobody took much notice. After all he was always up to something nobody else had thought about. For years now he had been running motor lorries as charabancs to Aikey Brae and Mintlaw Games, and horse buses to Boddam Station and Cruden Bay; nothing in that to affront the directors of the old and respected G.N.S.R.—indeed he had been aiding them by supplying a road link between the Peterhead and Boddam rail terminal. But now he had something else in mind, for he would take his passengers all the way to Aberdeen in motor-buses, and as the railway from Boddam ran almost parallel with the road all the way to Ellon he would drain the L.N.E.R. from two sources, from the Maud route as well as from Boddam, and from providing a road link between Peterhead and Boddam to the railway's advantage he would branch out on his own.

And there was this big green bus that came through from Rosehearty every Sunday morning in the summer months and stood
in the Broadgate in Peterhead, just under the eye of Earl Marischal
Keith on his granite pedestal and the townhouse clock. It had
solid rubber tyres and a flat roof and a huge starting handle held
up with a leather strap. Quite a crowd gathered to have a look
at this monstrosity that had come through from the Broch, and
some said it belonged to a Mr. Simpson who was running a bus
service between the Broch and Rosehearty, but there didn't seem
to be any name on the thing. Some of the more venturesome who
could afford it paid their fares to the driver and climbed on board
for a trip to Aberdeen, returning in the evening while it was still
daylight. The service was suspended during the winter because
nobody it was thought would want to go to Aberdeen on a winter
Sunday when all the shops were closed. But Jimmie Sutherland
cared as little for the shops being closed as for the kirks being
open, and he would give everybody the equal chance of going to
Aberdeen any day of the week, summer or winter, early or late,
at 3/6d. return fare, while the railway charged the ridiculous sum
of 10/-, and their last return left the city at seven o'clock, ten
o'clock for the buses, three extra hours in the city, and the trains
didn't run on Sundays.

Sutherland's first motor-bus also had solid tyres, and maybe
just as well, because that lad MacAdam hadn't yet been up here
with his tar boiler. He was on the way but so far the Buchan
roads were still surfaced with rough red or blue stone and gravel
from the local quarries. Great heaps of stone still lay by the roadside, with men in wall-tams and mufflers breaking them into chips
with hammers, each man to his bing, bicycle and dinner bag; the
equivalent of the surfacemen who spread the stone chips between
the sleepers on the railway line. But the red Daimler with the
white windows didn't have long to wait for a load. Passengers
paid their fares to the drivers because 'clippies' hadn't been heard
of and nobody bothered with tickets. Perhaps Jimmie Sutherland
owed much of his success in the new bus venture to the honesty
of his drivers—but there is nothing new in the Pay As You Enter
buses of the 'seventies; indeed they are back where they started,

without conductresses. In this first trip Jimmie Chalmers was at the wheel, a man who spent his lifetime with the firm and ended up as a yard gaffer, which was not uncommon with Sutherland's employees.

But one bus wasn't enough to cope with all the passengers who wanted to travel to Aberdeen so cheaply. So Jimmie Sutherland bought another red bus, a Leyland this time, and had his name printed on it in large white letters and No. 2 on the back. Within a year he had reached number six, a small Fiat with balloon tyres and piercing head-lamps that could pick up passengers in the dark.

The directors of the L.N.E.R. began to scratch their heads. They were extremely embarrassed. The Boddam line hadn't yet paid a dividend and the red and white buses were running alongside the track and picking up most of the passengers; farm folk at their road ends, cottars and villagers, they just didn't bother to go to the station when the bus went past their doors, stopping at the garden gate, because there were no organised stopping places. Sutherland's cattle floats and flat-leafed motor lorries were also beginning to depreciate traffic at stations as far out as Maud and Strichen. Farmers became reluctant to rise early and drive their fat nowt to catch the first goods train at the nearest stations, often in the dark with paraffin lanterns and all the gates open by the roadside. It was much easier to give Jimmie Sutherland a bang on the 'phone (or write him a post-card) and he'd send a cattle float the morning you wanted it. A motor float would take the stots direct to the mart gates or the slaughter-house. All that shunting at the railway sidings wasn't good for a man's beasts anyway, though some drivers were cannier than others, but with all that banging about the creatures could hardly keep their feet in the wagons, and by the time they reached the sale rings they weren't the same animals that had left your byre in the morning, or at least they didn't look the same: drooping headed, narrow-bellied creatures and such a mess of sharn you wondered that the butchers put in a bid for them at all. Na na, just ring Jimmie Sutherland. This was the general attitude, with sheep as well as cattle and pigs, and if you wanted a horse cab, a hearse or a taxi, or a mull tae thrash yer crap, Jimmie had it; or a puffn'-

billy (steam-wagon) for yer flittin' at the term, and ye only had to load corn once on a lorry, nae chauvin with it on horse carts at the station.

But of course Jimmie Sutherland had competitors in trying to beat the railways, both in passengers and in freight. He had been first on the Buchan roads with a regular bus service but others were soon to follow. His first and most serious rival was William Forsyth, who had a garage in Peterhead where the Playhouse Cinema now stands. Forsyth actually forstalled Sutherland on the Peterhead-Fraserburgh road and very soon had six buses running, orange coloured Fiats mostly, and he drove a bus himself. Forsyth did well on this run because it cut out the rail journey to Maud junction for Fraserburgh, and it was extremely popular with the fisher folks.

Cordiners of Boddam had three buses on the road, some folk called them Baker's buses, I don't know why, but they were dark green with white windows. Shire Motors had three more, grey clumsy vehicles; Park's of Boddam had two blue buses, and Whyte's Motors of Sandford had two of light green with cream windows, and all these ran in direct opposition to Sutherland, not only on the Boddam, Cruden Bay, Whinnyfold roads, but right through to Aberdeen they challenged him. Cruickshank & Ross of Newburgh ran a small fleet of lovely fawn-coloured buses to Aberdeen and Kerr ran a service from Methlick. Clan Forbes of Sandhaven did the Rosehearty, Fraserburgh, Aberdeen run, pale-green coaches with lush upholstery and they had a band in Forbes tartan painted around them just under the windows. These were the first luxury coaches on the Buchan roads, far superior in comfort to anything that Sutherland or the others were running, perhaps excepting Cruickshank and Ross of Newburgh, and it set a new standard in passenger comfort to attract customers. Clan Forbes were eventually taken over by Simpsons' Motors of Rosehearty, and they in turn were swallowed up by Alexanders. Goodall's of Strichen ran a service and James Daniel did the Udny run and several private firms served Aberdeen itself, like Rover, Bydand and Radio, but here we are overstepping the boundaries concerning Buchan transport and its effect on the railways.

THE LAST JOURNEY

Alexander Burnett of Mintlaw began the Stuartfield, Peterhead run round about 1925, mostly picturegoers at week-ends until he organised a regular service, which eventually embraced Maud, New Deer, Cumminestown, New Byth and Turriff. Sandy Burnett actually left the plough at Lunderton Farm, near Peterhead and bought his first second-hand bus, an old square van with cut-out windows and after several years of service it finished up as a hen-house in somebody's farmyard. His father, old Arthur Burnett, was a retired shepherd who lived in a cottar house at Wellbank Farm, in the Peterhead area. It would appear that in those days the Road Commissioners as an authoritative body of men just didn't exist, because Sandy Burnett started running his bus from Mintlaw to Peterhead like it was nobody's business, and throve every day after it, though he told me personally many years later that he had to work hard for a living against fierce competition before he managed to establish himself. Punctuality and a regular service was the general aim, but until this was established, and especially in the very early days of bus rivalry, time-tables were a bit haphazard, sometimes even non-existent, depending on how soon you got a load for departure, as compared with your competitors. But eventually the police were forced to intervene to protect the public from exploitation and to ensure them of a regular and dependable service on the Buchan roads.

Sandy used to take the wife and bairns with him from Old Deer and Mintlaw and drive a load of picture-goers into Peterhead, where he emptied his bus in the Broadgate and drove out with his family to his parent's home at Wellbank, where they spent the evening until the pictures came out, when they would return to Peterhead to pick up their passengers. But this led to bigger things and Burnett's Motors of Mintlaw survived Sutherland's onslaught, as did Simpson's of Rosehearty, and both firms actually outlived Messrs. Sutherland into the days of nationalisation, finally merging in the name of Alexander's of Falkirk, as a Northern division of this transport marathon.

Burnett's began as they ended in chocolate brown colours and always modified their fleet by replacing their numbers: by this I mean that they never registered a bus more than they owned, so

141

that their newest replacement could still be number one. Sutherland never did this and soon ran into double figures, though they were never operating the number of buses registered. Burnett's were also unique in possessing the only six-wheeler bus on the Buchan roads, a vehicle designed to carry upwards of fifty passengers, but during the Hitler War conditions were such that 92 people have been counted leaving this handsome coach in the Broadgate at Peterhead on a Saturday afternoon, and as there were no police restrictions this vehicle must have proved a real money spinner for the firm. Indeed you were lucky if you got a seat in a bus in those days and on the shorter runs you mostly paid to stand, and the fact that buses couldn't be replaced profits were bound to rise, though spare parts were a problem in keeping a fleet of vehicles running. Being unable to purchase new buses Messrs. Sutherland spent their money on buying farms to keep down income tax, so that by the end of the war they owned no fewer than 27 farms, which were later sold and the money ploughed back into transport. By the end of the war the Buchan firms were buying second-hand double-decker buses which had been discarded from the streets of Glasgow and the bigger cities where tram-cars were still in use.

The most tragic of all the upstarts in the field of Buchan transport was William Thom (namesake of the Inverurie weaver poet). Thom married a daughter of a Mr. Saint, who used to farm Collilaw, in the Blackhills area of Peterhead, and with the help of his father-in-law he bought a new bus and borrowed Jimmie Sutherland's colours, gleaming red, and tried to pioneer a service on the country by-roads. He did well for a start, picking up schoolchildren and shopping housewives, until he was involved in an accident in which a little girl died on her way to school. It must have been the very first bus accident in Buchan—an unprecedented tragedy, and very few went on Thom's bus again and he soon faded into obscurity.

By 1927 or '29 most of the Buchan roads were serviced by bus and the road versus rail war was hotting up real good. This of course was happening all over the country, and the stalwarts of the competition still survive: Messrs. Alexanders, Scottish Omnibuses, S.M.T., MacBraynes, and so on, while Strachans of Ballater fell to Alexanders. Numerous small firms have sprung up in recent years with buses for hire, catering mostly for tourists and the picnic outing, and two of the old-timers have reappeared in this new profitable sideline—namely Simpsons' of Rosehearty and Eastons of Inverurie, the firm I believe who bought Burnett's six-wheeler after the war, but no doubt now on the scrap-heap.

But let us take another look at the Buchan railways. Back in 1924 Boddam Station was a shuttling hive of activity. At Cruden Bay they even had two single-deck tram-cars to take the golfing toffs from the station to the luxurious Grand or 'Big' Hotel on the bents which was owned and run by the railway company. A siding to the local brickworks enhanced goods traffic while farmers sent truckloads of sheep and cattle to Ellon and Aberdeen marts. As a boy I have gone with my father in the dark mornings droving fat cattle to Boddam Station, about a dozen at a time, and sometimes carrying a paraffin lantern in the dead of winter. There were sheep and cattle pens at most of the country stations and there was a brisk trade on market days: Ellon on Mondays, Strichen on Tuesdays, Maud on Wednesdays, and of course Aberdeen on Fridays, and both buyer and seller used the railways for transporting their animals. There were queues of farm carts at the country stations loading draff from the Speyside distilleries. Business was good in coal and fertilisers, grain and potatoes, milk and fish, iron and timber, farm machinery and cattle-feed, such as maize, oil-cake, bran and locust beans, besides groceries, flour and meat, oil and paraffin, indeed all forms of merchandise, newspapers, mail and parcels.

But besides the bus rivals Jimmie Sutherland was not alone in trying to capture a share of this vast flux in goods traffic. James Reid & Son was a serious local competitor, while William French of Fraserburgh and William Wisely of Aberdeen challenged him further afield, and numerous smaller transport firms sprang up all over the place, including Charles Alexander, who later became the whale to swallow all the Jonahs of road haulage, though not yet in a position to harm Jimmie Sutherland.

But despite opposition on the roads goods trains of over forty wagons were still common on the Buchan railways, right up to and including the war years, during which they maintained a regular flow of traffic. Of course in visualising the Buchan railways we should draw a line from Fraserburgh to Aberdeen, another from Peterhead to Maud junction, and one from Boddam to Ellon. The trains from Peterhead and Fraserburgh arrived at Maud junction at the same time, or within minutes of each other, one waiting patiently for the other if either was late, and sometimes arriving neck and neck, one on each side of the platform, standing abreast in friendly unison, panting away like breathless chargers, while the fireman from the Peterhead train uncoupled his coaches. If you had come up from the Blue Toon (Peterhead) you would watch for the Broch trainie on the other line, doing her damndest to be at Maud before you, and I suppose the Brochers watched for the Blue-Mogganers' train in the same way. But what's this happening now? Marischal Keith from Peterhead has shunted off and is now reversing on to the turntable in the servicing bay. And now my Lord Saltoun from the Broch steams up the line beyond the points with his carriages and comes back in reverse for the Peterhead coaches, which are coupled to his own, including the guard's van, and he sets off with the lot, eight to ten coaches, for he has the honour of hauling them into Aberdeen. Not only that but he gets another three coaches at Ellon from the Boddam line, so that by the time he reaches the Silver City he's clean out of breath with his load of passengers. Mormond Hill was bad enough but a sair pech or he got over the Rannieshill at Newmachar. And Marischal Keith from Peterhead would be shunting trucks at Maud or he got back from the city, and yon Donkey creature at Ellon standing on a siding doing nothing. But this wouldn't do on a Holiday Monday, or a Muckle Friday, when the country chiels cam' into the toon at the Term, for the carriages would be tramping full. So Marischal Keith gave Lord Saltoun a hand on Monday Holidays and Term Days, and the two of them would tackle the Rannieshill in great spirit, though sometimes slowed near to a trot, while the country chiels waved and shouted encouragement from the open carriage windows.

144

THE LAST JOURNEY

When the railways were really booming the engines on the Buchan line sometimes had a gie chauve with the long goods trains from Peterhead and the Broch, vans packed with fish and potatoes or grain, besides a great many empty trucks collected at the wayside stations, perhaps where coal or draff had been delivered—and how they managed to arrange it all says a good deal for co-ordinated effort from head office to local clerks, porters, guards and engine drivers, where to stop and shunt off loaded wagons and where to pick up empties—but anyhow the single engine usually had a sair trauchle on the gradients, and round the base of Mormond Hill the local folk had a language for the engine, a language I have heard in other parts of Buchan with a steep railway gradient, where the folk swore the engine was alive and complaining sorely of its tormentors. Approaching the hill the engine would puff slower and slower as if in apprehension of its task, and the smoke from the lum would get thicker and blacker as the fireman shovelled more and more coals into its flaming belly. 'Wull I m-a-n-a-g-e, W-u-l-l I m-a-n-a-g-e, W-u-l-l I m-a-n-a-g-e, W-u-l-l I m-a-n-a-g-e . . .' This was the rhythm of the engine on the steepest part of the brae, and to get its vocal effect you must repeat in slow slow motion. Half-way up and a regaining of confidence brought forth 'I t-h-i-n-k I w-u-l-l, I t-h-i-n-k I wull, I think I wull, I think I wull . . .' and on reaching the summit the chooking of the engine became an exhileration as it sped away on level ground with quickening pulse to the tune of 'I ken't I wid—I ken't I wid—I ken't I wid—I ken't I wid!'—and this one as fast as your tongue can go, for the Buchan folk had a proper rhythm for it.

At the height of the herring season as many as twenty-one fish trains left Fraserburgh daily, besides passenger and ordinary freight trains, and we may assume as many from Peterhead, all converging on the Maud junction, enroute for Aberdeen and the south. Special trains arrived with herring gutters from Inverness and the north, Heilan' quines who had quite a reputation in the Buchan toons while the herring lasted, and when the herring shoals moved south in the autumn, more specials steamed out of Peterhead and the Broch to take the women to Yarmouth, while local women accompanied them, married and single, besides coopers and freckled youths looking for a job in the curing yards, salting or putting lids on the barrels.

But by 1928 the engines on the Buchan line were having an easier time, especially on the Boddam to Ellon branch, where the train was often running with the guard as the only passenger, besides a few parcels, letters and newspapers. One of Sutherland's red and cream buses, crammed with day-trippers, would pass under the bridge at Mill of Waterton, with its twisted approaches, while the empty train thundered overhead. Now there was no need to hitch the three coaches on to the Fraserburgh train waiting at Ellon junction, as the few passengers from the Boddam branch could walk across the station bridge and find a seat in an empty coach, except perhaps on mart days in Aberdeen when there would be more farmers about, and Lord Saltoun would be waiting for them, panting out his white breath from the small valve at his side, the driver leaning from his cab, listening and watching for the guard to blow his whistle and wave the green flag; then he would give the steam whistle a shriek and Lord Saltoun would jolt you gently forward, then smoothly over the points and the bridge on Station Road, his steam scented breath spreading over the fields, his stainless-steel driving rods working like a weaver's shuttle, coaches swinging at the couplings, while he steams towards the viaduct over the Ythan at Esslemont. And the Gordon Highlander would be waiting for him at Udny Station, heading north with a goods train, but the nearest place they could meet with sufficient double track to let them pass.

When Lord Saltoun returned to Ellon from Aberdeen the Boddam trainie steamed away home with its three empty carriages, probably with Sandy Stewart at the controls and Alex. McIntosh with the coal shovel, shadowed by one of Sutherland's buses, just as the goods trains were accompanied by motor-lorries and cattle floats. Even by 1927, four years after Sutherland's stranglehold began, traffic on the Boddam line had so depreciated that the bigger engines had been withdrawn from passenger service and replaced by side-tank 0-6-0 shunters from Kittybrewster; two may have been in use, with one Kinmundy type engine retained for freight, which was also falling off considerably. These smaller engines never or seldom used the turn-tables, either at Boddam or Ellon, but ran in reverse one way, pulling the coaches by the front coupling. The same thing was done I believe from St. Combs to Fraserburgh, a small branch line which long survived the Boddam rail link, mainly because of the loyal support of the fisher folk from Inverallochy and Cairnbulg.

This reversing process was also practised on the Peterhead convict line, which was run by the Admiralty from Salthousehead Prison to the granite quarries on Stirling Hill, overlooking Boddam Station but providing no link with each other. The Admiralty line lasted for sixty-six years and was finally closed in November, 1958. It was used to carry prisoners and penal guards to Stirling Hill quarries and in transporting the granite to the piers for building on the Harbour of Refuge project in Peterhead Bay. Four or five side-tank 0-6-0 engines were used (beetle-crushers), all named after royalty, such as King Edward VII, Prince of Wales, and Duke of Kent, and green was the dominating colour, with brass funnel and dome. The prisoners were carried in open carriages, not unlike cattle trucks, fitted with wooden seats, and armed guards were mounted on every train. At Glenugie Distillery, on the south side of Peterhead, where the railway left the prison yard, there is some really beautiful bridge and parapet stonework, and from here the three odd miles of track can be traced by high embankment and deep cutting over Sandford Hill to the granite quarries. Several bridges are still intact where the line went under the road, all built of Stirling Hill granite (the same as the Boddam branch) but there were no stations on the convict railway. The Prince of Wales was the last engine in use, built in 1892, and driven by Mr. William Law of Burnhaven.

The passenger service on the Boddam line ceased 'as from Monday, October 31st, 1932,' although the then resident stationmaster, Mr. Paul Stuart later asserted that the last passenger train ran on a Saturday. Freight traffic was discontinued during World War II. But as late as 1944 quite handsome coaches were standing derelict at Boddam Station (on the site now occupied by the R.A.F.) while the rails rusted and grass flourished between

147

the rotting sleepers, a sad nostalgic memory. At the end of the war the Boddam railway had the regretful distinction of having the longest train in Britain, over ten miles in length, stretching from the outskirts of Boddam nearly all the way to Ellon, but with a difference in that it had 'breaks' at level crossings and over bridges, because it was a stationary train, comprising thousands of empty wagons from all over the country, parked on the derelict line awaiting repair after five years of hard war service and bomb attack. Now most of the bridges have been removed, leaving only the parapets of beautifully dressed Stirling Hill granite, a memorial to the engineers who built what must have been one of the saddest little branch lines in Britain, opened in 1899.

Just after the war the great hotel at Cruden Bay (sometimes called Port Erroll) was demolished and the tramlines were lifted from the streets. It is ironical to think that the building stones from the hotel were bought and used by one of the great transport giants who had indirectly helped to destroy it. They were purchased by Mr. Charles Alexander, the Northern Transport King, and removed (by road) to Brotherton Mains, Johnshaven, where he used them to build his farm house, a miniature replica of the great mansion which used to be the mecca of famous golfers on the bents at Cruden Bay.

The stationmaster's house at all the stations on the Boddam line still remain standing and occupied, though not of course by railway employees, but distinguishable from their familiar 'squat' type of railway architecture. There used to be a 'Halt' or 'Whistle Stop' at the notorious Bullers of Buchan, where travellers could alight and gaze in wonder at the famous 'Pot' or cliff cauldron, surrounded by walls an hundred feet high and in places only two feet wide, where the lame Sir Walter Scott walked round the giddy top and Dr. Johnson and Boswell sailed in through the arch in a rowing boat. On Stirling Hill the track ran quite near the cliff edge. Strangers must have shuddered as they gazed down at the awful chasms of water and the jagged rock face some two-hundred feet below the rails.

As memory serves me I recall that the station at Cruden Bay was destroyed by fire, or at least part of it, for it has been described as having two platforms. . . . 'The building on the down platform is set back (from the line) with a glass verandah supported on three columns in a manner similar to Ellon and Inverurie . . . while a typical old wooden bridge of G.N.S.R. style spans the lines. The staff at that time (1931) one porter.' Apart from this porter, and perhaps a few surfacemen, the line was run almost its entire length by the stationmaster from Boddam, as far as Auchmacoy, where the stationmaster from Ellon took over.

Mr. Stuart continues: "The signal cabins were all closed and replaced by ground frames. The instruments from the Boddam cabin were put in the booking-office, the branch being worked as one section. The cabin was sold for a mere nothing and I was sorry that I did not make an offer for it as it would have made a good greenhouse. I don't think all the loops were taken out in my time: these drawings which do not show the loops must have been altered after the date shown—1937. The locomotive and carriage sheds and the turntable at Boddam were there when I left and the R.A.F. took over in 1941.

"The daily freight came straight down in the morning to Boddam where the locomotive was turned and watered. I went up with it, working the necessary sidings: I always went to Cruden, usually to Hatton and sometimes to Pitlurg. I had a season ticket on Sutherland's buses and it was easier to catch them at Hatton.

"The Cruden Bay Hotel was still open as I can recollect it being used by troops in the 1939-'45 war. Ten to fifteen baskets were sent daily to the laundry and these were taken on one of the trams . . . I was hardly ever down at the hotel so that I did not see much of the trams nor the layout."

I myself have actually driven coals from Hatton Station by horse cart to the farm of Newton of Kinmundy, where I was employed as a youth. At Hatton you can still see the station platform from the bridge where the main road climbs and twists over the deep cutting and steep banks and the grass-grown track. Also at Hatton, a short distance from the railway bridge, on the branch road to Cruden Bay, one of the old tramcars from the 'Big' Hotel can be seen in a house garden; a small, ornamented, single-deck vehicle in a good state of preservation. Writing in 1972, several coaches from the Boddam line can still be seen on the cliff-top at Whinnyfold, used by the local fishermen to store their nets and gear, still intact with upholstered seating and with lovely coloured pictures under the luggage racks.

The main road again crosses the line at Birness. This time on a very sharp bend, and no doubt these bridges will eventually be dismantled and the road straightened for modern traffic, a facility which was originally sacrificed for railway convenience. From the bridge at Birness the old line can be traced like a dead scar across the brown loam and green knolls of Pitlurg and Auchmacoy, the only real beauty spot on its entire length, with trees around the old stationmaster's houses and along the railway banks. Here at Auchmacoy the trains emerged from the woods on the last stretch of open country towards Ellon, crossing the almost hidden bridge where the old road twisted under the railway like the letter S, an old danger spot even for careful drivers, yet marvellously free of accidents. This bridge was one of the first to be dismantled and the road to Ellon straightened in the late 'fifties of our present century.

Whilst on the subject of branch railways in Buchan perhaps the five odd miles of track between Longside Station and Lenabo are worthy of mention. The line was completed in 1916 and was used for passengers and goods until 1920. It was built at the behest of the Air Ministry and run by the G.N.S.R. to service the airship station at Lenabo. One of the local lairds, Major Hutchison of Cairngall, was paid £2,500 compensation for the land across his fields on which the railway was built. A few months later he received a second cheque for the same amount. On returning the money with an explanation that he had already been paid for the land the Major's honesty was rewarded with official silence and not a word of thanks. And but for Major Hutchison's honesty it just goes to show what a High and Mighty and careless Bureaucracy could do with your Income Tax.

THE LAST JOURNEY

Another extravagance of Lenabo was that by the end of the war building was still in progress and contractors were obliged to finish their contracts. Nevertheless the demolition squads were sent to work and while the train was used to bring up new material from Longside station it returned with truck-loads of scrap for the breaker's yards. No wonder that the local folks regarded Lenabo as a sprawling White Elephant, especially by those farmers who had been evicted from their land and peatbogs to make its construction possible.

The Lenabo railway was also responsible for Buchan's first fatal automobile accident. It happened in the last year of its existence (1920) while Lenabo was still being demolished, that a Peterhead business man and his wife, Mr. and Mrs. Patterson (drapers) of 'London House,' Chapel Street, were killed in their 'veteran' car on the level-crossing at Flushing, where the train emerged from the woods at Cairngall to cross the main road and the open fields to Lenabo. The engine practically wiped the road with the car and the occupants were unrecognisable. A tragedy in our own day but you can imagine what it was like in a community practically free from road deaths.

There were numerous level crossings on the line but no real bridges, probably because of the level nature of the land, or that the railway would only be temporary and not worth the expense of building parapets. Many of these crossing places gave access to fields and farmyards, but three of them were on public roads and without attendance, because the horse traffic of those days could be halted or frightened off immediately by the blast of a train whistle. The occasional motor car had not been reckoned with and the calamity happened like a thunderclap out of the blue.

Conventional engines of the 'Kinmundy' type 4-4-0 serviced the line and an extra signal lever was installed in the cabin at Longside to manipulate the points change, though no doubt this has long since been removed. The embankments and shallow cuttings can be followed for most of its five miles from where it crossed the river Ugie at Strawberrybank to Lenabo, now known as the Forest of Deer, since it was taken over by the Forestry Commission.

STRAW INTO GOLD

As a fee-ed loon at Auchtydore I have herded sheep on Lenabo, before a tree was planted on it, and while its two lonely smoke stacks still protruded from the underground hydrogen factory (helium was not then available) where the gas was generated to inflate the airships. By the time of Hitler's War the tall chimneys were surrounded by fir trees and one German bomber crew thought it was a secluded factory of some significance (perhaps producing a hydrogen bomb) so they let fly with a basket of incendiary bombs, but the missiles went over the forest harmlessly and set fire to a nearby farmstead. On Sunday morning, October 14th, 1962, the crumbling 66ft. smoke stacks at Lenabo were brought down by army demolition experts and the lovely Athenian gateway was removed from the main entrance.

For those interested in aviation a propellor from one of the Lenabo airships can be seen in the Chapel of St. Jonn at Longside, where it commemorates the loss of its crew over the North Sea in action with a German U-boat, the only loss sustained by the R.N.A.S. in operating the 'Lenabo Soos,' as the locals nicknamed the airships.

In 1929-30 I worked on the farm of Nether Kinmundy and actually carted turnips and loads of sheaves on the old Lenabo railway, where it was used as a road to the farmstead, so I know its geography like the palm of my own hand and have spent many happy days in the vicinity. And incidentally, when World War Two started Longside was again chosen for an air station by the R.A.F., but on a different site, and this second aerodrome is not to be confused with the original Lenabo and its unfortunate little railway.

As a teenager my love for trains was such that I was seldom away from the windows, and used to select a corridor carriage, so that I could stand there without molesting anyone with a draught from the open window. Maybe I didn't stand all the way from Buchan but I got up at most of the stations when the train stopped, either to watch the people or the shunting of trucks on the sidings, or just to look at the tin hoardings on the platform, advertising Swan Vestas as 'The Smoker's Match;' 'Curr's Coffee;' 'Palethorpe's Sausages;' 'Fry's Cocoa;' or the posters in the station arcade, lovely pictures of far-away places I had never seen or could ever hope to see, but the morning prospect filled my young heart with hope and joy. Another feature of the old railway stations was the chocolate machines, where you put a penny in the slot and got a rather slim bar of Nestle's plain chocolate. There was also the printing machine, where you could squander another penny and stamp out the letters of your name on a strip of aluminium, which we used to tack on to our kists in the chaumers, just below the keyhole, so that a stranger knew the foreman's kist from that of the orra loon, and I still have my kist with the name on it. And if you wasn't sure of your weight you could dig another penny and weigh yourself in the waiting room, and if you were over twelve stone you was a hefty chiel in the chaumer, and could carry corn on your back at the thresh-ing mills, $1\frac{1}{2}$ cwts. in the bag, up a stair if need be; and after a day at this you could take your pull at the swingletree, or lifting 56lb. weights above your stupid head in the corn loft. Sometimes you'd time your pocket 'Ingersoll' with the station clock, and if the train was late you knew the driver would make it up between stations with a bit more speed.

Kittybrewster was a special attraction, what with all those polished locomotives taking on coal or water, panting with their white breath in the sunshine, their drivers and firemen fussing about them with oil-can and cotton rag; rows and rows of beautifully upholstered coaches with their brass door handles, First or Third Class marked on the doors (I never knew what happened to the Second Class) and 'Smoking' printed on the windows of the compartments where you were allowed to light your pipe or take a drag at a fag. And all of those trucks and vans being knocked about by the 'Pugs' or Beetle-crushers, the busy porters running after them with long poles to apply the side brakes on the vans, or couple or uncouple the wagons between the buffers, or shifting the hand points where there was no connection with the signal-box. The guard and the station clerks punched your tickets at Kittybrewster, before going on to the joint station, so there was always plenty of time to look around, and as there were no mini-skirts to distract your attention you were always fully pre-occupied with the railway side of the business. I always liked the smell of Aberdeen station: fish, stale fruit and steam smoke, an exciting combination and a welcome change from the sharn midden. And there was the brass model of Stevenson's Rocket under a glass dome, where for another penny you could see it working, and a heavy shell-case from the Great War, which stood on the platform, where you could drop in a copper for the war disabled, and then you were confronted with a notice which said 'Beware of Pick-pockets,' which made you feel your leather purse in your hip pocket, and you wondered if it was the safest place to have it, especially at the Term time, when you had just been paid for a six months' work.

My father was a railway enthusiast and I used to come with him on Term days and spend most of the afternoon watching the shunters in the south marshalling yards, which were even more exciting than Kittybrewster, and the posh red and gleaming L.M.S. coaches and Pullman cars at the platforms were a joy for the beholder, especially the First Class compartments with embroidered white lace on the blue upholstery and carpets on the floors. It was always a sore point with my old man that he had never travelled further than Aberdeen, and I think he used to watch these south bound expresses with a special envy. He was brought up with his Granny in Strichen, where, as a loon, he spent most of his spare time at the station, then a busy little place where the engines that passed through had brass domes and long funnels, and he was allowed to ride foot-plate to Maud and back with the friendly drivers, hiding from officials in the coal tender. In Strichen signal cabin he learned to pull the correct levers for incoming trains, though he wasn't fit for the long-distance signal post, being as the signalman said "Too light in the pooper!" and that he would have to sup a lot more brose for that job. But his Granny died when he was twelve, when he was forced to leave school and work on the farms, wasting his life like myself on a job that never absorbed his fuller interests.

For the old man and myself Aberdeen station was something of a Crystal Palace, because of the expanse of its glass roof, and we were not unlike the earth-bound farm worker who had been to the city and was asked next day what he thought of it. "Oh nae bad," says he, "a gie place, but a' covered wi' gless!" indicating the point of course that he had never found his way out of the station. But we were not quite so bad as that, for we found our way to Woolworth's, where we had high tea in the restaurant on the third floor, with a plateful of rich pastries between us, and when the girl returned with her note-book and pencil she looked at the empty plate and then at the pair of us in amazement, and my father found it amusing for days and weeks afterwards. He was convinced you see that you paid for these 'fancy pieces' whether you ate them or not; can't trust those city folks, so we made a feast of it to make sure we hadn't been cheated. Which reminds me of another farmhand who went into the Station Buffet and asked for tea. "A High Tea?" the girl enquired, whereupon the Buchan chiel looked the quine up and down and remarked: "Odd lassie, juist a fair hicht o' a tae!" perhaps expecting that she would serve him on a dunce's stool.

A ride on the trams was another treat, jolting along the full length of Union Street, and then down to the harbour to watch the stevedores unloading the cargo ships on to the wagons that stood on the rails on the quay, and were then shunted away to the Waterloo or Guild Street depots by the little Beetle-crushers that puffed along the streets among the horse lorries. Of course we knew nothing about the branch line that came down from Kittybrewster to the harbour area, and we were just as ignorant of the existence of the Deeside line, though I travelled it ten years later, in 1948, still in the days of steam, and once again in 1960 on a diesel rail-car.

Coming home from the city on a sunny summer evening provides another treasured memory, our engine giving a short blast on the whistle before entering the tunnels at Woolmanhill and Hutcheon Street, which always seemed a wonder to us country people, especially when someone told you that you were passing under 'The Royal Infirmary,' where people were lying ill or dying, and the train going so slow the tunnels seemed twice as long and dreadfully dark, and you had to close the windows to keep out the smoke, which perhaps was the reason for the whistle warning.

But gradually you emerged into broad daylight again and came gliding down to Kittybrewster, where the train stopped and someone asked for 'tickets please!' Most people had their tickets ready and the clerk put a final punch hole in your return half-ticket and slammed the door again. When the clerks had been through all the carriages you were off again, and as this was the last train home it stopped at most of the little stations on the way out: Woodside, Persley, Bucksburn, Bankhead, Stoneywood and Dyce, and sometimes you'd meet a 'Subbie' steaming back into the city on the other line. After Dyce junction the Buchan train branched off on a single track and you could only meet incoming trains at stations with a double line, so that sometimes you had to wait at a station platform or an expected train came in, goods or passenger; but eventually the signal light changed to green and you were off again, your leisurely engine steaming away out in front with its long line of swinging coaches, rounding a bend or crossing a bridge, picking up speed between the stations, but never long at high speed until the music of the wheels on the rail joints was slurred again by the grind of brakes as you approached a signal-box, where the signalman came down the steps from his tall cabin and stood at the line side, ready to swop tablet-hoops with your driver while the train was still in motion, which saved him a walk to the station platform. This was known as the Block System, ensuring that the line was clear between the stations, and the 'hoop' was merely an arm-catcher for the purse attached to it, containing the safety key which wouldn't fit the signal lock until it was 'buzzed' or coded from the next station, which indicated there was no other traffic on the line. Newmachar, Udny, Logierieve, Esslemont, Ellon—and each time you stopped people got on or off the train, newspapers and parcels were handed out from the guard's van to a porter with his trolley, and maybe a clatter of empty milk cans, your engine panting to be off again, waiting for the last door to slam and the green flag from the guard. Now you were gliding smoothly over the points from the sidings, away from the scatter of goods wagons, on to the main line again and steadily gathering speed, the white, steam-scented smoke from the engine floating across the green fields, now spangled with the gold of evening, while the cattle and horses cantered away from your noisy clatter. Arnage, Auchnagatt, Maud Junction, depends how far you were going, but again the slowing shimmer of latticed platform fencing; the flowers and posters, a glimpse of the station clock and the guard checking his watch: "Change for Fraserburgh," "Change for Peterhead!" Are you sure you are in the right carriage? If you are just sit still: if you are not they are just reminding you, and the engines will take you away. If you are going to the Broch you will travel by Strichen, Mormond, Lonmay, Rathen and Philorth; to Peterhead via Brucklay, Mintlaw, Longside, Newseat and Inverugie. You are approaching a bridge and you take your head inside just in case. You hear the swish of it in passing but it's getting colder now and you close the window with the leather strap and go inside and sit down contentedly on the red cushions. You'll soon be home now and your day with the trains is over. You won't have another joy ride for six months, at the next term, when you can look forward to another day in the Silver City. But tomorrow you will be back to breaking muck in the drills and the farmer will say that you have trains on the brain, because you can't speak of anything else. Maybe you are going to a new place and everything will be strange for a while. But a cinder in my eye eventually cured me of all this gaping from carriage windows, and though I suffered no ill effects from the hot missile perhaps it was a good thing that the diesels came to save my eyesight.

Besides the Flushing fatality there were two more accidents on the Buchan railways, both involving tractors at level crossings and killing their drivers. The first crash happened during the war, about 1944-5, when a north bound passenger train collided with a tractor on a level crossing a mile south of Longside, sweeping the mangled machine to the station while the driver lay dying in blood on the grass at the side of the track. The second calamity occurred at Udny, when in August, 1970, a south bound goods express hit a tractor and silage wagon on a level crossing and piled them up on the bank, killing a father of three in a mangle of steel and splintered wood. Both crossings were unattended farmways with barred iron gates for their users. Also during the Second World

157

War, on the farm of Crookedneuk, near Longside, two Italian P.O.W.'s employed on the farm were transporting a horse-drawn water-barrel on wheels for watering cattle in an outlying field. Crossing the railway, while the water-barrel was still on the rails, they started arguing about who would shut the gates, but before any decision was reached a passenger train sliced their barrel away from the shafts and sent it flying in a flurry of staves, wheels and water, clipping it away from the mare as with a shears, while she stood frightened but unharmed in the gate. People have placed all sorts of little obstacles on the rails: pennies, horse-shoe nails, keys, to have them flattened or welded together, but the strangest case was the man who placed his 'trigger' finger on the rails, so that he wouldn't have to go to Flanders—and he didn't. It took a bit of courage but it worked and you couldn't say that the man was a coward who dared the Buchan train to squash his forefinger.

During the Autumn Holiday of 1913, 2,000 people left Peterhead (about one-sixth of the town's population) by rail; 1,000 on the Saturday and 1,200 on the Monday. The following year, despite the Great War and bad weather two early morning specials carried 600 trippers out of town and 300 more on forenoon trains. Compare this with 1964 (last year in the life of the railway) when 13 adults and 5 children left on the 6.40 a.m. train, and 11 adults and 4 children by the 11.10 departure, while over 1,000 went by bus. Figures for Fraserburgh may not be available but they would probably be in the same proportion.

Jamie Sutherland started his business with a pony and spring-cart, which he bought at the age of twelve in 1876. This he used to drive sand from the beach at Sandford Bay to sprinkle on the earthen floors of the fishermen's hovels, and the venture was such a success that very soon he had a horse and lorry. In all this he was encouraged by his unmarried mother who worked the small farm of Newfield, about three miles south of Peterhead on the Gask road. By 1906 Sutherland owned a traction engine, to which was added a threshing mill and he hired out the plant to local farmers. This in turn enabled him to purchase two heavy duty wagons, which, in off threshing seasons were coupled to the engine to drive stones from the local quarries for building and road making. Eventually he owned five traction-engines and a fleet of wagons which were used in the construction of Lenabo, and this it is said really set Jamie Sutherland on his feet. He bought his first motor car in 1908, his first motor lorry in 1915. Red was his favourite colour, which applied to his buses, and though his transport lorries were grey they were identified by a red band and lettering on the cabs and leaf-work; even his own private motor car, which was chaeffeur driven, was painted a lurid red and known throughout the length and breadth of Buchan.

During the herring fishing season Sutherland could muster upwards of a hundred horse and lorries to drive herring from the piers to the curing yards, besides a considerable number of motor vehicles. About this time, in the early 'twenties, his depot and extensive open yard at Victoria Stables in St. Peter Street were worth a good look round, and as a boy I used to go there with my father on Sunday forenoons when we lived in the town. It was an old curing yard used as stables, with a huge roofed garage holding the buses, taxis, hearses and horse-cabs, while outside the yard was crammed with traction engines (Fowlers, Burrells and a Clayton), steam-wagons (mostly Foddens and Sentinels), threshing mills, wagons, motor lorries, horse carts and several gigs; almost everything connected with transport, and how the yard gaffers got all this stuff, or even a small part of it rigged out for work on a Monday morning says a lot for their management and good tempers, not forgetting the busy blacksmiths and their ringing anvils, repairing vehicles and shoeing horses in the workshops and forge at the back of the yard. Even the local Artillery availed themselves of Sutherland's Clydesdales to drag their heavy guns to the Roanheads for firing practice.

Jamie Sutherland was a batchelor and lived with his housekeeper on the farm of Sandford Lodge, which he had on lease, and where he died in 1931, leaving his business on trust for 21 years, which included the war years, and during which it still flourished as in his own day, though not without a little bickering among its directors, and one shooting incident. But 'James Sutherland, Contractor and Hirer' could still be read in gold letters on the frosted glass of the office windows at the corner of St.

Peter Street and Windmill Street, and the traditional Union Jack still fluttered from a flagstaff fixed to the chimney stack, high on the gable end of the building.

Prior to March 6th, 1950 (with two years in trust still to go) when the British Transport Commission took over, Messrs. Sutherland were operating 82 buses and 96 goods vehicles, besides owning 26 farms and employing 400 people. But it was a sad day for the late Jamie Sutherland's admirers when his buses were changed from red to blue and that Alexander chiel from Falkirk had his name printed on them. Some folk said it was a downright shame for a local man like Sutherland who had built up such a mammoth business with his own hands and brain. But even Willie Alexander & Sons Ltd. had begun as a cycle repair and hiring shoppie in Falkirk, though some said he got more aid from the Government and was favoured with railway co-operation. There is some confusion as to what happened to the transport side of the business. Some say that the lorries were absorbed by the British Road Services undertaking, with a depot in Fraserburgh, while others maintained that Charles Alexander & Partners had taken them over, but that they had been more considerate than Alexanders of Falkirk or the Transport Commissioners had been, in that they had left the name of Sutherlands of Peterhead on the firm's lorries, thus perpetuating the name of its founder and discarding the belief that there is no sentiment in business. But there are still others who say (and I believe them) that Sutherlands was completely wiped out, and that a group of Peterhead business men put their heads together and started up the firm again with one or two lorries, and because one of the contributors was called Sutherland, and for the purpose of attracting old customers they registered the new company in the old name.

One by one, over the years, Jamie Sutherland had swallowed up his rivals, and the representatives of James Reid & Son alone survive in name as an individual transport firm who were his contemporaries. Jamie Reid had his stables in the Royal Horse Bazaar, entered through an arched pend in Broad Street, which went right through to Back Street, where Buccochi had his fish and chip shop, and the stables were two-storeyed, where the horses climbed a ramp to bed after a day's work between the lorry shafts. Jamie Reid ran horse buses to Boddam, besides a horse taxi business, but apart from freight traffic he never opposed Sutherland with motor buses. Whytes Motors are still with us as carriers but had to give up their two buses in the struggle with the local giant. Gibbs of Fraserburgh were at one time associated with Sutherland's, and although still with us they cannot be easily classified, whether as victors or mere survivors, which in many cases means the same thing.

But as the end of the Buchan line drew nigh the buses themselves were faced with an embarrassment. Even at their moment of victory over the branch railways their own existence was threatened by the motor car. But Jamie Sutherland would have met the challenge, either with hovercraft or helicopters, for such was his nature.

The first passenger train steamed out of Peterhead Station one sunny day in July, 1862. Can you imagine the jubilation and excitement of that wonderful day? I don't remember the horse trams on the Port Henry rail-head, but I can recall the guard's van that used to stand just inside the level-crossing gate beside the stationmaster's house. I remember it from the days when I came in from the Lonmay district on the bar of my father's bicycle, when he would slow down and warn me to be prepared for the bump when we crossed the rails.

Later, when we lived two years in Peterhead the railway station became the mecca of my boyhood. I still remember the bustle when a passenger train came in, the hissing of steam and the slamming of carriage doors, the men in their jam-jar collars, tight trousers and jackets with narrow lapels, the women in their long flouncy dresses and rose-garden hats, and the children, the boys in knee-length breeks and the girls in long skirts and black stockings, their hair in pig-tails or hanging loosely down their backs. When the guard's van had been emptied on to trolleys the guard and a porter came along and checked each compartment, closing every open window with the familiar leather strap (not unlike the one on which my father used to sharpen his razor) and clashing all the doors with their brass handles. Meanwhile the fireman uncoupled the engine from the coaches while the driver watched from his cab, always it seemed with a handful of oily cotton waste. When the guard had gone back to his van and waved the green flag you could put your fingers in your ears, because the driver blew the whistle, a tremendous shriek under the glass roof, and the engine exploded in steam, threshing backwards out of the station, reversing the empty coaches up the Copland Hill, beyond the last points change, and while the brakesman held them there the engine shunted off the main line towards the coal and water sheds. But as you watched from the station entrance you could see that the carriages were moving again, for the guard had eased the brakes and they were sliding down the hill, steadily gathering speed, ever so smoothly, until they were back under the station roof, when the guard applied the brakes again before they hit the buffers or a fish van that might be standing there, to be coupled up for the next departure.

By now all the people had left the station, where the pleasant smell of steam smoke still lingered. Some had gone in taxi cabs, some walking, others in the yellow two-horse brake sent down from the Palace Hotel, or the one from the Northern, now all loaded up with toffs, their luggage on the roof racks, the slim-legged horses now spanking out of the station yard, the drivers in their livery of plain black coat or uniform, with hats to match, sitting up there on the dickie-board, leather reins in one gloved hand and a long thonged whip in the other, though seldom using it, but merely clicking their tongues in horse language that sent them off at the trot, down Queen Street into the town. Ordinary folks usually walked from the station, and sometimes you'd see a fish-wife with a creel on her back, having spent the day with it in the country.

Now the cleaner women got busy with their pails and mops and sweeping brushes, washing the windows and sweeping out the carriages, but a loon has little time for such palavers, so you nip round to the back of the engine sheds to see the engine being turned around on the turn-table, a man at each end with a lever, while the engine panted away quietly and pleased at being so fussed about, before moving off for a supper of coals and fresh

THE LAST JOURNEY

cool water. On Saturday forenoons you could watch the porters from the gates on Landale Road, shunting wagons and making up goods trains, while the signalman kept his eye on everything from his tall cabin, shifting levers to change points as required. All such fun for a boy in those days!

I hope May 1st, 1965 will be an eventful Last Journey to suit the memory, but signs are it will fade out unlamented and unsung. This perhaps the only epitaph!

FOVERAN AND FORVIE

THE A92 North from Aberdeen cuts through the heart of Foveran, past the school and the smatter of houses at Blairythan, and the traveller wishing to visit Newburgh, postal outpost of the parish, must strike off on the A975, at the A.A. box at the Rashierieve crossroads, down by the old church of Foveran.

Newburgh lies on the most direct route from Aberdeen to Peterhead, clinging to the coast due north instead of cutting inland to Ellon, which is the quickest way to Fraserburgh. Cruden Bay is also on the coast road, the Mecca of all good golfers, besides Slains Castle and the notorious Bullers of Buchan. And we are pretty certain this is the road that Dr. Johnson travelled with James Boswell on their tour of Scotland. Parts of the way are now cart track and farm road, particularly from Leyton and Hatterseat to Drums farm and Pitgersie, but from here on we are on the same road as the great lexicographer and his ebullient companion.

Foveran kirk lies in a lush green hollow, like a pearl in the palm of a satin-gloved hand, the finger-tips simulating the great dunes on the coast, and the space between forefinger and outstretched thumb is occupied by the vast tidal estuary of the river Ythan, which forms part of Foveran's eastern boundary.

Foveran in the Gaelic means 'the stream of springs,' and Foveran Burn runs through the hand like the Palmist life-line, from the inland wrist to the estuary, a distance of about five miles, and tumbles along beside the road from the kirk to Newburgh.

Foveran Burn has been commemorated in a poem by the late Rev. Wm. McWilliams, who was minister of Foveran during the first World War. He lost his only son in the trenches and his poems on this period are both poignant and touching.

The first Church of Scotland chaplain to give his life in World War II also came from Foveran. The Rev. Arthur Currie Gordon was minister at Foveran from 1932 to 1940, when he was killed in action in France on June 7 of that fateful year.

164

The church has a new manse, one of the finest in Scotland, and the site of the old manse has been cleared for a car park.

Across the road from the church and graveyard are the lodge and drive that leads to Foveran House, built in 1771 (three years before the church) and stands near the site of a former castle, for three hundred years the home of the Turing Family, the one-time baronial lairds of Foveran.

Before the days of Bruce this was Comyn Country, harried by the king in his scorched earth policy against his greatest rivals for the throne.

Even to this day the notorious Harrying of Buchan is in evidence, mostly in the peat-bogs, which were vast forests in those days, until the flaming sword of Bruce razed them to the ground.

Perhaps it could be said that the Buchan area of Aberdeenshire owes its lack of trees and its great number of peat mosses to the blazing torch of Bruce, where centuries of lichen, corrosion, decomposition and chemical processes have turned the trees to peat, and once in a while a fairly fresh tree is excavated by the mosser's spade.

Only last year we ploughed up a blackened trunk on arable land, hollowed to a tube of charcoal, a lone survivor of six centuries.

Where the mossers unearth a tree the peats are usually black; a crumblie peat, once it is dry, almost in the first stages of turning to coal; easily broken but excellent burning, probably because of the resin deposits in the wood, and the mossers refer to them as 'stickly peats,' and count themselves lucky to lease such a lair.

During the early stages of his campaign, from the murder of the Red Comyn in the church at Dumfries (1305), right up to the Battle of Barra (1308), near Inverurie, where Bruce routed the Comyns, the men of Buchan had been as a knife in the king's back, forcing him to fight on two fronts. Whenever he turned south to face the English the Comyns were on his back, terrorising his adherents and plundering his stores, until the king resolved to put the North-east of Scotland, his own dominion eventually, to fire and sword, incapacitating his foe beyond recovery.

Bruce established himself at Menie, where there is now a mansion house or 'Eventide Home,' administered by the Church of Scotland for the aged, about seven miles north of Aberdeen, and from here the king directed his forays into Buchan. The first torch was kindled in Formartine, which includes Foveran, and blazed across the Ythan and Ugie rivers to the uttermost reaches of the Comyn territory, even to Aberdour on the Moray Firth, to Kinmundy, Kininmonth and Pitsligo, the latter now world-renowned for the export of peat in whisky making.

That Bruce was reluctant to pillage and slay in Buchan is understandable, since the woman who dared to set the crown of Scotland upon his head came from that area. She was the Lady Isabella, Countess of Buchan, daughter of the Thane of Fife, wife of Lord John Comyn, kinsman to the traitor slain by Bruce; a patriotic and courageous woman who, in her zeal for the welfare and independence of her country, and in defiance of her estranged husband, even at the risk of setting the lives of her two children in jeopardy, had dared to crown Bruce at Scone in 1306, for which she endured long years of privation and imprisonment at the hands of Edward of England.

Isabella lived in the Tower of Buchan, what is now known as Old Slains Castle, in the estate of Erroll, where until recently the present Countess still resided (a direct descendant from Isabella) in a small chalet perched on the edge of a projecting precipice, near the ruined tower where Isabella of Buchan looked out across the North Sea.

By 1320 the king relented the Harrying of Buchan. He pardoned Bishop Cheyne of St. Machar's Cathedral, an old ally of the Comyns, and assisted him financially to build the Brig o' Balgownie across the Don, on the northern outskirts of Old Aberdeen, thus enabling the people of Buchan and Formartine to have easy access to the city.

The Comyn murder also weighed heavily on the king's conscience, and money left over from the bridge building was used in repair work for the 'Kirk of St. Machar.'

FOVERAN AND FORVIE

II.

Knockhall Castle is a ragged but picturesque ruin on a green knoll overlooking Newburgh village and the Ythan estuary. It was built in 1565 and destroyed by fire in 1734. In its latter days the castle was the property of the lairds of Udny, and Jamie Fleeman, the Laird of Udny's fool was sent to Knockhall to assist the resident housekeeper in running the castle. But she treated Jamie rather harshly, kept him scant of food, and her continual cry was "Peats Fleeman!" "Sticks Fleeman!" "Water Fleeman!" with the threat of eternal damnation, hellfire and brimstone in afterlife if he disobeyed her, until the poor man was nearly demented. On the night of the fire Jamie Fleeman roused the household (all except the housekeeper) and then broke into the strong room, where he rescued the charter chest or Deed Kist by throwing it out from an upstairs window, a feat which would have required the efforts of two men of normal strength.

Back on the ground, while he mingled with those who had come to help put out the fire, someone noticed the absence of the housekeeper and asked Jamie if he had wakened her. "Na na," says he, "she was aye on aboot the devil, so she'll get hell at hame the nicht!"

But eventually, and only just in time, even when the flames and smoke were at her bedroom door, Fleeman was prevailed upon to rescue his mistress. So he scrambled up the smoke filled stairs and woke her before she suffocated: "Come awa' ye jaad," he cried, "or ye'll get twa het hurdies!"

Newburgh lies at the mouth of the river Ythan, reputed to be the highest tidal river in Scotland, surpassing even the Tay in its inland flush of water. Of course it is much smaller than the Tay; its length is but 36 miles, including the bends, but in the last five miles of its course it falls only half-an-inch, and the spring tides lap the bridge at Ellon, six miles inland.

The Ythan is navigable to within a mile of the Ellon bridge and, in the days before the railways and road transport, flat-bottomed boats plied upstream to Waterton Wharf with cargoes of coal, timber, lime, bone-meal, oil-cakes and locust beans, and returned with grain, potatoes and wool, which were shipped from Newburgh at high tides. Until quite recently a small tramp steamer called at Newburgh.

A dangerous sandbar projects across the mouth of the Ythan. Only local fishermen, of whom there are a few, understand the currents and act as pilots for tramp steamers crossing the bar. The Newburgh lifeboat was discarded in 1965 because of the sandbar, which incurred serious loss of life in the crew, when men were pitched out of the boat into the sea. Swift changing currents endangered normal launching of the lifeboat from the slipway and it had to be towed by tractor through the town to a safer spot further up the coast. A ship in distress would have been in dire peril waiting for the Newburgh lifeboat and by the time it arrived on the scene a lifeboat from Aberdeen or Peterhead was often standing by. The Newburgh men then ran the risk of capsizing on the bar on their return, sometimes riding the waves in a piercing storm, waiting a favourable opportunity.

The Ythan is rich in salmon fishing, finnock, flounder, sea-trout and eels, and the estuary is particularly favourable to anglers, where stake-netting is also in evidence.

The oyster beds are less lucrative nowadays than they were in the past, perhaps because of the spates which have washed them from the river bottom. But the largest pearl in the Scottish crown was found in the Ythan, though no one nowadays can point out the place of its discovery.

The tide rises to six or seven feet at the river mouth, when the estuary spreads out to nearly half-a-mile. Crossing the bridge at Newburgh a stranger may think it incredible that such a small river should have such an influx of water. Above the bridge it widens to even greater dimensions, especially if the ingoing tide is met by flood water, so that a stranger may begin to question his geography, when he may stop the car to check with his map, looking for some loch or firth not yet charted there.

At this point the surprised visitor may also become aware of the enormous amount of wildfowl on the estuary, for it is a fact that the Ythan in its lower reaches attracts more bird migration than any other river on the east coast of Scotland. Web-footers flock here in their thousands, from Europe and Scandinavia, and during the Spring mating the estuary echoes a discordant symphony of bird sound.

There is abundant feeding on the slich, or Sleeks of Tarty, a salty marsh in the tidal basin, and the birds which visit the river at all times provide a varied list: Northern Penguin, Razorbill, Red-throated Diver, Auk, Gooseander, Pintail, Teal, Wild Swan, Heron, Oyster Catcher, Eider Duck, Little Grebe, Small Loon, Stubble Goose, Stormy Petrel, Snipe, Tern, Shell-drake, Sly-Goose, Guillemot, Gannet, Scrath, Sandpiper, Solan Goose, Pickerel, Water-rail, Brook-owzel, Pictarny, Golden-eyed Duck and Kittywake, besides all variety of gulls and local birds.

The Culterty Research Station is conducted by Aberdeen University while the neighbouring Sands of Forvie, which are on the other, or north side of the estuary, and the estuary itself have been established as a bird sanctuary and nature conservancy for the study and care of wild life.

About two hundred years ago Newburgh was described as 'a very dirty place in pleasant surroundings,' frequented mostly by sailors and smugglers and boasted seven ale-houses and one fishing boat, used mostly for piloting vessels up the river. Two stage-coaches ran daily to Aberdeen, one of them carrying mail. All that has changed, of course, and besides two excellent hotels there is an extensive golf course and lucrative fishing rights.

III.

In my last two articles we journeyed from Aberdeen to Foveran and Newburgh, via the A92 and A975, and we have just crossed the bridge over the river Ythan. Let us now park the car and walk down the north bank of the river, crossing the southern tip of the Sands of Forvie, where pre-historic man has left his mark.

Recent excavation has revealed the stone foundations of neolithic dwellings in the sand. Nine habitations were discovered, circular in design, the blackened hearths still discernible in the middle of the floor. The remains of a burial chamber were also uncovered, enclosing charred embers and fragments of pottery. The inhabitants were Flint Men and numerous examples of their 'flint-knapping' industries have been discovered on the higher ground. Tillage was favourable on the river haughs, before the sand encroachment, where the primitive 'strand-loopers' may have planted corn-husk, but it is more likely that spearing fish in the river supplied the staple diet.

If the moon is a dead world covered in lunar dust there is no better example to be seen anywhere as on the Sands of Forvie, where all human activity of past aeons has been hushed forever in the drifting sands of many centuries. The pre-historic village lies in a sheltered hollow about a mile from the shore. Here the dunes are spiralled into shapes of incredible phantasmagoria, windblown caricatures of lunar fancy, clothed in wisping spine-grass where the sand drift has been halted.

Whipping sand storms frequently change the pattern of the dunes, a sort of changeless variety in a static eternity, when the dunes become weird ghostly shadows barely visible in the stinging sand cloud, a whistling holocaust which daily increases or diminishes their size.

For days on end the North-west wind drives the sand back into the sea like smoke, where it is heaved ashore again by the next tide.

The inland dunes are of enormous size, covered with scree and a colourless heather; in early summer dappled with bright gold whin blossom, porous with rabbit warren and the poke of sand-martin.

These inland formations are many centuries old and have lost much of their salt deposits, so that contractors are using the sand for building.

On the farm of Drums, in Foveran, excavation work is in progress, and I wouldn't be surprised if the diggers came upon the skeleton of a Viking galley, buried with ceremony by the Norsemen nearly three thousand years ago.

But Forvie also has vast central stretches of smooth, wind-polished sand, miniature Saharalands surrounded by a skyline of frowning dunes, huddled in all directions and enclosing the visitor in a deathless, alien silence, broken only by the rumble of the sea or the wheeble of a passing snipe.

The wilderness covers an area of some 2,000 acres, now included in the neighbouring parish of Slains, although nobody can define the boundary or clarify the date of the union. The seaward regions are now a nature conservancy. for the protection of bird life on the Ythan estuary.

A more recent village existed on the northern tip of the parish, but this too was obliterated by a fearful gale and sand-storm in 1688. The wind rose from the south-east and sustained its ferocity for nine days, stripping the coast of sand and driving it inland in dark, blinding clouds. No one can say how many perished in the storm, either smothered in their homes or fleeing before the blast but, when the hurricane subsided and the dust had settled, the fertile lands of Forvie had become a desert.

The ruins of Forvie Kirk can still be seen protruding from the sand on the links near Collieston, a neighbouring village on the cliff-tops. Graves have been found around the kirk, and when these were opened human bones were revealed, which perhaps is the only certain evidence that a community existed here before the storm.

Various accounts of the calamity have been ventured, but the one most favoured describes the dying Baron of Forvie who left his estate to his three daughters, who, in those lawless days, were deprived of their inheritance by a scheming usurper. Thrown upon the world the hapless girls prayed that the lands of Forvie would prove worthless to their despoiler, and the great storm provided total retribution.

It sounds like something that Shakespeare would have liked to get his teeth into and but for the fact that he lived a century earlier we may have had a play on the tragedy of Forvie.

As it is we have an old rhyme which describes the damsels in their distress, and the sentiment expressed sounds more like a curse than a prayer, but the arid sands of Forvie provide ample evidence of its fulfillment:

STRAW INTO GOLD

Yf evyr maydenis malysone
Dyd licht upon drye lande,
Let nocht bee funde in Furvye's glebys
Bot thystl, bente, and sande.

It's time now that we emptied the sand out of our shoes. It's a long walk back to the car, and we might as well cross the bent to the main road, back to the bridge across the Ythan, where we started.

THE ST. FERGUS MURDER TRIAL

I T was the evening of Saturday, November 19th, 1853, dark, silent, peaceful, when the people of St. Fergus village were startled by a gun-shot, a sharp crack and a flash, then all was still as before. It seemed to come from the west end of the village, from the outskirts of the 'Kirktoon,' in the direction of Rora, where Rattray swings his beam of light across the patchwork of fields.

The silence of night was deeper in those days than now; there was no TV or radio, no motor cars, no trains or aeroplanes, so that most people heard the shot as if it were in their own backyard. "Fit was that?" neighbour asked neighbour, but nobody could tell.

Early next morning, in a field adjoining the village, the body of a young man was found in a ditch, a discharged pistol by his side—was it murder or suicide?

The victim was William Macdonald, a twenty-nine-year-old farm worker who lived with his mother and sister, and younger brother Robert on the small farm of Burnside, about two miles from the village.

Willie Macdonald had left home at the gloaming on Saturday to order a pair of haimes from the local saddler. His absence overnight had greatly worried his family, especially his mother, and at daybreak on the Sunday she sent young Robert to search for him, and to ask in the village if anyone had seen him.

Robert Macdonald had just recently left school, a lad in his early 'teens, and he strode out anxiously across the fields, towards the Kirktoon of St. Fergus. It was a short-cut to the village, and while leaping a dyke in his path he was horrified to find his brother in the ditch, about two feet down, lying in a few inches of muddy water.

Robert knelt in the ditch and shook his brother by the jacket, thinking perhaps that he was asleep, when he noticed that his face was dicoloured and spattered with blood. On realising that his

173

brother 'wis awa fae speakin',' Robert clambered out of the ditch and ran towards the village with the sad news.

He was sobbing when he reached the doctor's house and knocked on the door. Dr. Smith lived in the Kirktoon, on the outskirts of the village; indeed Robert Macdonald had been trespassing on one of the doctor's fields when he found his brother's body, so he didn't have far to run. The doctor did a little farming on the side, which was quite common in those days, just as the minister had his glebe, so he got hold of James Pirie the farrier, to whom he said "Come awa' man, Macdonald has been gotten deid up aboot Jamie Fordyce's"—and it is said that the doctor went straight to where the body lay.

Dr. Smith bent over Macdonald and shook his head. "Gweed preserve's," says he, "sic a sicht!" And a moment later Pirie saw him lift a pistol which was lying a few feet away from the corpse.

Finger-prints were of no importance in those days, so the doctor brandished the pistol quite carelessly: "Here," saye he, "Macdonald has shot himself, and here is the gun he did it with; at anyrate he has been partly shot and partly drowned."

St. Fergus had a doctor at that time but apparently no policeman, so that Constable John Hunter had to walk (or ride on horse-back) all the way from Crimond to investigate the case.

The body was carried to Jamie Fordyce's place, a croft on the edge of the field, where it was searched for powder and shot. Macdonald was wearing a polka-dot jacket, the pockets of which were too small to hold a pistol, and contained only a few matches and a snuff box.

Police Constable Hunter found that the dead man's face, particularly the right cheek, had been blackened by exploding gunpowder. Probing the wound with a straw he ascertained that it went in an upward and backward direction.

The worthy doctor took it upon himself to break the news of the tragedy to the bereaved women at Burnside, mother and sister to Macdonald. By now the kirk folk were on the road, hardly having patience to listen to the sermon because of the stir in the district. Mr. Moir was minister of the Free Church at Sheilhill and he met Dr. Smith on the way. The doctor informed him that

"Willie Macdonald had shot himself last night," and asked the Rev. Moir to accompany him to Burnside.

When Dr. Smith informed the mother of her son's death, implying that he "had done it himself," and that he "was partly drowned or suffocated," Mrs. Macdonald refused to believe it. She declared indignantly that Willie could not have shot himself, either by accident or otherwise, because to her certain knowledge he had never possessed a pistol. Besides, she said, he had nothing worrying him and was looking forward to getting married.

She did add, however, that she had heard her son hint that he had made an appointment with the doctor the previous evening.

Dr. Smith denied that he had made any arrangement to see her son on the Saturday. Mrs. Macdonald made it quite clear that she thought the doctor was telling lies about this, and he departed in a great huff, highly offended, with the Rev. Moir at his heels.

Constable Hunter eventually got from Dr. Smith a certificate, 'on soul and conscience,' stating the cause of Macdonald's death. This document further certified that 'the pistol must have been close to him, and from the direction the wound takes I infer it is not likely to have been done by any other than deceased.' This was in the doctor's own hand-writing.

Indignant though he was the noble Dr. Smith attended to all the funeral arrangements, a practice which was quite commonly performed by country doctors in former days. After the service he mentioned that if "Boyd, the procurator-fiscal at Peterhead, heard what had happened he would be coming out to St. Fergus."

Mr. Andrew Boyd did hear what had happened, from Constable John Hunter, and he wasted no time in coming out from Peterhead.

On visiting Burnside the procurator-fiscal quickly learned that Mrs. Macdonald and her daughter did not like Dr. Smith, and that they still resolutely refused to believe that "Willie's ain haun caus't 'is death."

Dr. Smith had been attending the family for close on ten years and still they didn't trust him. But why? And Mr. Boyd was further surprised to learn that Smith had had a lot of secret dealings—"traffickin' " Mrs. Macdonald called it—with her late son "aboot some kind o' insurance business."

Willie, who regarded the doctor as "a richt fine chiel," had been speaking in a way she did not understand about Dr. Smith being willing to let him have money at any time if he wanted to start a farm of his own when he married the girl he was courting, Mary Slessor, a domestic servant at Longside.

On returning to Peterhead Mr. Boyd made immediate inquiries at certain insurance agencies in the town. The startling fact was then revealed that Dr. William Smith held three insurance policies on the life of the dead farm worker, and would benefit, so the holder believed, to the approximate extent of £2,000 on the death of Macdonald. So much for the liabilities of the insurance brokers in the early days of its inception, the risks and frauds involved, until such time as both client and agency were protected by acts of Parliament.

A warrant was issued for the arrest of Dr. Smith and he was lodged in prison at Peterhead. Such immediate and dramatic action shocked the local community. That the 'hame-ower, genial Dr. Smith, a seemingly douce, upright man, aged thirty-three, living happily with his wife and two daughters' — that such a man should even be suspected of murder surprised everyone. The doctor was a popular figure in the district, and those who thought they knew him better were stunned with the idea that he should be accused of committing such an atrocious, cold-blooded crime.

But Smith's admirers were further astounded when it was ultimately revealed that he was also a 'Quack,' masquerading his services on an unsuspecting public; a man who had failed to qualify for his M.D. degree at Aberdeen University, and that while he pretended to be a member of the Royal College of Surgeons, London, his officially recognised qualifications, even as a general practitioner, were nil.

On March 13th, 1854, Dr. Smith was arrainged for trial at the High Court of Justiciary, Edinburgh.

During the second day's evidence a juryman became hysterical. He was medically certified as unfit to continue his duties and the jury was discharged. The second trial, which was opened on April 12th continued for three days.

The Judge Advocate submitted strong evidence of motive for the crime. The life of twenty-nine-year-old William Macdonald was insured with three different companies for a total sum of £2,000, in each case in favour of Dr. Smith. One of the policies, for £1,000, had been affected for one year only, expiring on November 24th, 1853, five days after Macdonald's death. Moreover, it was proved, the last premium on a £500 policy was paid by Smith on the day before the tragedy.

Insurance agents questioned stated that Macdonald understood nothing of insurances and appeared to take no interest in them. To one of the agents he had remarked: "The doctor's a richt fine chiel and I've always done as he bade me."

Mary Slessor, the girl to whom Macdonald was engaged, testified that he told her he "expected to get something off the insurance from Dr. Smith," but that he did not seem to understand the nature of the transactions.

Medical evidence proved that Macdonald was neither suffocated nor drowned in the ditch in which his body was found. A pistol bullet was embedded in the left section of the brain. Blackening of the skin by exploding gunpowder indicated that the pistol must have been fired at very close quarters, only a few inches from the face.

It was considered inconceivable that the bullet, travelling upwards and obliquely backward from the right cheek, could have been fired by accident. But the medical witnesses could form no precise opinion whether or not the pistol had been discharged by the deceased or by another.

Macdonald's relatives were unanimous and emphatic on oath that he had never been known to possess firearms of any order.

The prisoner denied having seen the fatal pistol until he found it lying in the ditch beside Macdonald's body. He further denied having possession of bullets or gunpowder, excepting an old pistol which he had broken four months before his arrest.

This was checked with evidence produced after a search of Dr. Smith's house at St. Fergus, where police officers found a pistol with a broken trigger and an opened packet containing one and three-quarters ounces of gunpowder.

Witnesses stated that about three months before the tragedy Smith bought a second-hand pistol for 4/6 from a shop in Peterhead, and that elsewhere in the town he had purchased two-dozen percussion caps. Shown the pistol found in the ditch, the man who sold the doctor a weapon could only say that it was of a similar make and design

It was further disclosed that on the eve of Macdonald's death, 'a little before dark,' Smith had obtained two ounces of gunpowder from a tradesman in St. Fergus village.

On being questioned on these discoveries Dr. Smith said he had bought the pistol found in his house about two years previously, and that he got the gunpowder to use in making up an ointment for a patient. He added that he had never opened the gunpowder packet.

Prisoner's statements about his broken pistol and the ammunition were plainly contradicted by the evidence. The prosecution sought to show that he possessed another pistol he had not accounted for, and that this was the murder weapon. Furthermore, it was learned that on two occasions prior to Macdonald's death the doctor had been seen practising pistol-shooting.

Adam Gray, brother to the then Provost of Peterhead, approached the witness-box for the defence. He flabbergasted the court and literally lifted the noose from the prisoner's neck.

Gray swore that, six years previously, on September 15th, 1848, William Macdonald introduced himself during a visit to Peterhead and said: "You pick up things at roups. Have you no gun that you could sell me?"

Witness (Gray) asked: "Are you going to poach?"

Macdonald replied: "Na na, it's tae frichten the craws frae the craps!"

Gray thereupon sold him 'a useless pistol' for 4/6d.

The pistol found beside Macdonald's body was then produced for Gray's inspection. He examined it thoroughly and startled the court with his reply: "From a notch which I remember seeing on the stock, which is whiter than pistol stocks usually are, it is my firm belief that this is the pistol which I sold to William Macdonald."

Macdonald was last seen alive when he left a shop in St. Fergus shortly before 7.30 p.m. Five witnesses fixed 7.35 or 7.36 p.m. as the time at which they heard the shot—some also saw a flash—coming from the direction in which, next morning, the body was found in the ditch.

How Dr. Smith spent all-important minutes that evening was a matter of sharp dispute between prosecution and defence—but the doctor's alibi was startlingly foolproof, even to the vital minutes in which the crime was committed. He was walking on a tight-rope which could so easily become a noose to hang him, one slip to right or left would decide, but he swung along on a hair-fine balance that impressed the jury.

On the night that Macdonald died the doctor was doing a round of visits to patients between 7 and 8 o'clock. Calling on one patient he took up a candle to look at the clock and drew attention to the time—it was twenty-five minutes to eight . . . .

This was testified by a witness in court. Now how could the valiant doctor be in two places at the same time, one indoors, one out?

He called on a woman about eight o'clock and moved his chair to sit behind her, so that she could not see his face. He wiped his face frequently and she thought his nose was bleeding. When he left the house the woman remarked to her husband: "I don't know what's wrong with Dr. Smith tonight!"

Another witness said he had seen Macdonald and Smith walking and talking together on the evening of the crime, just before dark —but he was jailed for bearing false evidence.

Summing up for the jury Lord Hope said that while the motive was strong on Dr. Smith's part, and that although he may have had the opportunity of killing Macdonald—"so had many other persons in the Kirktown of St. Fergus."

Unless the jury were to condemn Adam Gray for deliberate perjury it was impossible to hold that the fatal pistol belonged to Dr. Smith. Unquestionably, in view of Macdonald's character and cheerful disposition the moral evidence was all against the supposition of suicide. And he added: "It therefore remains a murder wholly unexplained."

The jury returned a verdict of 'Not Proven.' Eleven members favoured that verdict while four voted for 'Guilty.' Boos and hisses followed from a crowded courtroom. When Dr. Smith emerged from the court buildings the crowd showed such hostility that he was quickly ushered inside again. Not until the seething throng had dispersed was he discharged as a free man.

There was general dissatisfaction with the manner in which the trial had been conducted, and the verdict was sharply criticised.

The St. Fergus affair will ever remain, in Lord Hope's words: "A murder wholly unexplained."

BLACK KALENDAR OF ABERDEENSHIRE

WOULD you have liked to watch a man die on the gallows? The agonies on his face during the final moments of waiting? The anguish of his loved ones crouched around the scaffold? Would you have shouted or jeered or simply remained passive? Would you have joined the crowd for kicks in the days of public execution—itching for the drop and the death throes of the struggling victim, like a hen thrappled at Christmas?

Would you have queued to watch a fainting woman whipped through the streets by the common hangman, or drummed out of town by the local militia? Would you have mocked at some unfortunate felon in the stocks for petty theft? Spit in his face? Throw stones? Mock him with food or drink? Offer your sympathy? Would all this public savagery have proved a better sport for you than football or bingo or ten-pin bowling? You may search your conscience for an answer but if you had lived about 200 years ago these events were a common spectacle.

Public executions for the county were mostly carried out in the Castlegate at Aberdeen, or in the courtyard of the old City Chambers in Lodge Walk, and invariably they were witnessed by a large and motley crowd, whispering, jeering or booing, as the character of the victim or the nature of the crime deserved, or hushed into silence by the tragedy of someone who earned their sympathy.

In those days, as now, it was considered that the burial of executed criminals was a desecration of sacred ground, but relatives were allowed, after a period of time, to cut down the body of a criminal and take it out to sea and sink it from a boat. Sometimes the bloated corpses were washed ashore and picked up by beach-combers, who, for a few shillings carried them to the surgeons for dissection at King's College, to further the knowledge on medical science.

But as we read through the Black Kalendar of Aberdeenshire we find that all this butchery and callousness did not discourage crime; as year after year and page after page describes more crime and more punishment it seems that the prime deterrent incited a passion to defy justice. And there is something to be said here for the abolition of capital punishment.

In those days you didn't have to commit murder to make a spectacle of yourself in the Castlegate; you could get yourself hanged for sheep-stealing, or for beating your wife (if you did it often enough and loud enough to disturb the peace of the citizens) or merely for petty theft. And for the poorer classes in those days life was hardly possible without theft. Life was such a misery of poverty, hunger, dirt and disease that to make a martyr of yourself was the lesser of two evils. Desperation drove men to distraction and they sacrificed their cheap lives in a reckless gamble to live. Perhaps the gibbet in the Castlegate was a goal to be achieved if you were to live above your grovelling associates, a symbol of your status as a progressive criminal, and at least you went down in history with your name in the 'Aberdeen's Journal.'

One of the last citizens of Peterhead to die on the scaffold in Aberdeen was John Barnet, who lived in the Kirktoon early in the last century. John Barnet was charged with housebreaking and common theft and apprehended at the Bar. This was in 1818 and Barnet had already been in prison the previous year, but he had escaped with two other men. Barnet's wife was also in jail for theft. When he escaped he wrote her a letter informing her of his whereabouts and future intentions in crime. It appears that Barnet had a great affection for his starving wife, a sentiment which incurred great sympathy in the public during his trial and execution.

Barnet's letter to his wife was intercepted and opened by the prison authorities and in consequence of the information it contained he was arrested a second time and held in prison.

During his trial in Aberdeen, Barnet was found guilty of several but not all of the acts of theft libelled against him, and he was sentenced to be executed on Friday, 6th November, 1818.

Barnet was a wilful man with steel nerves and he listened to his doom without flickering an eyelid, glaring at his prosecutors with contempt and indifference. When he escaped from prison, prior to his second detention, a poster was issued advertising a reward for his capture. He was described as a stout man, about five feet nine or ten inches in height, with brown hair and red whiskers, and 'a downcast and thoughtful look.'

While he was in the death-cell many idle rumours were spread through Aberdeen about the terrible crimes which Barnet had committed, and frightful stories were told of the sights which were seen by a soldier on guard at the prison door. Probably Barnet had feined or attempted an orgy of suicide in full view of his goalers. He showed no signs of repentance but clergymen who attended him denied the rumour that he had refused their services.

Nevertheless, while awaiting the scaffold, Barnet troubled himself to 'set his house in order.' He wrote a cameo sketch of his life, stating that he had been in the army, first in the Northern Fencibles and then the militia, and maintained that for many years he had a stainless character, which was afterwards corrupted when he was press-ganged into the navy. On returning to civil life Barnet wrote that he had been harshly dealt with and stripped of his property by creditors and speculators, an example of which behaviour introduced him to crime and violence.

Barnet also wrote a confession on the innocence of a man named William Thomson, whom, at the time of his trial he had accused of being an accomplice to his crimes. He also declared that his wife had shared no part in his theft and housebreaking, a verdict which was already shared by the magistrates. On the Sunday before his execution John Barnet was visited by his aged mother, who had travelled all the way from Peterhead, probably walking, as she may not have been able to pay her fare by stage-coach. She stayed for several hours with her wayward son in the house of death. Finally, silent and heartbroken, the old woman took her last leave of her son and was led away sobbing by the guards.

STRAW INTO GOLD

On the scaffold Barnet was attended by the Rev. Mr. Thom, Professor Kidd and the Rev. Mr. Pennan, of the Independent connection. Barnet acknowledged the justice of his sentence and died with great composure.

After his execution his body was taken out to sea and sunk, but, within two or three days was cast ashore, near Balgownie, at the mouth of the Don, all bloated and discoloured, except for the hair and red whiskers.

At the beginning of last century, prior to the battle of Waterloo, and thirty years or so before Victoria became queen, although you could be hanged for sheep-stealing or house-breaking you could actually get away with murder. Apparently human life was cheap and insignificant in the callous days of 1800. Witness the case of James Carle, in the parish of Longside.

One Sunday morning, towards the end of June, 1800, a barbarous murder was committed. Margaret Keith, a widow, at the farm of Auchtydonald, between Longside and Mintlaw, had been courting a man called James Carle, a weaver, probably from Auchlee or Aden, by whom, at the time, she was supposed to be with child. Her body was found in the River Ugie near Crookedneuk.

She had been enticed out of the house at Auchtydonald that Sunday morning and had walked with Carle on the banks of the river. Carle took hold of her all of a sudden and threw her into the water. The poor woman, shocked and surprised, tried to scramble to the opposite bank, hoping to escape her assassin. But Carle was too quick for her, for when he saw she was likely to survive he ran up the riverside to a wooden bridge, where he crossed and ran back the opposite bank, and he reached the woman just as she was clutching at the reeds at the water's edge. While the frantic woman was struggling in the river, gasping for breath, Carle reached out with a stone and struck her several blows on the head. She sank without a gurgle, without a spasm, clean out of sight.

Carle made off but within a month, before July was out, he was arrested on suspicion of murder. He was imprisoned in Aberdeen, until his trial in September, when Mr. Gordon of Craig was counsel for his defence.

There was some confusion over Carle's identity, which displeased the jury, and they brought in a verdict of Not Proven. The evidence indicated that, on the Sunday morning, Margaret Keith, widow, living at Auchtydonald, in the parish of Longside, had been decoyed out of her house by James Carle, a local weaver, a fact which had been corroborated on evidence given by the children of the dead woman. Her body was afterwards found in the River Ugie.

A youth, who was herding sheep on a hill, saw a man, whom he could not identify at the distance, struggling to keep something down in the water, but he did not pay too much attention to this, as he thought it might be someone trying to drown a distempered dog.

The verdict of the Jury was unanimous but it did not give satisfaction to the public at the time.

But who cared about the public in those days? James Carle got clean away with murder; not even mention of a prison sentence.

Towards the end of May, 1743, three years before the battle of Culloden, James Robertson at Torhenry, of the estate of Lenabo, in the parish of Longside, and Alexander Hay, residenter in Rora, of the same parish, were brought to Aberdeen, under a strong guard, on a charge of sheep-stealing, committed a few days previously.

Hay and Robertson had lurked for several days and nights near the farm of Techmuiry, Strichen, occupied by Mr. George Allan. spying on his sheepfold. They retired to the Hill of Mormond for a day but returned to Techmuiry at nightfall, and, having forced open the door or gate of the fold, they stole away with six-and-thirty sheep. This was on the night of Friday, May 28th, or the morning of Saturday, 1743. They drove the sheep all the way to Dyce, where they grazed them over the weekend. On Monday, having crossed the Don by the road bridge, Hay and Robertson sold the sheep for ready cash to the Rev. Mr. Ragg, minister at Dyce, and Arthur Shand, servant to a Mr. Burnett of Kirkhill of Dyce.

A few hours after this transaction Hay and Robertson, who were armed with pistols, were apprehended while drinking in the house of a man named Chalmers, near Hatton of Fintray. The thieves put up a desperate resistance, short of using their pistols, but were finally overpowered and taken to Aberdeen, where they were securely locked in the Tolbooth. The money they had got for the sheep was found on the prisoners and promptly taken away from them. During his confinement Hay made a desperate attempt to escape, by cutting the bars on his cell window, but he was discovered in time and restrained.

On September 13th the prisoners were indicted before the Sheriff, John Thain, at the instance of George Allan of Techmuiry, and of the Procurator-Fiscal, James Petrie. The libel, as preserved in the Sheriff's record, is a curious document. The first charge is the general bad character of the prisoners, who are described as 'persons of bad and broken fame, thieves, and receptors of theft'; and Hay is stated to have been convened and convicted before the Baron Court of Inverugie, on July 21st, 1741, but to have absconded and fled from justice—this charge being so worded, that we are left to believe that the Laird of Inverugie had convicted Hay in his absence.

In the case of Robertson and Hay, the hour of night at which the theft was committed, and the fact that the prisoners were armed with swords and pistols, aggravated the libel in their disfavour.

For the prisoners there appeared, Thomas Mossman, Thomas Wilson and John Taylor, Advocates, who brought in written defences for their clients. These counsel, who appear to have done every justice to their case, stated various objections to the indictment. Counsel contended and quoted authorities to show that the Law of Scotland did not punish theft with death until the third offence, and it was denied (apparently with reason) that Hay had been convicted at the Baron Court of Inverugie.

With regard to the bad fame of the prisoners, counsel stated that fame was very deceitful, and seldom or never to be credited, for if persons were to be tried for simply being of bad fame, twenty Sheriffs instead of one would not be enough for the county.

The public prosecutor contended that theft was, 'by its own nature,' punishable by death, and to further damage Hay's character he reminded the court that he had not only tried to break out of prison, but that his brother, William Hay, had some time ago actually broken out and escaped justice. By the Jewish Law, he said, theft in the night was capital, and a man might lawfully kill a thief in the night-time.

Caution had been asked of the prisoners by Rev. Ragg and Kirkhill, the purchasers of the sheep, which the prisoners did not give, and so, by the Law of Scotland, they were thieves, and without other proof, ought to be condemned to the death.

A jury was then empanelled: William Abernethy of Crimmonmogate; Baillie Thomas Arbuthnot, merchant, Peterhead; Andrew Arbuthnot, Mill of Aden; John Arbuthnot in Fortrie; James Arbuthnot in Rora; Nathaniel Arbuthnot in Auchtydonald; William Scott in Nether Aden; James Barrack, Factor to Gordon of Ellon; William Milne, merchant in Ellon; John Petrie, merchant in Aberdeen; John Beagrie at Mill of Rora; William Moir, Bridgend of Cruden; Alexander Bruce in Tiffery; John Moir, Kirkton of Longside; and John Kidd in Rora.

The prisoners objected to all these jurymen, with the exception of John Petrie of Aberdeen, on the ground that they had all given information in this case, that they had advised the raising of the prosecution, and had contributed money to carry it on, and had declared to persons in the country that the prisoners were guilty. The prisoners maintained that the members of this local jury bore them malice and ill-will.

In reply, it was urged by Thomas Burnett of Kirkhill, who drew the libel, that he had got no information from any of these jurymen. He also insisted that the jurymen objected to were those fittest to judge the accused, because they were acquainted with the character and bad behaviour of the prisoners.

Counsel for the prisoners alleged that the jury members were biased against those at their mercy, and that it was a great pity to bring these gentlemen, in the busy harvest season, all the way to Aberdeen, when there were plenty of idle men in the town, fit to judge the case, and who had no harvest to attend to.

The Sheriff put the question of malice, and of having assisted in getting up the prosecution against the prisoners, to the oaths of the fourteen jurors objected to, and they all denied the allegations and swore to their own impartiality. The case was then remitted to their judgement.

In his summing up the prosecutor said, 'the prisoners are accused of stealing and driving away thirty-six sheep; they are accused of being guilty, art and part of receipt of theft; they are accused of having sold and delivered the sheep, and received the price of them; and, finally, they are accused as dissolute and wicked persons, common cheats and rogues, and pests in the country, ruinous to society, industry, and common honesty; all which, or any part of the same being proved, the prisoners ought to be punished with the pains of law, in other words, with the pains of death.'

The evidence consisted almost entirely in the identifying of the sheep sold to Ragg and Shand by the prisoners with the sheep stolen from Allan of Techmuiry. They had been marked on the horns with a hot iron, and, on being brought to the door of the courtroom, were identified by various witnesses. In the course of the trial, the evidence of a girl, Margaret Mitchell, was objected to on the ground that, by an act of the Justiciary Court, in August, 1661, the evidence of a woman was not to be received in criminal cases. Her evidence was passed over.

On the following day, at eleven o'clock, the jury, by their chancellor, Abernethy of Crimmongate, returned their verdict of Proven. The prisoners were brought again to the bar, where they were sentenced by James Chapman, Dempster of Court, 'to be carried to the Tolbooth, there to be detained till Friday, the eighteenth of November, and then, betwixt the hours of twelve and four, to be carried to the Market Place, and hanged by the neck until they be dead, and all their goods to be escheat by His Majesty's use.'

So James Robertson never smelled the scent of the heather on Torhenry again, and Alex. Hay never breathed the peat reek of Rora; but they were not hanged. Before the day of their execution came round their sentence was commuted to banishment—for life.

At the Spring Circuit, 1753, before Lords Elchies and Kilkerran, comes Francis Enoch Morris, a German by birth, for trial on a charge against His Majesty, King George II.

Morris was brought to Aberdeen by Lieutenant Backhouse and a party from Peterhead, on a charge of 'cursing the King, Prince George, and the Duke of Cumberland.' Three of His Majesty's paid servants, a serjeant, and two soldiers were the witnesses against him. In the course of the trial it came out that Morris was a German, unacquainted with the usage of the English language, and that he was drunk when the offence was committed.

The jury were divided eight to seven and returned a verdict of Not Guilty, on which the prisoner was dismissed.

'But,' says the anonymous author of The Black Kalendar, 'had the verdict been the other way, this poor ship-wrecked sailor, for uttering a parcel of foolish words, might, in those dangerous times have received a punishment fully as severe as a man now-a-days (1843) would get for housebreaking. We do not know how far the circumstances of his being a foreigner, and being in drink, and that the first words which a stranger learns of our language are our standard oaths, might have gone to mitigate his punishment, at a time, when the Court would have been anxious to shew its devotion to the heirs male of the body of the electress Sophia, being protestants.'

At the Autumn Circuit, 1827, John Lovie, farmer at Futteretden, near Fraserburgh, was tried before Lords Pitmilly and Alloway, for the crime of murder.

Lovie was an unmarried man, and had hired a servant girl, Margaret Mackessar, whom Lovie had often visited at her mother's home. Her mother had wished her to go to another service, but the girl preferred going to Lovie. She became pregnant by Lovie, and from evidence in the case it appeared that he had given her a violent purgative to bring about abortion.

On the morning of August 14th the woman was seized with violent vomiting, and after great suffering she died in the afternoon. During the summer months, while they worked together in the fields, Lovie had often conversed with his man-servant on the effects of various poisons. Lovie asked him if he knew what would cause abortion and he said that he did not. He asked, further, if he knew what quantity of jalap would produce purging, and how much would kill. He also inquired of the servant how much laudanum would make a person sleep. One morning, while they were hoeing potatoes, Lovie asked this man if he knew the name of a 'white kind of poisonous stuff,' and the other replied that he supposed he meant arsenic. This was more than a week before the girl's death.

On another occasion Lovie mentioned the names of two druggists in Fraserburgh, and he said he supposed they would sell arsenic. About the end of July Lovie called at a druggist's shop in Fraserburgh and asked for an ounce of jalap, which he got. On his remarking that it would be a good dose the lad in the shop asked if it was intended for a beast. Lovie said it was for a body and, when the druggist said it was enough to kill a person Lovie said he would divide it. Lovie then inquired if jalap was the strongest purgative, and what was best for rats? The druggist said arsenic. Lovie then went away, but came back on August 9th and said he would take the arsenic now as he was much troubled with rats. He got two half-ounce parcels away with him.

On the morning of the fourteenth Margaret Mackessar rose in her usual health and went to work. She took her breakfast about eight o'clock and soon after she was vomiting. Lovie's man-servant came in to breakfast, while Lovie remained at work in the fields. When the man went back to the field, he told this to Lovie, and remarked that his face grew red on hearing it. Lovie went home to breakfast. On returning to the field he told the servant that he had heard 'Meggy' vomiting. The servant said she might soon get better, on which Lovie said, that if she did not, she would not be "lang to the fore."

Lovie continued working in the field and, although Margaret Mackessar's mother passed three times within hearing, he never told her that her daughter was unwell. And he also forbade the servant to˙ tell her. In the meantime no medical assistance was got for the girl, though she lay in the greatest agony. About one o'clock she asked to see her sister and mother, but neither they nor the doctor, who was at last sent for, arrived till she was dead.

Lovie came into the house when she was on the verge of death. She called for a drink of water about half-past one o'clock and then expired. When Lovie heard that she was dead he said, "My God!" or "Good God!" He objected to having the body opened, as, he said, it would thereby become known that Margaret had been with child, and he urged Jean Mackessar, her sister, to tell her mother to object to opening the body.

The funeral took place on the Thursday, but the body was disinterred on the Saturday. Lovie asked one of the witnesses of the disinternment if the body would swell if the woman had been poisoned. The body was opened, and arsenic, in great quantities was found in the stomach and intestines. The woman was six months gone with child.

In his declaration Lovie stated that he had purchased some stuff to rub on his cows and heifers, after doing which, he washed the saucer, and flung the contents on the dunghill. It was proved that this story was false. The midden was searched, and nothing of the kind found in it, and it was discovered that the cattle had not been affected by any distemper. Lovie further stated, to a sister of the deceased, that he had never bought poison, and that someone must have got it in his name.

Such was the evidence, upon which a jury, after deliberating together for half-an-hour, saw fit, to the utter amazement of almost all who listened to the trial, to return a unanimous verdict of Not Proven.

And here the editor of the Black Kalendar states: 'In our humble opinion there was here furnished a specimen of presumptive evidence, against the accused, of the strongest and most perfect kind which it is possible to conceive. 'The jury,' says Mr. Alison, 'misled by the eloquence of Mr. Cockburn, found the libel Not Proven; but the Court were of opinion that the case was clearly made out—an opinion with which, it is probable, no man of sense, who considers the evidence, will be disposed to differ.'

In the month of August, 1756, Christian Clark, from Burnside of Philorth, in the parish of Fraserburgh, was tried before the Sheriff of Aberdeenshire, upon a most comprehensive libel, charging her with 'bringing forth two bastards, keeping a disorderly house, entertaining men as well in the night-time as in the day-time, and sailors upon Sundays, and of being habit and repute a harlot and a loose woman, and of keeping a bawdy-house.' She was found guilty, and was banished the country for life, with a warning that if, at the end of a month from the passing of her sentence, she was found in Aberdeenshire, she would be publicly whipped at the Market Cross by the common hangman, and again banished. At the same time, her sister, Ann Clark, was indicted for similar offences, but had fled from justice.

On Tuesday, April 15th, 1768, James Cullen, Junior, residing at Mosstown of Crimond, was committed to prison, charged with the horrid crimes of incest and rape, committed on the person of his step-mother, and with cursing and beating his parents. It may here be mentioned, that by an Act of the first Session of the first Parliament of Charles the Second, it was ordained that 'what son or daughter, above the age of sixteen years, shall beat or curse father or mother, not being distracted, shall suffer death without mercy.' James Cullen was indicted for all these crimes at the Circuit Court opened by Lord Kames in May following and pleaded Not Guilty. His step-mother came forward to give evidence against him. She was the principal witness to prove the rape, and, of course, the incestuous connection, and, it might be added, the adultery involved in the crime. Her testimony was objected to by the prisoner's counsel, on the 'ground that she had expressed the most inveterate malice, and a determined resolution to have the prisoner banished the country; and that at a time previous to the alleged rape.' The prosecutor insisted on the necessity of admitting her evidence, owing to the nature of the crime. The Court, however, decided that the prisoner should be allowed to prove the malice. The prisoner's Counsel contended that this prosecution arose entirely from the gross falsehood and malignity of this cruel step-mother, who wished to prevent the prisoner from bringing a wife into his father's family, whereby she might loose the power of embezzling the effects. Evidence having been called, the Court found the objection proven, and refused to receive the witness. The evidence of the father was such as cleared the prisoner of the other charge of beating his parents, and the Advocate-Depute having given up the case, the prisoner was dismissed.

As the malice of the step-mother was held by the Court to be established, there is certainly a high probability that the prisoner was not guilty of the rape and incest of which he was accused.

William Philp very narrowly escaped the gallows. He was a farmer at Stodfield of Skelmuir and was apprehended on a charge of horse-stealing. In the Spring of 1769, he was removed from Aberdeen, by an order from the Lord Justice Clerk, to be tried before the High Court of Justiciary. Having been found guilty, he was sentenced to be executed at Aberdeen on the fifth of May. This sentence was, however, afterwards remitted, on condition of the prisoner going into perpetual banishment.

Philp would now have been set at liberty, had not one John Davidson, in Waterside of Ythan, given in a petition, and made oath, that he was in dread of bodily harm from him. On this, Philp was imprisoned till he should find caution to keep the peace, which he afterwards succeeded in doing, and was liberated in order to go into exile.

STRAW INTO GOLD

On Friday, October 19th, 1764, John Hutcheon, farmer, at Cranabog of Carnoustie, was brought a prisoner to Aberdeen, under a strong guard, who had great difficulty in keeping him in custody, as he made a vigorous resistance. This man, who had at different times called himself Wallace and Gray, had committed numerous depredations.

John Hutcheon was placed at the bar, in May, 1765, before Lord Kaimes and Lord Coalston, charged with various acts of housebreaking and theft; and especially with having, in December, 1763, broken into the house of Mr. Fullerton of Dudwick, and stolen a gold watch, fifty pounds, and a bill due by himself.

From the existence of this bill we are led to suppose that Hutcheon must have been a person of some credit in the country —at any rate it is not usual to take bills from people who are reputed to be thieves.

Hutcheon was farther charged with having stolen from a person of the name of Moir a sum of money, amounting to thirty-six pounds fifteen shillings. The act, however, which led to his arrest, was committed on Sunday morning, October 7th, when he stole five head of cattle from the lands of Waterton. Three of the cattle, and the gold watch which he had stolen from Dudwick, were found in his possession when he was apprehended.

Having been found guilty, he was sentenced to be hanged on Friday, the 28th of June. This sentence was duly carried into effect. Having been brought down to the Laigh Court-house, and urged to confess his crimes, he denied being guilty of everything charged against him, except simple theft. He persisted in the same declaration when he was brought to the gallows. After praying some time, and reading on a book of devotions, he was thrown off, and his body, after hanging for some time, was cut down, and was taken away by the surgeons.

ON KEEPING A DIARY

H AVE you ever received a diary as a present for Christmas or Hogmanay? If you have, remember that you could be handling a lethal weapon, dangerous as a nail bomb, or a poisoned arrow pointed at your breast, psychologically speaking. Diaries have been read in court and have been instrumental in sending people behind bars, or even to the gallows. On the other hand you could become a future Charles Dickens, with the pleasant fields of literature awaiting your conquest.

Keeping a diary diligently over a period is one of the very best ways of learning to write. It teaches the diarist to think with words, to analyse human nature, to study character, to describe scenery, and if the chronicler is an apt pupil he will find that in a reasonably short space of time he will develop a power of perception and observation which otherwise had remained dormant in his nature. He will achieve an individual style of writing and a flair for his special subject, besides providing him (or herself) with an admirable hobby and endless enjoyment.

But of course it is useless to start a diary on the first day of January and abandon it in three weeks. You have to be persistent; you have to persevere until the habit grows on you. At first it may seem as bad as trying to give up smoking, but as you go on and your entries accumulate and become memories you will warm to the task. Three to five years of consistent scribbling is the minimum term of apprenticeship, unless of course you are a genius or have natural talent, in which case you should get cracking on a short story or full-blooded novel right away.

All this of course is sheer enthusiasm, which, after all, is the spice of life, and not to be compared with the drab aspect of financial reward. Dr. Johnson once wrote that 'nobody but a fool would ever write for anything but money,' but don't you believe it, for there is just as much fun to be got with a pen as with a

195

paint brush (painting word pictures) or with a fishing-rod or a sports rifle, a set of golf-clubs or a tennis raquet, depending as always on your chemical make-up, and if you do happen to become professional (or strike gold) the remuneration can be really quite astounding.

Keeping a diary may be compared with printing your own private newspaper, and even though the diarist himself is the only reader it is a colossal circulation: every brain cell, every nerve-end, every duct and gland, and every one of his five senses is concentrated on the perusal of his daily jottings, and there isn't a newspaper in the country that could compare with this reception, for it is like every single member of the population reading a national journal, which is far more than any reasonable editor could ever hope for. So do not be discouraged though nobody reads your diary but yours truly. Remember poor Anne Frank, who died in a German concentration camp, and who, before her capture wrote her diary as a letter addressed to herself every day, which on discovery after her death provided the reading world with a most remarkable document. The diarist (unlike the editor) can be ruthless and indiscriminate in print, and provided he keeps it private he has nothing to fear from libel or the Lord Chamberlain.

But you may take great pains in keeping your journal a secret, even to writing it in code, like Samuel Pepys or Beatrix Potter. which to me seems pointless, for their is little fun in being an artist without an audience, and you might as well be an actor on the stage of an empty theatre.

Nobody wants to read your diary until you are dead in any case (if you are to exclude Aunt Martha or a snooping wife who used to be your sweetheart — or vice versa of course) certainly not busy editors or a preoccupied public. But there is a posthumous snag about diaries that is worth considering: Supposing you have confided in your book what you really think of your associates, and have written down the foibles and follies you know them to be guilty of, in other words slandered the neighbourhood with a scandal sheet comparable with PEYTON PLACE and you suddenly have a heart attack before you've had a chance to burn it.

Think of the responsibility you have saddled your family with, especially if it is a work of art they have no wish to destroy, although they may have the good sense to suppress it. Consider what a cad you might appear to be in the eyes of your grandchildren—perhaps they may be reading your very inmost secrets, your shameful confessions, your vices and your weaknesses, learning all about your carousals and your flirtations, complexes and guilty thoughts you never intended others to read about, code or no code. This is something you have to make up your mind about for a start: how far you are prepared to go in a private diary, and at the same time avoiding restraint to the point of becoming a bore; for unless you reveal yourself to some extent, in other words "let your hair down," so to speak, it isn't really much worth while, and unless your personality gets on to the page it is lacking in human interest.

At the same time you could become a posthumous John Evelyn or a Fanny Burney in spite of yourself. When James Boswell died his journals gave his family such a red face that they banned his publishers from using them. They hadn't the heart to burn them either, but stuffed the mass of papers into trunks and boxes and hid them in lofts and cellars. As generation followed generation in the Boswell genealogical tree James's daily jottings were lost and forgotten. One would have thought that this would have been the end of the worthy James Boswell—actually it was only a prelude to his greater fame . . .

James Boswell died at 55 in 1795 and 45 years later shopkeepers were wrapping their goods in his foolscap pages. How this came about no one knows exactly, but it began a search for Boswell's paraphenalia which, punctuated by periodical discoveries of his letters and diaries, culminated at Fettercairn House in Kincardineshire in 1930, 135 years after Boswell's death. How they came to be here is one of the great riddles of literature, especially when you consider that Boswell was an Ayrshire man, the son of Lord Auchinleck.

Ten years earlier, in the summer of 1920, Professor Tinker of Yale University, U.S.A., learned of the existence of an ebony cabinet in Malahide Castle, near Dublin, entirely filled with Boswell's papers.

STRAW INTO GOLD

Claude Colleer Abbott was visiting Fettercairn House, near Stonehaven, on a quest for something else when he stumbled on Boswell's documents quite by accident in 1930. Professor Abbott, of Durham University, was enamoured with his remarkable discovery, and with great care he catalogued and edited Boswell's correspondence and prepared it for the press. All the Boswell secrets were removed to America and publication of his works began at Yale University in 1950. British publication rights were secured by Heinemann's of London and we had our first glimpse of Boswell's remarkable *London Journal* in the summer of 1951.

It is really one of the most delightful diaries I have ever read. But I can't give quotations because if our editor printed them here he would probably be horsewhipped, both for pornography and infringement of copyright, though I will give a snippet in a moment to show what I mean. Boswell reveals himself in his Journal as a dude, an amorous, bragging dandy, and one doesn't have to read far to understand why his family suppressed its publication after his death 'I fanned the flame by pressing her alabaster breasts and kissing her delicious lips. I then barred the door of her dining room, led her all fluttering into her bedchamber, and was just making a triumphal entry when we heard her landlady coming up.' He also mentions the 'preventative sheath' in sexual intercourse, nearly two centuries ago, and we are left to imagine it as a pretty crude affair. Hitherto I had always thought of the contraceptive as an invention of our own times. Despite these lustful outbursts, Boswell is amusingly philosophical and entertaining, and I only wish I had possessed his foresight and practical outlook on life at the same age. Boswell's Dutch Journal has unfortunately been lost, but others have appeared from time to time and are still being printed.

Boswell met Flora MacDonald and in one of his later, more genteel, entries he gives us this account of her: 'She was a little woman, of a mild and genteel appearance, mighty soft and well bred. To see Mr. Samuel Johnson salute Miss Flora MacDonald was a wonderful romantic scene to me. We had as genteel a supper as one could wish to see, in particular an excellent roasted turkey, porter to drink at table, and after supper claret and punch. But what I admired was the perfect ease with which everything went on. My 'facility of manners,' as Adam Smith said of me had fine play.'

Samuel Pepys wrote his diary in a crude form of code or shorthand and bequeathed it at his death to Magdalene College, Cambridge, where it lay for 115 years until it was deciphered by a clergyman named John Smith and published in 1825. Pepys and Boswell are the gossips of literature and while Boswell gives us a newsy account of the social elite of his day Pepys records its history in graphic detail: the Great Plague and Fire of London, the Dutch Wars, ten sensational years packed with incident.

On November 14th, 1666 Pepys gives us our first glimpse at a primitive form of blood transfusion: 'Dr. Croone told me, that at the meeting at Gresham College tonight there was a pretty experiment of the blood of one dog let out (till he died) into the body of another on one side, while all his own run out on the other side. The first died upon the place, and the other very well, and likely to do well. This did give occasion to many pretty wishes, as of the blood of a Quaker to be let into an Archbishop, and such like: but, as Dr. Croone says, may, if it takes, be of mighty use to man's health, for the amending of bad blood by borrowing from a better body.'

But perhaps you have no desire to become a Pepys or a Boswell. Maybe you'd rather become a Barbellion and watch yourself die. W. N. P. Barbellion analysed his disease and watched it gnaw into his spine until his life hung by a thread. He announced his death on the last page and cheated his readers by two years. He lived to read in print what he had written by hand and gloated over its success. Otherwise Barbellion was an honest man and a genuine sufferer. He made amends by writing another *Last Diary* from his death bed. At the end his wife or his nurse wrote while he merely dictated, because by then he was almost totally paralysed. We take Barbellions' hand to the very edge of the grave; not pathetically or engrossed in self-pity, but emanating a spirit of courage and resignation to fate which is almost Christ-like in its dedication of soul. The ever present prospect of death gives him an introspection on life far beyond our seeing and we are left trembling on the brink of revelation.

Hear him on the last terrifying phases of his illness; defiant it seems but accepting the inevitable with indomitable spirit and clarity of vision: 'I am not offering up my life willingly—it is being taken from me piece by piece, while I watch the pilfering with lamentable eyes . . . What I have always feared is coming to pass, love for my little daughter. Only another communicating string with life to be cut . . . I take my life in homepathic doses now.'

Barbellion died at thirty in 1919 and left us *The Journal of a Disappointed Man*. And while he stripped his soul to shreds Katherine Mansfield was wasting away with tuberculosis. She doesn't pick her bones quite as thoroughly as Barbellion. But her diary is a touching one, poignant and revealing, a record of thwarted love and approaching death that could well be described in one of Robert Burns' least known verses:

> Fairest flower, behold the lily,
> Blooming in the sunny ray—
> But let the blast sweep o'er the valley,
> Then see it prostrate on the clay.

But not all diaries are sad. Indeed *The Diary of a Nobody* is one of the funniest things in the English language. Written by brothers George and Weedon Grossmith, a pair of London theatrical personalities of the late Victorian era, it gives such a delightful picture of a London middle-class household you get a giggle on every page. The only trouble is it is supposed to be fictional.

Fred Bason's diary is also very amusing, and apart from the political 'Dictionaries' which appear from time to time it is one of the latest published diaries of note. Bason collects autographs, mostly the signatures of the famous, and his efforts to obtain them are painstaking and ingenious, especially when he unintentionally secures the signature of a murderer.

There are as many recorded diarists in the English language whose names would cram a page or more of this book. And there are war diaries: Haig, Count Ciano, Allanbrook, and many others, all pages of history which posterity will cherish.

ON KEEPING A DIARY

The century in which we are now living is the most exciting and eventful in recorded history. Current events make it more worthwhile keeping a diary than ever before: what with space flight, man on the moon, the development of hydrogen weapons and atomic power, the jet age, the permissive society, the savagery and violence of our world environment, guerilla warfare, hijacking of aircraft, assassination of national figures—it's time someone got cracking writing it all down for posterity. So if you do get that diary for Christmas or Hogmanay don't waste any time.

And, who knows, writing a diary may keep you out of mischief with less chance of landing yourself in jail than otherwise.

PETER STILL
THE BARD OF UGIESIDE

ON March 3rd, 1842, after some apology and acknowledgement to his subscribers, possibly for some delay in publication, Peter Still, the Bard of Ugieside, begged his readers, while perusing his *Poems and Sangs*, to bear in mind his low station in life and lack of opportunities which his existence afforded him in the way of writing poetry. He also stressed the fact that he was a deaf poet who wrote and lived in a silent world, and he prefaced his little volume of verse with the following lines, seemingly borrowed from another source—one who:

> —*never hears the song of birds—*
> *The humming of the bee—*
> *The music of the mountain wind—*
> *The murmur of the sea.*
> *and to whom*
> *All nature unharmonious lies,*
> *All silent and all still,*
> *As if creation tuneless slept*
> *On valley, stream, and rill.*
>
> *Millbank, Longside, March 3rd, 1842.*

Apart from his poems Still wrote several songs which have come down to us almost as traditional balladry: songs like *The Glen o' the West, Jeannie's Lament*, and, most important, *Ye Needna be Courtin' at Me, Auld Man*, which, sung to the air of John Todd, comes very near to the best of our truly Scottish songs, or to something in the nature of *The Wee Cooper o' Fife*, or *The Barrin' o' the Door*, or to Hector Macneil's *Come Under My Plaidie*, and several other compositions whose authors are known to us.

Peter Still was born on New Year's Day, 1814, the son of a farmer in the parish of Fraserburgh. At the time of Peter's birth his father was fairly well off, but a protracted law suit forced him

202

into adverse circumstances. He was obliged to leave his farm, so he moved to the parish of Longside, where he employed himself as a day-labourer, and young Still enjoyed a few fruitful years at the local school.

At the risk of being labelled an amanuensis I shall endeavour to let young Still give us his own story in as few words as possible: 'About the seventh or eighth year of my age, I was sent to school by an uncle, a brother of my mother, who died soon afterwards, and I had scarcely ceased to bewail his loss, when I was taken from school; my parents being unable to continue my education any longer. My education on the whole amounted to nothing more than what is common to almost all the peasantry of Scotland—a few years of tuition at a country school, often interrupted by bad health; for I have been from my infancy subject to frequent attacks of headaches, and also to pains in my ears; accompanied at times by a partial defect in my hearing; which latter complaint has terminated in complete, and it may be, incurable deafness.'

Like Beethoven Peter Still never heard the sound of his own music. And for six months of his adult life he was as blind as Milton. Perhaps in the loss of his faculties Still concentrated on word music, lyrics that jingle in the mind like the sleigh-bells in a child's idea of Christmastide.

The Bard of Ugieside was born for adversity: poverty, ill-health, hard times, and, for the most part, obscurity. Wm. Walker, in *The Bards of Bon-Accord*, page 482 says: 'Peter Still was indeed one of nature's noblemen, one of the few choice spirits whom adversity could not break, nor prosperity spoil, but who possessed his soul in all its integrity and manliness in poverty, penury, and obscurity, ennobling by his character and life the humble lot he moved in from the cradle to the grave.'

How many people know that the following famous lines, perhaps equal to anything in Gray's Elegy, were written by the Prince of Poverty (so he styled himself) on the banks of the humble Ugie river, a mile north of Longside village?

STRAW INTO GOLD

I saw the widow's bosom bleed;
I heard the orphan beg for bread;
I saw ambition's godless greed
  Tax every loaf;
Then praise the patience of the dead,
  Whom want cut off!

Echoes of the Corn Laws or the Bread Riots of the Industrial Revolution. The theme of Mrs. Craik's nineteenth century novel, *John Halifax, Gentleman,* condensed by Peter Still to a verse of six deathless lines.

Everyone knows (to use a popular expression) that the village of Longside is the last resting place of Jamie Fleeman, 'The Laird o' Udny's fool,' and hundreds of sightseers have visited his grave over the years in the old parish kirkyard; the more knowledgeable move a few yards further on and examine the headstone of the Rev. John Skinner, noted poet author of *Tullochgorum,* and *The Ewie wi' the Crookit Horn;* and there the pilgrimage ends, leaving Longside's two other poets almost completely forgotten.

About a quarter of a mile from the village, on the Ludquharn road, John Ross Imray, Longside's 'homespun' poet lies buried in the New Cemetery. The little house, Ivy Cottage, where he lived, can still be seen in Armoury Lane. But John Imray doesn't concern us here, except in the lines below, where he is standing on Ardlaw Hill, to the north of the village, overlooking the site of Peter Still's 'hallan,' or cottage, near the farm of Millbank, on the Ugie river.

O sweet Longside, a gem thou'rt set
By Ugie's wimplin' burnie,
Wham pageant blooms the meadow queen
At ilka crook an' turnie.

The meadow green wi' dewdrap clear
Upon ilk leaflet clingin',
I've wannert ower in early morn,
Aboon the laverock singin'.

THE BARD OF UGIESIDE

An' aft fae Ardlaw's wooded hill
I've watched in simmer mornin'
The gowden sun rise in the East
Dame Nature's face adornin'.

Of all Buchan villages Longside is the most richly endowed in poetic lore. Most people will say the village had one poet, meaning Skinner, a few will tell you it had two poets (although Imray could hardly be compared with the former), but not a soul in the village will mention the greatest of all three, the poet-laurate of Buchan as a native of Longside, Peter Still, the sensitive, passionate, gentle-hearted ploughman brother of the soil who wrote the sequel to Burns' *Cottar's Saturday Night*, namely—*The Cottar's Sunday*.

When eleven years old Peter was taken by his father to the feeing market at Longside, where he was engaged to herd cattle for six months on the rough moorland overlooking what is now the great forest of Lenabo. The young poet was nearly five miles on foot from home, heart-weary, dejected, sometimes soaking wet and almost weeping for home and the green banks of Ugie. But he tells us his master and mistress were kindly, understanding folks, and that eventually he spent many cheerful days on the heath under smiling summer skies and couldn't have felt happier in Paradise.

'At times, indeed,' he says, 'I was cold and wet, but a contented mind has the jewel of happiness within itself. Martinmas came, and I found myself by my mother's side, tendering her my scanty half-year's wages. That was, indeed, a happy moment to me. Where were the wet, the cold, and the comfortless days now! All forgotten in the smile of love she cast upon me. O there is no smile like a mother's smile!'

Who else was better qualified to write *The Cottar's Sunday*. Like Sir Walter Scott Peter Still was fortunate in having a grandmother imbued with folk-lore and anecdote which she imparted to the boy throughout his happy childhood, and it is to the great loss of folk-lorists that he didn't live long enough to hand them down to posterity. But from his granny and the scarce books he walked many miles to borrow young Still acquired the rudiments of education he needed to bequeath us a volume of poems to rank with William Thom or Robert Tannahill, or even in his finest moments to rival Burns himself.

I have often heard it lamented that Buchan never produced a poet of the calibre of Burns, and even Gavin Greig himself has blamed this deficiency on the uncompromising nature of the climate and scenery. And yet, on one of Buchan's bleakest patches, about a mile upstream from the meeting of North and South Ugies, in the barren, misty Haughs of Rora, near the old Lint Mill of Auchlee, and about a mile from Longside railway station, Buchan's greatest lyricist worked and lived and wrote his finest verses.

The following lines are anonymous but they paint a graphic picture of Still's environment in relation to society:

> *North Ugie said to South Ugie—*
> *Where shall we twa meet?*
> *—Doon in the Haughs o' Rora*
> *Where all men are asleep!*

But Peter Still has immortalised his beloved Ugie as sweetly as any poet has ever sung of his native river, as witness the following:

> *Roll on—roll on, thou mem'ry-stirring stream!*
> *Thy daisied banks are deeply dear to me:*
> *I gaze upon them, and again I seem*
> *A schoolboy, bathing gloriously in thee!*

> *Swift as the wind, again my unshod feet*
> *Pursue by thee the gaudy butterfly;*
> *Or on thy banks, with wild flowers scented sweet,*
> *At sunny noon, imparadis'd I lie.*

THE BARD OF UGIESIDE

In childhood's glee, they throng thy pebbled shore,
But, turning round, the dear delusion o'er—
My offspring, frolicsome, around me play;
In childhood's glee, they throng thy pebbled shore,
Such as I was, when in my early May.
Roll on, my Ugie! though I'm young no more,
Yet will I love thee till my dying day.

Peter Still married his 'Bell' before he was out of his teens, but in his poems he refers to her as his 'Tibbie.'

My Tibbie, blythesome, at my hip,
Gars spinning'-jenny nimbly trip,
Or, some auld seam that's tint the grip,
She seams anew;
While on Parnassus' tap I sip
Poetic dew.

After his marriage Peter left regular farm service and employed himself as a day-labourer—cutting peat, breaking stones for road-making, cleaning ditches and digging drains, from five in the morning till seven or eight at night, often without milk in the house for months, with a wife and bairns to keep, yet devoting the spare hours which broken weather or ill-health sent him, to poetry and the muses!

Despite sporadic attacks of migraine and crippling rheumatism Peter tells us that, from 14th April to June 21st, 1841, he had cast 14,000 barrowloads of peat, and he had some 2,000 barrowfuls yet to wheel out on the lairs. He further informs us that he was paid eightpence for the first hundred barrowfuls and one-shilling-and-fourpence a day for the rest to individual farmers, each perhaps requiring on average 800 to 1,000 barrowloads.

Rora was the moss nearest to Peter's abode, but he may have gone further afield to the peatbogs of Kininmonth, Kinmundy or Crimond, always on foot, wherever work was to be found. But Peter thought nothing of walking overnight to places like Aberchirder, to visit a brother poet, and the best of his work is contained in the epistles he wrote in verse to his varied and numerous correspondents, comprising the titled laird and the humble fisherman.

Almost from the start of his married life Fate began to tighten the screw on poor Peter Still. The first few years of bliss were soon spent and he was assailed by sickness and unemployment and the poverty of his family resulting from his misfortune. But his spirit couldn't be broken and it appears that in his misery and despair he sang the sweeter:

> *Yet dark December broodin' o'er*
> *The snawy plain, the surgy shore,*
> *Brings joy to me a countless store,*
> *When gloamin' gray,*
> *Somewhere about the hour o' four,*
> *Seals up the day.*

> *Wi' joy unfeign'd, ye needna doubt,*
> *Frae some wet ditch I clam'er out,*
> *An' buckle on my auld surtout*
> *We freedom's pride;*
> *Syne through the snaw I tak' the route,*
> *To Ugieside.*

> *An' there my wee bit cantie ha',*
> *Peeps oot frae 'mid a wreath o' snaw,*
> *Whilk hauds the frosty win' awa';*
> *For there it lies,*
> *Till safter gales in pity blaw,*
> *Frae warmer skies.*

> *My half-seen hame once mare I view,*
> *My happy heart loups licht, I trow,*
> *To see the "wee things stacher through"*
> *The lairy snaw;*
> *Ilk smilin' face, says, "Here's him noo,"*
> *An', "Come away!"*

THE BARD OF UGIESIDE

The youngest ane—a wee bit lammie—
Rins ben the hoose to tell its mammie;
An dancin', says that first it saw me—
    Syne to the door
Again it rins, "Tit-ta" to ca' me,
    Wi' a' its power.

Wee innocent! its blythesome smile,
Nor mask'd wi' art, nor stained wi' guile,
Repays my ilka care an' toil,
    To keep it cozie;
I'm truly blest when prest a while
    To its leal bozie.

Afore I sing my hindmost sang,
An' lay my weary banes amang
The lang-forgotten, mould'rin thrang,
    In yon kirkyard;
I hope to see't, maist sax feet lang,
    My toils reward.

But, as I said, when gloamin' gray
Seals up the murky winter day,
I "hameward plod my weary way"
    Through wreaths o' snaw;
Syne to my lyre without delay,
    I gleesome fa'.

Or ower some weel-tauld, witchfu' tale,
'Bout some angelic Arabelle;
An' hour or twa we baith regale,
    (Minds maun be fed)—
Syne ask a blessin' on our kale,
    An' gang to bed.

The wee things, beddit lang afore,
In ithers oxters soun'ly snore;

209

STRAW INTO GOLD

There's nocht ado but bar the door
An' rest the fire—
Till mornin' then, lat Boreas roar,
Until he tire.

While blest wi' health, an' meal an' kale.
My humble lot I'll ne'er bewail;
To ilka breeze I'll spread my sail
An' steer awa',
Nor coward-like flee frae ilka gale
That haps to blaw.

Why has Buchan allowed the memory of her greatest poet to perish in obscurity within a hundred years of his inglorious death?

Surely Buchan's true poet of the soil, and no man fitter than he to write *The Cottar's Sunday*. But how few people in Buchan even know that poor Peter Still ever existed. By superhuman effort he published, between 1842 and 1844, two volumes of verse, now mostly in the hands of collectors, and by these alone he survives for us. But no Immortal Memories or Haggis Suppers for the lone Bard of Ugieside; no busloads of worshippers to the site of his turf-roofed hovel; not a knowing finger to point out his grave.

From a moral point of view here is a man more deserving of our homage than the debauchery of Burns. He endured the same poverty and degradation, even moreso, for Burns had a chance and destroyed it, whereas Still was never feted in Edinburgh or introduced to the nobility; his candle never had a chance to gild the thrones of greatness, and it was snuffed out in the remoteness of hardship in which he existed, leaving no trace of its brightness. But because Peter Still was divinely honest the ensuing hardship was more severe; but he fought it with hard work and unflinching endeavour, and never sought loose-living as an antidote. He never once left the narrow path for the wider avenues of self-destruction. In this he was more courageous than William Thom of Inverurie, the Weaver Poet, with whom he was contemporary, and who shares a similar fate, which may soon be remedied by a revival of his works. Thom and Still were friends, but so alike was their genius that some of Still's poems, when unsigned, were taken for the work of Thom. The Weaver Poet knew that Still was stealing some of his thunder, that 'water was going past his mill,' but it made no difference to their friendship.

On the whole, however, Still's style is more like that of Burns than of Thom; so much so that Still has been blamed as an imitator, much as he has denied it. He is less original than Thom but more musical and easier to read, which perhaps is not the best kind of poetry to survive among the serious students of the art, who are in the best position to reproduce it.

No one can deny the similarity to Burns in *The Cottar's Sunday*. But who among the experts can read Burns without visions of Ferguson? Most art is imitation and making comparison is a wholesome part of the entertainment.

For their 'Cottar' poems Burns and Still both used the Spencerian stanza. In my opinion Burns was the original creator (after Ferguson)—and Still was the improver, the polisher of the rough stone, the almost tearful perfectionist. From the mediocrity of Burns' so-called Immortal poem Still produced a masterpiece, and it was written on the banks of Ugie

In the stanza below we get a glimpse of the granny who taught Still in his childhood, and who shared his ingle until her death in advanced age:

> *Beneath a load o' three-score years an' ten,*
> *Wi' staff in hand, an' earthward bendin' sair,*
> *Auld grannie now comes hoolie creepin' ben,*
> *And seeks the neuk where stands her auld armchair,*
> *A cushion, saft and clean, awaits her there,*
> *An' doun she sits; the wee things show their pride*
> *By welcome words an' warm affection's air—*
> *The language o' the heart that winna hide—*
> *For blythe are they, I trow, when seatit by her side.*

STRAW INTO GOLD

Wi' palsied hand she strokes ilk little head,
An' tells them how to spend the holy day,
That Jesus rose victorious frae the dead,
To conquer sin an' death, an' live for aye;
Her earth-sick heart delights to lead the way
To that blest land where all her hopes repose;
The life to them that seems so sweet and gay,
To three-score years an' ten seems full o' woes,
And all her thoughts are fixed beyond its earthly close.

It is communion sabbath and the cottar and his wife go to
church, leaving the bairns in the care of grannie. In those days a
sacramental service lasted all afternoon, and in the evening we
get a picture of the parents returning home, the bairnies running to meet them, while old grannie watches from the cottage
door.

Meanwhile, wi' ashen locks, the age-bent dame
Stands in the evening sun before the door,
An' while the bairnies welcome mammie hame,
Recalls to mind the happy days o' yore,
When she, fu' blest, wi' him that's now no more,
Returning frae the holy house o' prayer,
Had wont to meet her ain blythe infant core,
That now are parted far, some here, some there,
Some in the green kirk-yard, an' some she kens-na-where.

Sad wi' the thought, she seeks the ingle neuk,
An' heaves a secret sigh unkent to a',
Syne bids the cottar bring the holy book,
An' read the text an' psalms ere gloamin' fa';
Close to her chair he willingly does draw,
The soul-inspired mandate to obey;
The wee things, standing in a ruddy raw,
Their leal-loved grannie's reverent leuks survey,
As down she bends her ear, attention deep to pay.

THE BARD OF UGIESIDE

Health and weather permitting, Still slaved all summer in the fields and peat-bogs, storing his mind for the dark winter nights when he wrote his poetry. Here there was no profligacy of spirit, no dissipation of energy; but a robust, almost stern, adherence to duty, and a worship of the muses that lightened the task. Conscience wouldn't allow Still to neglect his work for poesy while he could make a sixpence outside. But even in his direct poverty he wouldn't accept charity, which perhaps made it doubly hard for his wife and bairns. He wept over them in their hunger and distress but his spirit would not yield to begging. When a well-meaning farmer's wife collected money in the neighbourhood to ease the suffering of his family he sat up in his sick bed and sent his wife back with the donation.

The lady sniffed at his selfish pride and told Bell to take the money and say nothing about it. "Na! please peace I winna—I wad seener work thae ten fingers to the stumps than tak' a bawbee o't," said Still's wife, and returned to her duties at the sick man's bedside.

When the poet had recovered sufficiently he printed a bill and stuck it up on the door of the old Lint Mill at Auchlee, where the weavers and passers-by could see he would not accept money he hadn't worked for, either with pen or with spade.

The only beneficence Still would accept was through the publication and sale of his poems, and it was about this time that he began his search for subscribers. He collected his miscellaneous pieces (some of them had already appeared in various newspapers and magazines), and, in the end, through the concerted efforts of Principal Jack and his lady, of Aberdeen University, and several other interested parties, Still began to make money. His book found a ready sale and he removed to Peterhead and sent his family to school. After the charity campaign he could no longer endure Millbank, and there were those who admired and supported his independence of mind.

The quest for subscribers to his second book of verse took our poet as far south as Edinburgh, where he wrote home that he was richer by £23 (a lot of money in those days) and that the publication of his second volume was assured. In this journey Still had

213

been obliged to discard the slate he usually carried with him everywhere, to assist him in his deafness, and he engaged a communicative companion for the search, which perhaps was more conducive to collecting signatures than the dumb slate.

The second volume appeared in 1844, two years after the first, and it contained some of his most delightful compositions. These were the most fruitful years in Still's life and the work he now produced was far superior to anything he had written before 1840. The second edition of his poems brought wealth to poor Peter Still beyond his wildest hopes. His destitution was so much relieved that he could afford a pilgrimage to Ayrshire, where he paid homage at the shrines of Burns.

Years before, Still had dreamed of this pilgrimage. Now that it was a reality he shed the devotion of his short lifetime on the idol of his gushing heart—on the poet who had died just 17 years before he himself was born, to the same hard, cruel, insensitive world—the world of Robert Burns.

> *Anon, at Beauty's witching shrine,*
> *Thou pour'st thy numbers, half divine,*
> *Stealing a heart in ilka line,*
> > *Wi' magic power,*
> *Till frien's an' foes alike are thine,*
> > *Braid Scotlan' ower.*

> *Thou dipp'st thy pen in tears of woe,*
> *And sweetly sad thy numbers flow,*
> *Like virgin's prayers, when kneeling low,*
> > *Wi' streamin' eyes,*
> *Beside the bed where, pale as snow,*
> > *Her lover lies.*

> *Still glowing with seraphic fire,*
> *Thou strik'st a loftier, holier lyre,*
> *Amid the cottar's humble choir,*
> > *On bended knee,*
> *While angels hovering round admire*
> > *Thy minstrelsy.*

THE BARD OF UGIESIDE

From the banks of Ayr Still also sent his most beautiful tribute
to Ugie, the native river of his dreams. But it is sad to think that
it was one of his last songs, and one can almost detect a premoni-
tion of approaching disillusionment in the lines: in phrases like
'leafless November' and the 'shaken love rose'; beautiful as they
are these words are deceptive in a poet who we imagine to be at
the zenith of his power.

> *Dear stream of my heart, thou art far, far away,*
> *And long have I sighed to be near thee;*
> *For naught, save the pang that recalls me to clay,*
> *From the folds of my bosom can tear thee.*

> *Ah—there thou art blended with all that I love*
> *In my moments of thought to remember—*
> *The joys which were mine in my April grove,*
> *Ere I thought of my leafless November!*

> *But her voice no more my closed ear*
> *From its silence deep can awaken;*
> *And why am I dreaming a dream so dear*
> *When the leaves of that love-rose are shaken?*

There are only three beauty spots worthy of mention on the
meandering water of Ugie: one on the North Ugie at Strichen,
another on the South Ugie at Old Deer, and the loveliest of all
at Inverugie about three miles west of Peterhead, after the meeting
of the waters. Here the river is smooth, wide and deep as it steals
quietly by the old ruined castle of Ravenscraig, Norman keep of
the Cheynes and Cummynes of Buchan, perched high on a
buttress of red rock and peeping from the trees for miles
around. Here indeed are the pinks and gowany braes of which
the poet sings, and no doubt he had this romantic stretch
of Ugie in mind when he strode on the banks of Ayr.

One of our modern poets sings equally sweet of this famous
beauty spot, if I may be privileged a verse from our own Peter

Buchan of Peterhead, describing the scene as viewed from 'Mount Pleasant,' overlooking the river:

> *The old grey bridge, the lazy stream;*
> *The ivy-covered castle wall;*
> *The lark's clear, lilting joyous theme*
> *Above it all.*

From Ayr, Peter Still returned to Edinburgh where he embarked by sea for Aberdeen. He arrived home in time to witness the death of his father at the advanced age of 85. The Stills had always stuck together as a family and honoured each other's marriages and funerals and family crises with the fidelity of the Jews for the Fathers of Israel.

But the screw was tightening on Peter Still; on his return to Peterhead the last iron thread of his life was being wrenched into the socket of his existence. The long years of wet ditching, back-breaking toil and malnutrition had at last crushed the spirit that had sung so sweetly. He hung his harp upon the wall and in four years we scarcely hear a song from him.

He had taken the Blackhouse Toll Bar, at that time about half-a-mile from Peterhead on the Fraserburgh turnpike. The Toll Bar was paying fairly well, but he had a hankering for a croft and the quieter life of former years, where he might with ease combine his study of the muses with more leisurely, self-directed employment. On looking at one croft of some promise he was heard to explain: "Oh but for ten more years to make an Eden here!"

About this time the waning poet wrote what is believed to be his last poem, an incomplete fragment which he scribbled on the back of a letter to his brother. One can detect in the lines a glimmering revival of interest in the poet's surroundings, a struggling rejuvenation of spirit in one who is weary of the world, a mind striving for the light against physical weakness, pain, depression and disappointment. The poem has only once previously been published, in the Edward's Collection of 1881.

There's sunlight on the earth again,
There's music in the sky;
There's beauty on the brow of May,
And glory in her eye.

She smiles benignly as of yore;
Her mournful days are gone,—
Rejoice again ye fruitful fields,
Put all your beauties on!

Bloom on the braes ye daisies dear;
Bloom on the meadows green;
Ye cowslips yield your golden cups
And mingle in the scene.

Ye bluebells and ye panzies pure
O sweetly gem the plain;
There's glory in the eye of May
And light on earth again.

But it was not to be, and a persistent spitting of blood gave signs of an early grave for our poet. He still frequently struggled to assist his family in collecting road dues but, in June 1847, he ruptured a blood vessel which rendered him practically helpless until his death the following March. On the twenty-first of March, 1848, he died in his chair by the fireside at Blackhouse, aged thirty-four, and thus was silenced forever the finest poet Buchan ever had.

Thirty-three years later, in 1881, when a sample of Still's work was included in the Edwards' *Collection of Scottish Poets*, his widow was still alive, employed, says the biographer, as a washer-woman, from house to house.

Bell had been neglected but her son, young Peter, fared better. On the death of his father, the young lad, to ease the distress of his mother and family, was sent to work for two years on the land. Fortunately at this stage he was taken in hand by the professors and Principal Jack of Aberdeen University and received a thorough-going education. He proved to be an apt and eager scholar and eventually became a schoolmaster and poet in his own right. For seven years, until his health broke down, he was rector of Peterhead Academy, where he improved the curriculum and revolutionised the methods of teaching.

But poor Bell survived both poets, father and son by many years, and shed tears for both. Young Peter was twelve when his father died and he himself was laid to rest on February 9th, 1869, one year younger than his father.

BRITHER SCOTS AND ENGLISH MEN!

A Parody On Burns

Noo brither Scots and English men
And Commons in the Lobby,
Anither Scot now wields the pen—
But his name is nae Robbie.

Noo wi' a gun I'm little use,
As little wi' a graipe,
But gie's pen tae write abuse
And faith I'd gar ye gape!

The only thing that I hae got
In common wi' the Bard—
The circumstances o' my lot
Like his, were unco hard.

Likewise born beneath the thatch,
In biggin' made o' clay,
I never thocht his powers tae match,
Or sing so sweet a lay.

I canna sing o' Banks and Braes,
Or sigh the loss o' Mary O!
But likewise I've had blithesome days
Among the rigs o' barley O!

For there I courted Maggie Jane,
My winsome country maid;
Her folks were cottared at the Mains
When she and I were wed.

Noo I can write in sober prose,
And even verse when e'er I can—
And still content tae sup the brose,
I'll pu' a neep wi' ony man!

219

STRAW INTO GOLD

Noo brither Scots and English men,
And a' that drink the toddy,
Anither Scot now wields the pen—
But his name is nae Robbie!

FRUSTRATION

I live in a lone world
Where there are few that trespass;
A lone pilgrim
On a dewless ecstasy,
But joining in the full symphony
Of orchestrated art.

Oh joy of soul unending
Soothe me with thy enraptured melody—
To a softer cadence of the poet's song;
Lull my senses deep,
Deep in the sleep of living bliss.

Roll me in the dead leaves that lie
Knee-deep in wind-scythed woods
Of dead summers' vanished memories—
Down the leafless lanes of hopes unrealised
Unhappy harvest of a summer gay.

Oh Spring that heralded joys complete,
Now enshrined in winter's tinselled frost.
Nature's marble wonderment
In a mocked ecstasy of dreams.

And mark my wing-singed search for ethereal fire,
Searching the Infinite;
Feeling and seeing where few have touched
The dew made molten gold at the sun's forge.

FRUSTRATION

Oh send a comet down,
That I may use it as a scimitar,
A flaming arc to slash and hack
The barriers down
Between those daisied fields
And my leisured hours of long desire.

(First published 1970)

SHADOW OF A DOUBT

God is Father of the earth,
We all in Him have life,
The sun in heaven is His hearth,
Dame Nature is his wife.

But God bequeathed His powers to man
To last for all eternity,
And gave assurance for each one
A moment of sublimity . . .

Some may think this price too high
This glimpse of Heaven that gives us life,
When each one so soon must die—
Martyred for a world in strife.

Earth is but a carnal tomb
Where Death strews all our bones,
For souls in Nature's teeming womb,
At birth, must have new homes.

For we must go that others may
Enjoy the sun of Love's sweet smile;
If here we could forever stay
How could Death old Time beguile?

221

STRAW INTO GOLD

Is this then our promised bliss?
Our hopes of immortality!
Must Heaven be baited with a kiss?
Or witnessed in a baby's eye?

Must we to our hopes still cling?
Nor look for portents in the sky—
Content to hear the angels sing
In a new-born infant's cry.

Had Nature been a barren wife
And God could spend His time at play
There would be no use for life,
And we would still be clay.

But God he has a farmer's pride
And all the fields are tilled,
And Nature is a buxom bride,
So all the graves are filled.

God's purpose in ourselves we see,
But still undaunted let us sing:
"O grave, where is thy victory?
"O Death, where is thy sting?"

(1963)

POOR LITTLE RICH MAN!

Poor little rich man indeed! For
In the lip of the marigold I can find gold pieces,
In the Sunflower I can find wealth.
I can hew ingots from the sunbeams—
Even from the flimsy gossamer
I can spin a linen banknote.
The clouds are galleons laden with bullion,
Breathed along by a wind
Fragrant with incense.

222

POOR LITTLE RICH MAN!

But I am not a Titian,
Therefore I cannot, mix my colours
With the juice of flowers.
But in the aurora-borealis I taint my brush;
The rainbow is my paint-box—
The dawns and sunsets are my copybooks.

I am gifted with a camera-eye.
The lightning is my flashbulb;
The eclipse of sun and moon are by exposures.
On foggy days I dip my prints in gloom
And show them to the angels in the starlight:
That is when you see the Milky Way—
'Tis the reflection of Heaven
When the gates are open.

The crescent moon is my gondola,
And I paddle through the spheres.
With a comet for an oar,
And the stars are twinkling lights
From my own Venice.

Now upon a meteor I streak
To earth once more,
Where every leaf and blade of grass
Suspends its drop of silver for my gathering.
And when the Hunter hangs
His lantern in the sky
They are turned to lobes of gold—
Poor little rich man indeed!

(1968)

AN ADDRESS TO PETERHEAD

In Which Town And Its Environs I Spent Most Of My Youth.

I like the toon o' Peterheid,
I like its bonnie lasses
In tartan slacks and strings o' beads,
Shakin' oot their basses—
Wi' faces flushed and hair untrussed
Throwin' oot their ashes.

I love yer halls, twa spires sae tall,
The evenin' curfew tollin',
Yer flowery public gairdens all,
Yer statue and yer column;
I've played wi' bools at your fine schools,
And prayed in kirk sae solemn.

I adore yer picture palaces,
They thrilled me as a loon,
Whaur Indians focht wi' Palefaces,
And Garbo wore her goons;
There stars o' screen I've aft times seen,
And heard Bing Crosby croon.

The Auld Pretender landed here—
And though the toonsfolk warna keen
The bailiffs met him on the pier
And he got lodgin's o'er the Queen;
Above the door whaur Jeems did snore
The Stewart crest may still be seen.

Next day in Inverugie's halls
The Prince sat doon wi' Marischal Keith,
They briefed the war and forth did call
On every laird and Highland Chief,
On the Braes o' Mar they proclaimed war
That ended in their flight frae Leith.

AN ADDRESS TO PETERHEAD

Ye had some fame in byegone days
For chasin' Greenland's mighty whales,
But nooadays that doesna pay
So noo yer nettin' smaller tails—
We spread the mead, the soil tae feed,
Wi' their entrails!

Noo yer puttin' soup in tins
And sendin' 'em far Sooth;
Abroad ye send yer barrelled fins—
Yer cash for beef tae Booth,
Wi' some tae slake the Auld Kirk plate—
Preservin' faith and truth!

The tins are made at C. & B.'s,
See their tall lum smoke;
When Goerin' doon the bombs did toss.
He fairly gar'd it rock.
But like the throng it stands among
It still survived the shock.

Noo aft ye heard the siren toot
When Hitler started war,
And mony a sodger ye sent oot,
And mony a jolly tar—
Defendin' all oor aims and claims
In oor Dominions near and far.

Upon the Links by the Kirkyard gate
The War Memorial stands,
For noble sons who for the State
Have died in foreign lands:
For those who bled, the glorious dead
Reposing now in angel bands.

225

STRAW INTO GOLD

Yon Lib'ral Monument on Meethill
Still marks the Corn Laws' repeal;
I've seen the grindstones near Stonemill
That ground the townsfolks' meal;
But Toried corn, since I was born
Did ay reduce oor yield.

In prison fast, across the bay,
And up in Stirlin's quarries grim,
The brooding convict spends his days
And toils a lifetime for his sin;
Transforming rocks tae concrete blocks—
They have built a harbour trim.

Machinists noo are fashionin' drills
Whaur cairters' horses used tae graze;
There's a graveyard noo upon the hill
Whaur ploomen sang in former days;
Whaur fishers' nets were dried on yetts,
Hoosewives noo hang oot their claes.

Whaur stands yon braw new housin' sites
That far extend yer suburbs,
Lang syne I used tae fly my kites
And gaird'ners planted rhubarb;
Frae Windmill Brae roon tae the Bay
There's hooses noo but nae a pub!

I dinna like yer pubs noo pals,
The whisky is owre dear,
I'd raither be at Aikey's stalls
Drinkin' ginger beer!
But stout or rum, noo by gum,
There might be something here!

226

AN ADDRESS TO PETERHEAD

Noo last, not least, there's your Press,
Thy famed OBSERVER leaf—
Wi' hints on whaur tae buy oor dress,
And a' the news in brief;
Wha's stirks tae sale, or straw tae bale,
And whaur they catched the thief!

Noo my freens my stroud must end—
In winter I pu' neeps;
Doon my weary back I bend
While tired nightwatchmen sleep,
In spring tae sow, in summer hoe,
And in the autumn reap.

But, kind freens, if ye should bleat
Tae thank me for my pains—
Yon Palace in Hanover Street
I'd like tae ca' my ain;
But as I've been told, the place is sold,
I make no further claims.

(1960)

A GRATEFUL TRIBUTE TO THE
ARBUTHNOT MUSEUM PETERHEAD

I admire yer Public Library,
its clocks and its braw tower,
For there in greatest liberty
My muse it found its power—
Tae garner lore, still in store
Tae cheer my darkest hours.

227

STRAW INTO GOLD

Ye hae a fine museum there
Stuffed wi' birds and 'looms;
But strangers note: it's up the stair!
Nae in the readin' rooms—
Though there grey hairs beguile their cares
In silence sweet as doom.

Late dignitaries o' the toon
In painted portraits wi' their names,
Wi' faces stern and sable goon
Are hangin' here in gilted frames:
But in between can still be seen
Some works o' art o' wider fame.

In sculptured marble here essayed
Stands woman in her fairest form;
Now were yer daughters like arrayed
Such walks they would adorn!
To see such maids these walks I'd tread
Each even and dewy morn.

A Highland stag frae wolves at bay,
A pheasant 'neath a fox's paw,
A vulture's tallons on his prey,
A trout in otter's bloody maw,
A crocodile frae the banks o' Nile
Spreadeagled there upon the wa'.

A snake it seems alive in grass,
A weasel at the throat of hare,
Embryo sealed in jars of glass—
From regions wild a polar bear;
In scenes like these raw nature breathes,
And shows survival is her care.

A GRATEFUL TRIBUTE TO THE
ARBUTHNOT MUSEUM PETERHEAD

And there's a little hairy musk,
You'd like tae stroke its hair yourself;
Besides a pair o' walrus tusks
And boaties on a shelf—
Built tae scale, o' steam and sail
Wad tempt the seaman's hand tae pelf.

There's sea-shells, fossils and giant crabs
That look like stones tae layman's eyes;
Insects and beetles pinned tae tabs,
And lovely wing-decked butterflies.
There's birds' eggs too, of every hue,
Dipped in Nature's wonder dyes.

There's a meerchaum pipe, an auld snuff mull,
And flintheids frae the heath;
There's a boney pate, an ancient skull
Which still retains its teeth;
A spinnin' wheel, a fishwife's creel,
And pearls frae the coral reef.

Noo there's a rustic hobby-horse,
Ye'll see it frae the street,
And there's a mantrap there, of course,
For prowler's stealthy feet;
And there's a mass o' minted brass
Wad gar the miser greet.

There's claymores broad and swords twin-edged,
Whaur Mr. Rust has nibbled,
And stony slabs where learnèd sage
Wi' patient art has chiselled;
And scrolls unrolled and hides of old
Whaur musin' poets have scribbled.

STRAW INTO GOLD

The Marischal's clock, a prized antique,
Stands hidden in a neuk;
His pistol's there for ye to seek,
Likewise an Eskimo prayer beuk:
Ye're a learned man if there ye can
Find a chapter frae St. Luke.

Moccasins frae the frozen North
With paddles and a real canoe,
And whalebone trinkets here set forth
As fashioned in the far igloo.
There are some busts to gather dust
And fishes under glass in view.

Ye'll see the strangest wooden plough
That ever turned furrow,
But from that prim'tive frame I trow
Our fathers did ideas borrow.
The tractor race may there find place
On some distant morrow.

There's ram-loaders and blunderbusses,
Most excellent for sparrows,
And for the duck among the rushes
There's the bow and arrows;
There's harpoons, spears and claspknives here
Wad pierce ye tae the marrow.

I've travelled far in search of lore,
Frae Gretna Green tae Inverness;
But in Peterheid I saw such store,
I found it worthy of my verse:
In gratitude for all that's good—
My thanks tae you I now rehearse.

GLOSSARY

abeen — above

aneuch — enough

antrin — occasional

agyaun — agoing

backet — shaped wooden box, open at one end for carrying peat, potatoes or turnips

bade — told

bairn — child

bannocks — pancakes

barfit — bare-footed, without shoes or stockings

bass or basses — rugs or mats

ben — through, other end

big — build, to build, but also means large or muckle

bing — heap

binks — brickwork, mostly at fireplace

birn — bundle

bools — marbles

boll — in oatmeal ten stone

"bone-davie" — manure distributor, used originally for ground bones from the slaughterhouses

boreas — northern storms, from aurora borealis or "northern lights"

bothie — Men cooked their own food and lived in the bothies, whereas chaumers were merely sleeping accommodation, the men feeding in the farmhouse

bozie — bosom

braw — grand, stylish

brazen — bold, "brazen hussies," bitches or whores

breeks — trousers, breeches

breid — oatcakes

briest — breast, bosom

brocht — brought

Broch — defence tower of stone used by the Picts against the Norsemen, but also the local name for Fraserburgh, probably because of a famous broch which may have stood there

brose — oatmeal mixed with boiling water, salt and pepper, taken
　　　with cream or milk, sugar or treacle optional and milk may
　　　be substituted with stout or "porter" ale
bugger — swear word

ca' — call or drive
canny — slow, cautious, wary
cannier — more careful than others
canned — slang word, drunk
caperin' — antics, playing tricks on somebody, clowning
casten — changed or soiled, cast off
chakie — haversack
chap — knock, hammer-blow, but also fellow or young man
chaumer — sleeping chamber
chauved — hard struggle
chauvin — struggling
chiel — man
claes — clothes
clart — smear
click — large crochet hook used with woollen rags in rug making:
　　　sometimes applies to shepherd's crook
cloart — Scotch expression: in this case obesity, "fat cloart"
clootie-dumplings — plum-duff or Christmas pudding boiled in
　　　cloth or towel
cogie — small wooden bucket for feeding calves with milk
cole — hay-cock, small mound of hay
coulter — turf cutter on stem or beam of plough
coup or couped — topple or empty out
cottars — married workers in tied cottages on the Scottish farms
craps — crops
craws — crows
cronies — comrades
cuddle — hug, fondle
cozie — warm, comfortable
dab — let dab, told
darg — dig
daundered — ambled, to walk
dawdling — bouncing, diddling
deem — girl, kitchen lass, as distinct from the English verb

dermititis — udder infection
ding — throw or push out
dominie — schoolmaster
douce — quiet, well-meaning
doup — buttocks
dour — heavy, sullen
dracht — draught, twin-load or consignment, but can also imply
    draught or wind
dreich — wet, cold
dresser — old-fashioned kitchen sideboard with back
drookit — soaking wet
dross or drush — peat crumb
dubs — mud
dubby — muddy

earie — weird, pertaining to the supernatural
earth-closet — dry lavatory

farrier — veterinary surgeon
fee-ed — engaged for work; unwritten contract, barter
firlet — $2\frac{1}{2}$ stone or $\frac{1}{4}$ of boll in oatmeal
fleer — floor
fleerish — steel knuckle-duster for striking fire from flintstone,
    probably from flourish.
frichen — frighten
fluffert — flurry
fooshinless — without substance
frail — weak
fule — dirty, soiled

geets — bairns, children
graips — short cross-handled forks
greep — byre or stable floor

hach — spital from the throat
haflin — young man, male teenager
hame-ower — home-loving, plain, domesticated
hames — iron frame fixed over horse shoulder collar with hooks
    for drag-chains

hangman cheese — cheese curds pressed into gauze cloth and hung
    outside on the wall to drain off whey and harden
hankering — longing, craving
haugh — mud flats, river bed
haun — hand
harn — rough sacking
hantle — big quantity
haverin — joking
hefty — strong
heftet — over ripe
hey — hay
hicht — height
hinder — delay
hirple — cripple, hopping gait, hop-a-long
hirst — numerous
hish — shoo, chase off
hooch — to shout or ejaculate from the throat while dancing a
    jig or reel
howes — valleys
hurdies — backsides, hind-quarters
hurlie — trolley
hyow — hoe

ilka — every one
ilk — every one the same, kindred, similar

jammy piece — slice of bread and jam

keek — peep
kist — chest or trunk, mostly of wood
kinch — wind or tie up
knack — sound of wooden cartwheel when sounded wilth hard "K",
    as opposed to knack, meaning skillful, with soft K

lairy — soft, sinking
leal-loved — well loved
leuks — looks
limmer — girl of loose moral behaviour
loup — leap

martingale — nickle-plated harness decoration, worn on a strap fastened to a horse's girth to keep its head down.

mesmerised — fascinated, astonished, hypnotism

mirk — shadows

muffler — big spotted handkerchief tied round the neck, cloth scarf

natter — argument, nagging

neeps — turnips

new-fangled — up-to-date

nicked — pregnant

nicky-tams — leather straps with buckles worn below the knees by workmen

nocht — nothing

nowt — cattle

oxter — breast, bosom, armpits, armful

peewits — lapwing, teuchat

perquisites — provisions instead of money, barter for work in the cottar system, probably of feudal origin

powin — pounds stirling

prigged — pleaded, begged

pucklie — small amount or quantity

quines — girls

randie — variation of limmer; bitchy, girl of loose moral behaviour

rashes — bulrushes

ravel — ruffle

reek — smoke

rennet — curdling substance extracted from the stomach of a calf. Used for "yerning" or curdling milk and cheese making

richt — right

rickling — piling or stacking up on ends

rig — to fit out

rig or lea-rig — sections of a field in ploughing

riled — angered

rucks — corn or haystacks

roup — sale

rouse — anger

rosette — imitation of a rose in coloured material, mostly ribbon and used by horsemen in decorating their harness

sair — sore, painful

saltpetre — nitrate of potassium: when soaked in newspaper will ignite and smoulder from spark after drying

saps — milk and bread sops

sark — shirt

scutter — loiter, delay

sharn — cow dung

shim — light implement for removing weeds from between turnip or potato drills

sic — such

sicht — sight

sieven — seven

siller — money, silver

skelp — walloping, a thrashing

skelves — shelves, sounding the K

skirling — screaming, yelling

skweel — school

spleiter — pelt of rain, splatter

sneck — hasp or latch

snib — catch or fastener

sort — repair or attend to

spunk — spirit

stickly — peat embedded with resin or rotted wood

stilts — plough stilts, plough handles

stime — glimmer

stirk — steer or heifer, half-grown cattle

stite — nonsense

stoup — spout

stot — castrated male ox, bullock

stroud — screed, poem, song or monologue

surtout — coat, mostly black, frockcoat

suppie — small drop, trickle

swey — hinged or swivelled gantry over the fireplace

swines' hoose — pig sty

tanzie — ragwort, field weed with yellow poisonous flower
tatties — potatoes
teem — empty, opposite of teeming in English
teuchat — lapwing
thole — endure
thrawn — stubborn
troch — cement watering trough for cattle and horses
tick — credit
trauchle — weary, struggle, hard unrelenting task
travis post — divisional post between stalls in byre or stables
trysts — meeting place for lovers, also tryste — to tempt or persuade

wannert — wandered
wall-tams — same as nicky-tams
wark — work
weevil — worm or grub
werd — word
wheeble — piping call of the lapwing or the curlew, also an
    expression for whistling
whundyke — whindyke
wull — will

yerned or yerning — yerned milk, milk in the first stages of
    curdling
yett — gate
yoke — wooden spar for pulling plough. Shoulder spar for carrying
    water
yoking — a period of work
yoking time — starting time for work